A VERY ARCH ANGEL

The buzzing in his arm reached its peak and Clayton said to it, "I want the Archangel Michael brought here. I want him right now." And then the room became dark, much like the darkness in Paolo's limbo, and there was a shape in the darkness that was darker still.

"Hey, what the heck! I was in the middle of a meeting!"

Clayton kept his arm in front of him. "Are you the Archangel Michael? That's who I called for."

The dark shape leaned toward him a bit. "Yeah, that's me. Who the heck——? Say! It's Pinkes, right? The one Raphael calls Pinhead? Pleased to meet you, pal."

"Paolo is . . . Raphael is refusing to help me. So I need you."

"You mean you've seen him? Raphael?"

"He's where I sent him. He could come back, but he won't."

The shape shrunk back a little. "Where you *sent* him? Holy cow. Ho-lee cow."

An angel who said "Holy cow"; Clayton was amused.

"I want to find God. I need your help. Do I get it?"

"Sure. Sure you do. In fact, pal, I'd be delighted."

PROPHETS FOR THE END OF TIME

MARCOS DONNELLY

PROPHETS FOR THE END OF TIME

A Baen Books Original

Baen Publishing Enterprises
P.O. Box 1403
Riverdale, NY 10471

ISBN: 0-671-57775-1

Cover art by Stephen Hickman

First printing, November 1998

Distributed by Simon & Schuster
1230 Avenue of the Americas
New York, NY 10020

Typeset by Windhaven Press, Auburn, NH
Printed in the United States of America

To S. L. Spotts,
Who Insisted We Think.

Book I:
The Age of Innocence

"And the angel answered me, and said,
Know ye not what these be?
And I said, No, my lord.

"Then said he, These are the two
anointed ones, that stand by
the Lord of the whole Earth."

Zechariah 4: 13-14

Prologue

These are the generations of Clayton Pinkes, one of the Lord's two anointed; protégé of the Archangel Raphael; Prophet for the End of Time:

Levi Cohen begat Samuel Cohen during the reign of Abraham the President. This was at the beginning of the Age of Machines, and throughout the Earth noble men of great stature began to gather unto themselves devices and machines; and those who possessed devices and machines were spoken of with reverence for their nobility and stature. Levi Cohen himself never personally owned a machine of any note.

His only-begotten Samuel Cohen *did* own several machines, including electric light bulbs, which he was not operating the night he begat Tobiah Cohen, several years prior to the anointing of He Who Was Called (No, Really) Grover. Samuel Cohen also begat Kenneth O'Mally, quite by accident and unbeknownst to him, on the night he realized a tremendous return on early industrial investments and was celebrating with much wine in a Brooklyn house of frolic.

1

And Michael, Prince of Angels, was displeased with the splitting of this bloodline, which had not been part of the plans for how the End of Time would happen; and in a snit, he almost called the whole thing off.

Kenneth O'Mally begat Myra O'Mally, and Myra, albeit a bastard of the bloodline, comported herself admirably and with compassionate nature. She worked for Catholic charities, and danced and sang into a machine that made soft voices loud so that gold could be gathered for the Second of the Great Wars. Myra O'Mally knew Harold Pinkes, and together the two of them begat Daniel Pinkes.

And the Archangel Michael called forth two angels to carry to the face of the Earth the Urim and the Thummim of old to be hidden among men. And the angels gazed upon the ancient objects of the Lord, saying, "Where, O Prince of Angels, shall we hide the Urim and the Thummim of old on the face of the Earth among men?"

And Michael, Prince of Angels, said, "Oh, who cares? Just anywhere," for he was still peeved about the Samuel Cohen begetting incident.

And the angels went forth from Michael's presence to beseech the aid of the Archangel Raphael who, alone among angels, could touch what men touched and be physical as men were physical. And Raphael consoled the angels, assuring them that Michael was just being pettish, and that they should proceed with Heaven's original plan. "Praise unto you, Raphael," the two angels sang in unison, "for you have come to our aid in the labors of Heaven."

And the Archangel Raphael rebuffed their praise, saying, "C'mon, guys, knock it off. I'm just a working stiff like the rest of you."

On Earth, Tobiah Cohen begat Zachary Cohen according to the true bloodline. Zachary, who was raised to maturity during times of gayness and frivolity, begat robustly and with great vigor. He begat eleven times by eight women, and among the fruits of his begetting was Lisa, whose surname was not Cohen but Gerard. Last names were often confounded that way throughout the last century of that millennium.

Then there was sent to Earth the Archangel Gabriel, who intervened on behalf of the majesty of the Archangel Michael, Prince of Angels, lord of cherubim and seraphim, the Holy One of holy ones, by introducing Daniel Pinkes to Lisa Gerard in a Syracuse bar. These two communed regarding occupation, income level, and past attempts at begetting—for these were the days of Richard-Who-Fled, the beginnings of the Begetting Plagues—and soon they joined in ritual wedlock.

Michael, Prince of Angels, was pleased with the rejoining of the bloodline, and decided to go ahead with the End of Time after all.

And it came to pass in the second year of the forth decade before Christendom's third millennium, that Daniel Pinkes knew his wife and begat Clayton Pinkes, one of the two Prophets for the End of Time.

And there was great rejoicing among the angels of Heaven, except by Raphael, who didn't even make an appearance at any of the best parties.

ONE:
1976, In the Rochester
Suburb of Brighton

On the second verse of the *Memorare*, Dickie Lanpher's right foot kicked Clayton Pinkes' ankle out from under him, and Clayton fell to the tan linoleum of the classroom floor—a sound *smack!* on the word "you" in the phrase, "Inspired by this confidence, I fly to you, O Virgin of virgins, my Mother." Sister Leo Agnes—who could not have witnessed the assault, since she stood devoutly eyeing the cross at the front of the room during the entire prayer—waited until the recital ended to lift Clayton from the floor with one hand, half by his shirt collar and half by his hair. As he rose, Clayton, who was thirteen, saw himself at the age of thirty-nine, saying to a blonde-haired woman whom he could clearly visualize but whom he had never met: "That's how life is, Elizabeth. That's just how it is."

Clayton had grown used to these flashes of himself doing things years from now. They didn't bother him as much as they had at first. He'd decided they were something that everyone went through but nobody talked about, like new growths of hair on unmentionable parts of the body. So the flash only distracted him for a moment, and he heard Sister Leo Agnes finish her scolding with the words, " . . . without playing the clown! Just once, Clayton, try to behave during prayers. Do you think Our Lord is happy looking down at you and seeing you horsing around while the rest of us are honoring His Mother?"

Clayton agreed with Sister Leo Agnes that God would not be happy if He saw Clayton horsing around during the *Memorare*, and Clayton decided to rig Dickie Lanpher's chair during recess so it would fall off its stem when Dickie sat down after grace for lunch.

Which would have been hilarious, and great revenge, except that Sister Leo Agnes caught him in the empty classroom at recess time.

"Clayton Pinkes, what do you think you're doing?" The question came from behind him, thin and pointed like an icicle, and he felt its chill shoot straight across the room, hit him at the bottom of his neck and trickle down his back, shrinking every inch of skin on his arms and legs a size too small. Well, what did she *think* he thought he was doing, crouching on the floor with an adjustable wrench (stolen from the janitor's closet) in one hand and the bolt from Dickie Lanpher's swivel chair in the other? "Praying," he said, knowing even as he said it that it was the worst possible answer, although at that very moment true. Sister Leo Agnes cuffed his ear and towed him by the shirt sleeve to the principal's office.

That was a stroke of luck. The principal was Sister Assumpta, a woman who, unlike Sister Leo Agnes, radiated with the love of God, His Mother, and His angels, and who thought Clayton was the most adorable nuisance on Earth since young Saint Augustine stole apples from the orchard. By the time Sister Assumpta returned to her office from lunch, Sister Leo Agnes had gone back to the classroom to supervise students returning from recess. This gave Clayton time to work up a faceful of tears. Sister Assumpta crouched down beside the chair he was sitting in and pinched his cheek. She was smiling.

"Clayton Pinkes, what kind of trouble have you gotten in now?"

So Clayton explained about the squeak in Dickie Lanpher's chair, and about how Clayton hadn't been able to concentrate during prayers because of the squeak and was afraid the squeak would distract him during the afternoon math test, so that was why he stole the wrench from the janitor's closet, to fix the squeaky chair for Dickie, although now he knew that was selfish since he wasn't really fixing it just for Dickie but also so Clayton could concentrate during the math test. Clayton managed one last tear and told Sister Assumpta how Sister Leo Agnes would probably hate him because she didn't understand the whole story.

Sister Assumpta shook her head and hugged him. She took a tissue and wiped his eyes and nose. "Clayton Pinkes," she said, "you have the devil's own knack for walking into trouble." Then she wrote a note to Sister Leo Agnes that said, "I've taken care of the situation. Please move Dickie Lanpher to an empty seat for the rest of the day." Clayton read the note on his way back to class.

When Sister Leo Agnes read the note, her face showed nothing, unlike Dickie Lanpher, whose face showed hurt, betrayal, and finally suspicion when he was made to sit in the empty desk in the far back corner of the room.

Julie Ward leaned across the aisle while Dickie was being escorted to the new seat, and whispered, "Smooth, Pinkes. However you pulled that off, real smooth."

Clayton's stomach lifted a bit, since Julie Ward was the best-looking eighth grader in Sister Leo Agnes's classroom, and he almost said, "That's how life is, Elizabeth. That's just how it is." But Julie was not named Elizabeth, and she had brown curls, not long blonde hair, and saying that would sound stupid. So he said nothing and smiled at her, which he realized was just as stupid. Clayton's palms were very, very wet, and he checked them nervously to see if any hair was growing there.

As Clayton was leaving the classroom at the end of the day, Sister Leo Agnes stopped him. "I suppose this little matter of truancy, theft, and potential violence now includes a healthy dose of lying, Mr. Pinkes. If Sister Assumpta can't penetrate your charade, I'm certain Father Dorman can." Then she smiled, much the way Sister Assumpta always smiled at him.

If there was anything at St. Catherine's parish more frightening than Sister Leo Agnes, it was Father Dorman. The nervous joke among the eighth grade boys was that Father Dorman had personally carved all the "nots" in the original Ten Commandments. So after dinner that night, Clayton asked his parents if the three of them could go to Saturday confessions the next morning. His mother was surprised, and even his father lowered the evening newspaper. "Well, sure, Clay," his father said, and his mother gave an approving nod.

The answer to question four hundred and nineteen of the *Baltimore Catechism No. 2, New Revised Edition* from Benziger Brothers, Inc., 1962, said, "A sense of shame and fear of telling our sins to the priest should never lead us to conceal a mortal sin in confession because the priest, who represents Christ Himself, is bound by the seal of the sacrament of Penance never to reveal anything that has been confessed to him." Clayton, who along with the rest of his classmates had been made to memorize all four hundred and ninety-nine catechism questions during fourth, fifth, sixth, and seventh grades, confessed the entire truth to Father Dorman the next morning, without shame or fear. Clayton told him his name to make sure Father Dorman knew just whose confession he shouldn't be revealing.

Father Dorman was quiet for quite a while, and Clayton tried squinting through the mesh of the confession screen to see if the priest was still there. Father Dorman's silence told Clayton that he'd been right—if Sister Leo Agnes came and tried to tell Father the story, now the priest couldn't even discuss it with her.

"Clever," Father Dorman finally said, and Clayton jerked back from the screen. "You're a very clever little boy, Clayton Pinkes. But God is not a game, young man. For your penance, you are to go to Sister Assumpta and tell her the entire truth about this escapade. If you refuse to carry out your penance, this sin will continue on your soul in the eyes of God." He paused, Clayton supposed, for the full impact to hit Clayton.

What did hit Clayton was another of his flashes— at first the tingling in his right forearm and the cloudiness behind the outer edges of his eyes, and then the clear picture of himself standing before a seated old man who was dressed in white robes, a red cape, and a skullcap. "I realize Your Holiness finds this amusing," Clayton was saying to the old man, "but it's my *life* we're discussing." As the flash disappeared, Clayton gripped the elbow rest of his kneeler to steady himself against the returned darkness. He made his Act of Contrition and left the confessional to sit in the pew beside his parents.

Clayton was very angry, partly because his plan wasn't working, but mostly because of the *reasons* it wasn't working. What was supposed to be one quick prank for revenge on Dickie Lanpher had been passed up through Sister Leo Agnes, on to the principal, then to the priest, and now through the priest up to God, whom Clayton had never planned on trying to outmaneuver. The whole thing had gotten way out of hand.

"Where are you going, Clayton?" his mother asked.

"Back to confession. I forgot one sin."

"C'mon, Clay," his father said, "I'm sure you're good for one lousy sin until next—" But Clayton's mother gripped his father's forearm, and his father looked away with his hands folded on his lap.

"Father forgive me for I have sinned," Clayton said, squeaking his voice so it would sound different to Father Dorman. "It's been a short time since my last confession."

"And what are your sins, my daughter?" Clayton hadn't realized he'd been squeaking his voice that well.

"I didn't do the last penance I was assigned."

Father Dorman said prayers and, as a new penance, assigned two Hail Marys and three Our Fathers, which Clayton fulfilled and then doubled, just to be sure, before his parents drove him home.

Since third grade at St. Catherine's, Clayton had received straight A's in Religion.

That evening there was a telephone call from Heaven. Clayton picked up the phone, because his parents were out at the movies seeing *The Paper Chase*. Heaven must have been waiting all day for Clayton to answer, because his father had twice gotten the phone earlier that afternoon and been hung up on. Clayton knew the call was meant for him, because after he said hello the woman on the other end of the line said, "Good evening, Clayton Pinkes, this is Mandi calling from Heaven, Management Information Systems division. How are you tonight, sir?"

Clayton said he was good, thanks. The woman's voice sounded the way a kindergarten teacher's voice sounded when she talked to you in school, even if you weren't in kindergarten, even if you were already in eighth grade. Clayton wondered if Sister Leo Agnes were stooping to prank phone calls.

"Mr. Pinkes, we're doing a Quality Inspection Survey for our Major Account customers, and I was wondering if I could have a few moments of your time to ask you some questions about your level of satisfaction with the services we supply. Would this be a good time for you?"

Sure, Clayton wasn't doing anything much, except that *The Six Million Dollar Man* was coming on in twenty minutes and he wanted to see it.

"This should only take about ten minutes, sir."

Even if this was a prank—Dickie Lanpher had an older sister, he remembered, and this was about Dickie's style—Clayton was enjoying the "sir" stuff. He told Mandi from Heaven that she could go ahead and ask her questions.

"Question one: Mr. Pinkes, have you received training in the new Direct Contact Management Program?"

Clayton said he didn't know what that was.

"Have you received training in the new Direct Contact Management Program, Mr. Pinkes?"

Clayton explained that since he didn't know what that was, then he probably never had received training for it.

"Question two: How long ago did you receive that training, Mr. Pinkes?"

Since he hadn't received it, Clayton couldn't say how long ago, but Mandi from Heaven repeated the question and he told her it was zero months ago.

"Question three: In which modules of the DCMP did your managing angel train you?"

Clayton had never heard of a managing angel, although he had heard of guardian angels who help us by praying for us, by protecting us from harm, and by inspiring us to do good, numbers forty-two and forty-three in the *Baltimore Catechism No. 2, New Revised Edition*.

"Would that be modules forty-two, forty-three, and number two, then?"

Clayton was upset that Mandi from Heaven didn't seem to be listening to him, and repeated, loudly this time, that nobody had trained him in any program whatsoever, that he didn't know what a managing angel was, and that if this was a prank it was really a stupid one.

Mandi seemed to listen to him that time, because she put him on hold and returned to inform him that he was being transferred to her boss.

"Hello, Clay? Bob here, supervisor for Heaven,

Management Information Systems division. How are you today?"

Clayton suggested Bob should ask Mandi how Clayton was today, since Clayton had already answered that question. Bob sounded older than Mandi, and Clayton wondered how Dickie Lanpher could organize such an elaborate prank. He couldn't. Father Dorman, then? Would a priest have the nerve to pull telephone pranks?

"Listen, Clay," Bob said, "Mandi tells me you've never been trained in DCMP. Is that true?"

That was still true, yes.

"This is bad, Clay, bad. We'll find out who's responsible and get right to the bottom of this."

Clayton was very grateful for that.

"Now, Clay, if you'll just give me the name of your managing angel, we'll make sure he starts making his regular contact immediately."

And how would Clayton know the name if he'd never been contacted?

"Right, right," Bob said. "I'll track that down for you, Clay, believe you me. This is terribly embarrassing for us."

Clayton was sorry if he'd embarrassed them, and wanted to know if a managing angel was the same thing as a guardian angel.

"Not at all, Clay. Whole new program. End of the world and all that." Bob chuckled. "Quite a heyday up here in Heaven, this end of the world stuff. An administrative nightmare."

Clayton was very sorry about that, and asked if he could talk to God.

Bob laughed. "You Major Accounts always have the best senses of humor. That's what I love about this job, Clay. Listen, you'll have that angel in no time. Believe you me. Oh, and Clay—great move with the confession this afternoon. Negotiating for a reduced penalty, and then doubling penance for good measure. I love it! Those kinds of things are the reason I love this job."

Bob hung up. Clayton wondered, How had he known about the double penance?

Clayton's home was about two and a half miles from St. Catherine's school, which meant Clayton had to ride the school bus every morning. He resented that. Almost every one of his classmates had been walking to school by fifth grade, and the school bus was filled with brats who were three, four, even seven years younger than Clayton. It was all his parents' fault. If they had gotten a house closer to St. Catherine's, or if they had let him go to Brighton Junior High, the public school, he wouldn't be faced with the humiliation of standing at the bus stop every morning while the neighbors left for work and waved at him, more than likely thinking what a cute little boy he was, traveling with all those little children in the big, yellow school bus, wearing his dark pants, white shirt, and blue clip-on tie, like a little gentleman, isn't he? and if only our children looked so nice going to school, why it's a shame all the schools don't have dress codes.

Years later, Clayton would learn that his hometown's border was precisely 666 miles due east of the small town of Hell, Michigan. He would use that as a way to explain his difficult childhood.

This morning, though, Clayton suffered with his back to the street so he wouldn't have to see the neighbors drive by. There was no way, no way, he would go to St. Ignatius Loyola Catholic High next year. Three miles away, four more years of buses. And not just nuns in the classroom . . . priests, Jesuits. He wrinkled his nose at the thought. Jesuits, of all things.

Maybe the St. Catherine bus wouldn't come this morning. But, no, the bus would come. The bus always came. Even winter mornings when he heard on the radio that Brighton Junior High was closed for a snow day, the St. Catherine's bus would come, right on time. That school never closed. Clayton supposed that if St. Catherine's were to burn down overnight, Sister Leo

Agnes would be standing in the ruins with the class in front of her, teaching how beneficial tribulation was for the soul.

Clayton's flashes usually came when he was excited or nervous, so it surprised him that one started now, right there at the bus stop. It was a different sort of flash, with no tingle leading it in, and it was the first time a flash ever scared him. He saw all blackness, and something just a touch blacker than the blackness that said, "Pinkes, right? The one Raphael calls Pinhead? Pleased to meet you, pal." Then it ended, and he was back at the bus stop, but Clayton was shaking. He prayed by instinct, a prayer they'd had to learn in third grade: "Angel of God, my guardian dear, / To whom His love entrusts me here, / Ever this day be at my side, / To light and guard, to rule and guide, Amen."

When Clayton prayed it, he had not said "guardian," but "manager." When he realized that, he laughed, and he was still laughing when the bus came.

Clayton didn't know it, but at that very moment the Count of the Faithful, as recorded by the Population Numerics Data Base in Heaven, Management Information Systems Division, read as follows:

FAITHFUL [DEFINED IN THIS CONTEXT AS THE RAW NUMBER OF THOSE WHO HAVE BASED THEIR LIVES, HOPES, OR BELIEFS ON THE WORDS OF CLAYTON PINKES]:

ROMAN CATHOLICS:	0
PROTESTANTS:	0
ORTHODOXED, ETC.:	0
OTHER CHRISTIANS:	0
TOTAL:	0

TOTAL PERCENTAGE OF WORLD POPULATION:
0.00%

TARGET PERCENTAGE FOR URIM/THUMMIM:
2.76%

At the bottom of the screen, a priority memo from the Executive Council flashed in bright red letters:

BOB: THIS IS IT. START THE COUNTER.

Three years after that morning, this is how Clayton would explain the event of first meeting his managing angel: "I arrived at school," he would say, and Elizabeth would lean closer to him, expectant, recognizing the suppressed passion for faith in his tone and in the way his eyes stared beyond her into the past. "It was like any other morning, nothing special about it." He would leave out the part about the previous evening's phone call from Heaven, which at that time would still strike him as absurd. He would leave out the vision of blackness at the bus stop, which would still terrify him. "And as we were sitting in Religion class, an angel of the Lord appeared to me in disguise. After revealing himself to me, he commissioned me to serve as the Prophet for the End of Time." And Elizabeth would believe him.

That version of the story would be thematically true, although Clayton would be editing some of the substance. For the angel appeared to everybody, not just to Clayton, and the angel certainly never used phrases like "commissioned to serve."

Clayton took his seat amid Monday morning noise from the class. This was one of the few times during the day that the class could speak freely, and Clayton, rather than joining in, felt vaguely annoyed by the screeches of girls and the cracking voices of boys who spoke too loudly to be heard over one another. The voices echoed hollowly off the cinder-block walls, the linoleum, the ceiling. He half-hoped somebody, maybe Julie Ward, would come over to ask him what was wrong; the other half of him just wanted to be left alone to think. He didn't even acknowledge Dickie Lanpher thwapping his ear once when Dickie took his seat across the aisle from Clayton.

Precisely when the first bell rang, a tall, thin man with curly black hair and a suit coat entered the classroom door and dropped a stack of books on Sister Leo Agnes' desk. He carried a bright, obviously new, brown leather briefcase in front of him, hugging it with both arms and covering his abdomen. "I'm Mr. Kallur, and let's get one thing straight," he said. The class immediately dropped to thick silence. "A substitute teacher is not a target. A substitute teacher is not a vacation. A substitute teacher is a dedicated professional who assumes the role of a permanent teacher when the permanent teacher has taken ill. Any questions?"

Clayton had questions like, What is Sister Leo Agnes ill with? and, What did we do that you're already mad at us?, but he wasn't about to ask them, and neither was anyone else.

"Good," Mr. Kallur said, "then let's get down to business. Mr. Clayton Pinkes, please lead the class in morning prayer."

Clayton's skin buzzed, and everyone looked at him except Mr. Kallur, who stared over everyone's head, his arms before him, holding the briefcase, waiting. How did Kallur know his name? The attendance book, Clayton decided. The guy just pulled a name from the attendance book. That was it.

Clayton stood and opened with a Hail Mary, which went well even though Kallur stared straight at him the whole time, not piously facing the front-wall crucifix the way Sister Leo Agnes did. During the Our Father, however, Clayton fumbled through some of the phrases because Dickie Lanpher was whispering the recital along with him, changing words: "Our Fatter, Who fart in Heaven, hollow pee on Clay, Thy kinky come . . ." Clayton was as irritated by the attempt to trip him up as he was astonished by Dickie Lanpher's lack of respect even for prayers. Before the prayer ended, Clayton saw Julie Ward's hand shoot up.

"Mr. Kallur," she said, "I can't concentrate because

Dickie Lanpher keeps whispering dirty words during the prayers."

Clayton hardly had time to feel proud of Julie, because Mr. Kallur walked straight back to Dickie Lanpher's desk and said, "When you die, Mr. Lanpher, you'll go straight to hell."

Wow, Clayton thought, and then a few seconds later, still not sure what to think, again thought, Wow. Clayton saw Dickie Lanpher's face turn red, and Dickie Lanpher's lips pressed together tight. Clayton had never, never seen Dickie disciplined so quickly and totally—one sentence, and Dickie was wiped out. Kallur was like a bolt of lightning, a shooting bullet, an avenging angel of God. Clayton thought about that, the angel of God part. He was still thinking about it when Mr. Kallur turned to Julie Ward and said, "You'll be right there in hell with him, missy, if you think tattling is how you go about getting things done your way."

Kallur walked back to the front of the room. Clayton saw Julie starting to cry, but it was a silent cry, strong, just a couple of tears from one eye and her face like stone. Clayton wanted to reach across the aisle and touch her arm. No he didn't. Yes, yes he did, he just wouldn't. He couldn't do that.

Clayton faced forward, toward Kallur, and thought, Wow.

Kallur finished morning prayers by leading them himself, and immediately started first period, Religion class. He finally set down the shiny, leather briefcase and pulled out a worn copy of the *Baltimore Catechism*. Then he closed the briefcase again and locked it. The briefcase had a separate combination lock for each of its two gold latches. "Today we'll begin a four-day review of the *Baltimore Catechism*. We will focus on reviewing ten lessons per day, with the last day including two of the Appendix lessons. The review will take the form of recital from memory. I suggest that if you're weak in that area you take your catechisms home for study each evening. Any questions?"

Clayton wondered whether Kallur really expected questions, or if the phrase was a nervous habit.

"Good. We'll begin; no books allowed." Kallur himself opened a copy of the catechism to ask the questions. That annoyed Clayton.

"Question one: Who made us?"

God made us, the class told him.

"Question two: Who is God?"

God, everyone answered, is the Supreme Being, infinitely perfect, who made all things and keeps them in existence.

"Question three: Why did God make us?"

God made us to show forth His goodness and to share with us His everlasting happiness in Heaven.

"Question three-and-one-half: So if God is such a Supreme and Perfect Being, why does He hide from the things He created?"

"God hides from the things He created," Clayton recited from memory, although the rest of the class didn't, "because deep down, God is afraid that maybe He screwed up."

The world suddenly became eyes for Clayton: the eyes of the class, for the most part studying the linoleum; Julie Ward's eyes smiling at him as if he had pulled some joke on Kallur to avenge her; Dickie Lanpher's eyes wide, saying, Pinkes, you're a lunatic, you saw what this guy did to me! Kallur kept looking down at his catechism, back up at the class, down again, up, down. "Tell me something," he said at last. "Did this class memorize from the *New Revised Edition*, Benziger Brothers, Inc.?"

A tingling in Clayton's forearm, then, and a voice in his head not at all like Kallur's that said, "You've had twenty-six years to think about it, Pinhead. I'm just the angel, you're the prophet. Your world, not mine; your choice, not mine. Is it the End of Time?"

The flash ended in less than a second, and the classroom door opened. The principal, Sister Assumpta, walked in, her hand on the shoulder of a short, skinny kid with dark skin and black hair. He looked Indian, Clayton thought, or maybe very, very Italian. "Excuse me for interrupting, Mr. Kallur," Sister Assumpta said. Kallur looked guilty; he lowered his head a bit and once again picked up the leather briefcase to cover his abdomen. "Class, this is a new student," said Sister Assumpta. "Paolo Diosana. His family just moved into the area, and he'll be joining us to finish up the school year."

At that point, Dickie Lanpher groaned aloud. At first Clayton thought it was another prank, but when he looked he saw that Dickie's face was pale. Dickie jumped from his desk and ran toward the door, saying a quick "Excuse me" to Sister Assumpta as he pushed past her into the hall. Clayton heard him heaving in the hallway, and cringed. Vomiting in school, which Dickie had just done, was an embarrassment Clayton wouldn't wish even on his worst enemy, which Dickie Lanpher was.

"Oh, dear," Sister Assumpta said before she and Mr. Kallur ran into the hall. "He must have the same flu Sister Leo Agnes came down with."

Normally there would have been a commotion from the students in a situation like this one, but the last twenty minutes had been far too strange for anyone in the class to even think of reacting. The only movement was that of Paolo Diosana's casual saunter down the aisle to Dickie Lanpher's abandoned desk. After sitting, Diosana leaned across to Clayton and said, "Well, I guess this spot is available."

Clayton looked at him and said nothing. Diosana smiled. "Loosen up, Pinhead. You ain't seen nothin' yet."

Which is the full story of Clayton Pinkes' first encounter with his managing angel.

TWO:
Seven Years Earlier, and
Someplace Entirely Different

Roland, who did all the cooking and cleaning, set aside his mop and greeted Henri Elobert at the breakfast table. As usual.

"Good morning, Henri," he said with his bright smile and empty eyes, eyes which never seemed to fully connect and left Henri with the feeling Roland was studying his neck.

"Good morning, Roland." Henri stood, stretched upward, and clapped a hand on the janitor's shoulder, returning the smile. It was a ritual, this morning greeting; Henri, who had only six years of age, liked Roland very much, almost as much as he liked old Dr. Elobert himself. The two of them, Henri and Roland, had performed this greeting ritual for as long as Henri could remember. The few times Henri had stayed in his bed chambers sick, perhaps with influenza or a sore throat, Dr. Rousas had been in an uproar the next day, complaining that Roland kept walking away from his daily chores to stare down the cafeteria hallway, waiting.

"Beautiful day, no?" Roland asked.

"*Oui, c'est belle.*" Of course, Henri did not know whether the day was beautiful or not; he rarely was allowed outside the compound, and never by himself. But this was the way he and Roland always did the greeting.

"It does not seem as if it will rain, does it?"

"Not at all, Roland."

"No, it certainly does not."

"Certainly not."

Roland took his mop and slushed a final wide arc across the red and black mottled tiles of the cafeteria. He then proceeded to wash his hands in the side-wall sink before preparing Henri's breakfast. "So," said Roland, as always, "how is all the studying?"

"Mesmerizing."

Roland nodded, and said, "Good, good." Henri had always been curious what it was Roland thought "mesmerizing" meant.

"Oh," Roland said, a very dim glimmer coming to those absent eyes, "Dr. Rousas was looking around for Dr. Elobert this morning. Have you seen Dr. Elobert? Dr. Rousas looked very upset."

A tautology, Henri thought, to say Dr. Rousas looked upset. He realized their greeting ritual had just been skewed by a variable, and a variable introduced by Dr. Rousas at that.

Henri felt uncomfortable. He, much like Roland, preferred his days to be typical: rise at 7:00 and wash himself clean; eat breakfast at 7:30 after greeting Roland; practice math studies with Dr. Rousas from 8:00 to 10:30; do microbiological and biochemical lessons with Dr. Bernardin from 11:00 to 13:00; eat lunch from 13:00 to 14:00 with Dr. Elobert—kind, old Dr. Elobert, whose second name was the same as Henri's—and then go with Dr. Elobert right into lessons on microphysics and applications; and finally, from 16:30 to 19:00, in with Dr. LeFavre to do studies in astrophysics and cosmology.

After that, dinner with the doctors, discussion of the day's studies, and back to his sleeping chambers by 21:00.

That had been Henri's typical schedule for as many of his six years as he could remember. Today, he feared, was not going to be typical, and that made him nervous.

After breakfast he walked to Dr. Rousas' study room. Dr. Elobert was there. The two doctors were yelling at each other, so they did not notice right away that Henri had entered.

"If you have lost faith in the project, just say so, and you are free to resign!" That was Dr. Elobert.

"I have not lost faith in it!" Dr. Rousas shouted back. "I am simply relating to you the concerns of the Société. We have worked for three years here, and there is concern that we will never generate revenue to justify the investment."

"This is long-term!" Dr. Elobert punched his fist on Dr. Rousas' desk. "They *knew* results would be a decade in coming."

Dr. Rousas began pacing in front of the chalkboard. He ran his hand over the bald spot in the middle of his head. "We cost a lot, Javier," he said in a smoother tone. "A great deal."

That was when Dr. Rousas saw Henri. He stopped pacing. Dr. Elobert also turned and looked. Henri wondered if it was bad not to have told them he had been standing there. He was going to say he was sorry. Dr. Elobert walked over and put his hand on Henri's shoulder, so Henri realized that he was not in trouble.

"Generate revenue," Dr. Elobert said to Dr. Rousas in a quite angry voice. "Fine. If that will appease them, fine." Then he said to Henri, "Sit down, please."

"I have my mathematical studies right now, Doctor."

"Not today, child. Today we generate revenue."

Henri did not know what that meant, but he was too anxious about the sudden schedule change to ask any questions. Dr. Rousas sat down also and rested his chin on his hand.

"Fiber optics, Henri. Laser communication. Have we discussed the topic?"

"The doctors have discussed it often at dinner," Henri said. "I have never been asked to join the discussion."

For the next two hours, Dr. Elobert explained the nature of a laser source transmitting photonic signals through the core of glass fibers. He detailed the process of signal encoding by opto-electronic controller hardware, and final reception of the signals by a similar opto-electronic decoder.

"The problem is attenuation; the laser signal grows weaker over long distances. Solve the problem, Henri. How can the glass fiber be modified to produce reliable transmission over great distances?"

"If you please," said Henri, "why would there be a need to transmit over long distances? No point inside the compound is more than a kilometer in distance from any other point."

Drs. Rousas and Elobert glanced at each other.

"We work with a theoretical situation, Henri. Solve the problem."

Henri nodded. "Then if you please, Dr., I believe you wish to first consider not glass purity, but a flaw in your initial structure. You do not want to use simple laser light broadcast."

Henri spent the next three hours explaining how a light-emitting diode would be preferable to pure laser, sending a less focused but more stable photonic signal with decreased attenuation, provided that 1) the fiber core be increased from Dr. Elobert's theoretical 8 microns to Henri's suggested 50 microns, and 2) the light emitting diodes broadcast at a wavelength from 800 to 850 nanometers. This did not mean, of course, that laser light was not an option, or that glass purity need not be improved. This was simply Henri's quickest solution to the attenuation problem.

They worked through lunch. Dr. Elobert took copious notes. Dr. Rousas checked Henri's math but found no errors. By 16:30, Henri had countered all their arguments and constructed on the chalkboard a practical schematic of a LED source fiber optic communication system, along with supporting equations. He felt very hungry.

Dr. Elobert thrust his notes into Dr. Rousas' hands. "There," he said, and Henri could tell Dr. Elobert was still angry after all these hours. "Tell your precious Société to sell this to Bell or Corning or AT&T or whomever the hell they want. It is worth a few million, I suppose."

Dr. Rousas was pale.

"If you please," said Henri, "could we return to our schedule tomorrow?"

Dr. Elobert smiled and rubbed his hand through Henri's hair. Henri felt warm. He really liked Dr. Elobert and was distressed that the doctor was so angry today.

"Yes, Henri," Dr. Elobert said. "Tomorrow we will return to schedule."

Henri smiled now, too, and he felt calmer than he had all day. Perhaps it was not right to feel confused by unscheduled changes. Perhaps, like the laser light, his own tight focus would cause attenuation.

But Henri's whole world covered just a few square kilometers. He did not need to travel as far as beams of light.

THREE:
Back to 1976 Again
with Clayton and His Angel

For four weeks after he first arrived, well into the beginning of June, Paolo Diosana said nothing to Clayton Pinkes or, as far as Clayton could tell, to anyone. Outside at recess, Diosana would stand alone, bouncing a small, blue rubber ball against the red bricks of St. Catherine's school, catching the ball with one hand, the other hand shoved always in his pocket. Clayton watched him do that for a few days, debating whether or not to go and talk to him, and always decided against it.

"What do you think about the new kid?" Dickie Lanpher asked Clayton once. Dickie had become a lot nicer to Clayton lately. While Dickie was out ill, Clayton had yelled at Ben Raymond and Mike Delveccio for referring to Dickie as "The Puke-faced Wonder" and "King Vomit." The story had gotten back to Dickie.

"Paolo Diosana?" Clayton asked.

"Only new kid we've had all year. What do you think?"

Clayton shrugged. "How'm I supposed to know? How's anybody supposed to?"

"Yeah. Not a talker." A burst of shouts from the grass playing field made Dickie turn his head. "Hey, they're playing Smear the Queer with the Football. The lunch mother must not be paying attention. You wanna play Smear the Queer with the Football?"

Clayton was still watching Paolo Diosana. Paolo looked in their direction just then, and Clayton smiled and waved his hand over his head. Paolo nodded once and returned to his endless ball-bouncing.

"You wanna play Smear the Queer with the Football?" Dickie persisted.

"Yeah," said Clayton.

That afternoon in Social Studies—Sister Leo Agnes's flu was still dragging on, and Mr. Kallur seemed to have taken on the status of permanent substitute—the class began a review study of the Civil War. "It was a war that divided this great nation in two," said Mr. Kallur. He hugged his leather briefcase, paced around the room. "Brother against brother, father against son, testing the strength of the noble experiment called Democracy. By the end, it had cost the lives of tens of thousands of Americans."

Clayton was writing "tens of thousands of Americans" in his notebook when he heard Paolo Diosana say, "Hundreds of thousands."

Kallur heard, too. He walked to the front of Diosana's aisle. "Pardon me?" he said, in a way Clayton knew really meant Paolo should be the one asking pardon.

"Hundreds of thousands," Paolo said.

Kallur's lips were a tight grin. "I heard what you said. I was alluding to the fact that your comments weren't offered in a way standard to this classroom's rules."

Paolo rested his chin on one hand and limply raised the other arm. "Hundreds of thousands," he said. "Five hundred twenty-nine thousand two hundred and sixty-eight."

Kallur sliced off the rising chuckles by cutting a swath with his eyes from the door to the windows. Then he set down his briefcase, tugged at the elbow of each sleeve on his suit jacket, and leaned forward with his palms flat on the front desk of the row. "You're a Civil War enthusiast, Mr. Diosana?"

Paolo sat up straight and focused his eyes directly on Kallur's. It was the first thing Clayton had seen Paolo fully focused on since he'd arrived, except for that little blue ball he always tossed against the side of the school building. "I follow wars in general, Mr. Kallur."

"World War I?"

"One hundred sixteen thousand five hundred and forty-two Americans dead."

"World War II?"

"Four hundred five thousand four hundred and twenty."

"The Vijayanagar battle at Talikota?"

Paolo Diosana opened his mouth as if he were going to answer, but after a sidewise glance at Clayton he sat back and dropped his focus from Kallur. Mr. Kallur remained leaning on the desk, smiling, then broke to continue his lecture on the Civil War. Every few minutes, after stating some fact, he would say, "Am I right about that, Mr. Diosana?" or "Please correct me if I'm wrong, Mr. Diosana." But Paolo seemed untouched by the sarcasm; he had again withdrawn into himself, as if nothing had happened. But right before the end of the class, Paolo slipped Clayton a note that read:

TROOPS PRESENT, BATTLE AT TALIKOTA—
FOOT SOLDIERS: 703,129
MOUNTED SOLDIERS: 32,612
ELEPHANTS: 551
PROSTITUTES: 12,483

Clayton looked over to see if Paolo was kidding, but Paolo sat slumped and disinterested as always. Clayton slipped him a note that said, "Don't worry, you're smarter than him," but Paolo Diosana didn't answer.

Clayton kissed his mother—on the cheek, quickly—and called "G'night" to his father. His father grunted from behind the sports section. His mother said, "Good night. Sleep tight. Don't let the bedbugs bite."

"Clever, Mom," Clayton said, and went upstairs. He knelt by the side of his bed and slowly, word by word, went through a Hail Mary, an Our Father, and the Act of Contrition. Then he added, "If you really are my managing angel, appear to me now." He opened his eyes and looked around the bedroom. Off-white walls, two throw rugs, a bookshelf half filled with Hardy Boys mysteries, no angel. "God," he said, "if I really do have a managing angel, show me some sign . . ." He paused, because it seemed more respectful to give God extra time to answer " . . . *now*." A bare ceiling light bulb, the closet door, the window that looked out over the slanted roof of the garage. Silence.

Clayton waited about three minutes more. He stood up and took off all his clothes. After he'd climbed into bed he got up again and put on his underwear, just in case a sign or an angel were late in coming. How long did prayers take to travel? Ten minutes later he took the underwear off again, figuring God knew what he looked like naked anyway. He lay awake. "C'mon, Paolo," he said. "Please."

Half an hour later he was still awake. Nobody was coming. No signs, no angels. Bust. Zilch. Harassed by Heaven and then ignored. Fine. Okay.

In the boredom of waiting, he started playing one of the stories in his mind, one of the night stories. It started playing itself, really, but he closed his eyes, put his hands under the bedcovers, and let it play.

In this night story, there's been a nuclear war. Somehow only he has survived. He's never worked out the details on how that could be. But the school is in rubble. He's alone, except—yes, he hears crying, over there behind that pile of rubble. He investigates and finds Julie Ward. Her brown curls are stringy, a mess, her face is dirty, and her shirt is torn and shows part of her bra. Her eyes are blue. He helps her up, he is strong and reassures her, and he takes her to a place where they can have shelter for a while; he finds food—Clayton rushes the story at this point—and the first evening it's cold, so they share a blanket together. "You've always been special to me," Julie says. "And now we're together. Clayton, could you hold me?" Clayton holds her and feels her arms, her legs. "And kiss me?" she adds, and he feels her lips, her hands touching him, her naked skin, and et cetera and et cetera until Clayton is alone again back in his room and sweating, rolling over and feeling guilty, believing he is sick in his head somehow, thinking God must despise sick people like Clayton Pinkes.

At recess Clayton walked right between the brick wall of the school building and Paolo Diosana. He snatched the little blue ball out of the air. Paolo crossed his arms and smiled.

"You don't talk much," Clayton said.

Paolo nodded.

"People aren't gonna like you. Why don't you talk much?"

"I don't have a lot to say."

"Bull. You're smarter than Kallur, and he always has a lot to say."

"He does have a lot to say."

"Yeah, he does."

Paolo reached in his trouser pocket and pulled out another blue ball. He walked a few steps down from Clayton and went back to bouncing the ball against the school building.

"But you're smarter than Kallur," Clayton said.

"Yes, I'm smarter."

"But you don't say anything."

"I'm quiet. I'm smart and I'm quiet."

"Yeah," said Clayton.

Paolo rolled his eyes and stuffed the second ball back into his pocket. "This chat is starting to sound like Hemingway dialog."

Clayton couldn't think of anything to say to that. He didn't know what Hemingway dialog was.

"I'm quiet because if I start talking, Pinhead, I sound like a maniac. Ideas come at light speed and I'm a barrage of non sequiturs oscillating between the mundane and the bizarre. I turn hyperkinetic, I make remarks too sophisticated to be grasped by healthy people, and I sacrifice the James-Dean-slash-Gandhi facade of cool and wise for a vaudevillian charade."

Clayton couldn't think of much to say to that, either, so he said, "Are you an angel?"

Paolo Diosana said, "Yeah."

Well, thought Clayton. That's what he'd wanted to know, and now he'd asked it. Well. How about that? Well.

"Which angel?" Clayton asked. "Gabriel?"

Paolo's body jerked a little. "Oh, please," he said. "Gabriel? Am I that bad at this? How obnoxious do I look? One lousy luck-of-the-draw two thousand years ago on the Mary Had A Little Lamb shift, and Gabriel hasn't let anybody forget it since. Every time he walks into a room it's, 'Hail, guys, are you all full of grace?' and 'Blessed art thou, old sport.'" Paolo sneered. "You know, we hold an annual convention in Stockholm, and each year Gabriel jumps on a bicycle in Oslo to make the trip, and he goes out of his way to cut through the city of Hell, Norway, just so he can arrive at the hotel and say, 'I went through Hell to get here, ha ha.'" Paolo Diosana snorted and leaned a shoulder against the brick wall. "And each year, everybody laughs. Am I Gabriel? Spare me, Pinhead."

Clayton decided that Paolo was right: he did sound

like a maniac once he got talking. "Are you the Arch-angel Michael, then?"

Paolo's face changed, just for a second. His eyes widened at the same moment his eyebrows lowered. He shifted a glance quickly to the left, as if someone were watching, and bit his lower lip. "No," he said, "not Michael. I'm Raphael, okay? My name is Raphael."

Raphael sounded like an angel's name. Clayton thought he'd heard it before but wasn't sure. "How do I know—" Clayton stopped, because if Paolo were a real angel he wouldn't want to insult him.

"Know what?" Paolo was smirking.

"That you're not the devil?"

Paolo laughed. "There is no devil. Demons are just a thought experiment used to shift blame. Besides, who needs demons?" Paolo reached out and patted him gently on the side of his face. "You've got us. You've got angels."

Then there was a scream from the grass playing field, and Dickie Lanpher's voice yelling, "Oh, shit! Oh, shit!" A group of the boys who had been playing Smear the Queer with the Football were gathered in a circle, and Dickie was lying on the ground next to the loose ball.

By the time Clayton got to the field, the lunch mother had also gotten there. "Stay away from him," she said. "Nobody move him."

"My shoulder, oh shit!" Dickie kept yelling. His arm was twisted the wrong way, his elbow forward although he was lying face up. Dickie was crying.

"Now you don't need to curse and swear!" the lunch mother hollered. "Who did it? Who tackled him?"

"I didn't do nothin'!" Ben Raymond yelled. "I just tackled him normal! He fell wrong, it's his fault!"

"Oh, Jesus," Dickie said, a lot quieter because he had looked down and noticed his elbow facing up.

The lunch mother grabbed Ben Raymond's shirt collar and shouted back, "You do not talk to me in that tone of voice! Don't you talk to me like that!"

Clayton knelt beside Dickie. "You'll be all right, Dickie. You'll be okay."

"Hey, Clayton," Dickie said, and then he glanced down at his elbow again. "Isn't that weird? Shit, that's weird."

The lunch mother hauled Clayton back by yanking his arm. "I said to stay away from him and not touch him!" She turned back to Ben Raymond and said, "My job is to watch all of you, and now look what's happened. How do you think this makes me look?"

"I didn't do nothin'!" Ben Raymond yelled again.

Paolo Diosana had slipped in at some point. He kneeled next to Dickie. "How's it going?" Paolo said to him. "Been a rotten month, no?"

Dickie closed his eyes and inhaled in short gasps.

"Don't sweat, Dickie. Be glib. All the best heroes are glib when they're in pain."

"I don't know what glib means," Dickie said. "Oh, shit."

"Glib? Uh, glib?" Paolo rolled his eyes upward, as if he were reading the definition of "glib" off the top of his eyes sockets. "James Bond is glib when they're shooting at him. Spiderman is glib when he fights Doc Ock." He looked back down at Dickie. "Yeah, Jesus was glib, hanging on the cross saying, 'Hey, can't a guy get some water up here?' and 'Where's Mom? Anybody see Mom?' "

Dickie made a chuckle that turned into another sob. "Guy walks into a bar," Dickie managed to say, "and asks, 'Do you serve Italians here?' "

"That's the spirit," Paolo said. The lunch mother was still ten feet away arguing with Ben Raymond. Clayton wanted to yell at her. Shouldn't she get the school nurse? Call an ambulance?

Clayton looked back at Paolo and saw him rolling up the long sleeves of his dress shirt. That image stayed with him for years—Paolo slowly folding up one sleeve, just above the elbow, then turning to roll up the other, so concentrated on that one act that you would have believed it was the single most important thing that had ever occurred on the face of the Earth. The gesture first struck Clayton as extremely adult, way more adult than anyone on the grass playing field that day, including the lunch mother. But immediately after that first impression, the gesture didn't seem to have anything to do with acting adult. Paolo's intense fix on those sleeves, the calm importance of that act to Paolo, meant something about believing and about really really knowing what to do when nothing could be done. Not a "Well, I guess I'll do this" sort of knowing, but an "I must do this" sort. For Clayton, Paolo's focus on rolling up his sleeves eclipsed in importance even the act of healing that Paolo performed on Dickie's shoulder and arm.

The lunch mother finally saw Paolo beside Dickie, and repeated her order for everyone to leave him alone. She yanked at the back of Paolo's shirt collar, but small, short, skinny Paolo Diosana didn't jerk backwards the slightest bit. She yanked harder, and this time she managed to rip part of the collar from its seam. Paolo reached down and took hold of Dickie's arm. He made a quick half-twist of the arm, then shoved forward. Clayton heard the faint popping sound. Paolo kneaded Dickie's shoulder through the shirt.

"Jesus, that feels all right," Dickie said.

Paolo glanced back at the lunch mother. "Take two aspirin and call her a bitch in the morning." Then he looked over to Clayton. "That's all right to say in the 1970's, isn't it? I mean, it's a little sexist, but it's glib."

Paolo walked away, back toward the school. The lunch mother was yelling after him, then yelling at Ben Raymond again when she got no response from Paolo, then yelling at Dickie to stay down and not move, even though Dickie was swinging his arm around and saying, "It's okay. It feels great. It was just popped out. He popped it back in."

Clayton stayed on the field for a minute, and then

he went up toward the school building. He found Paolo crouched down around the corner by the side of the building that faced St. Catherine's church itself. Paolo's knees were bent up to his chin. His arms were wrapped in front of his legs, making him look like a tight, little ball up against the brick wall.

"I believe in you now," Clayton said.

"Yeah."

"You really are an angel."

"Christ," said Paolo, "I hate theatrics."

Clayton lost sight of Paolo after school. There was the normal rush across the parking lot by the older students, Clayton standing with all the younger ones waiting for buses, and although he scanned most of the faces as they passed, he missed Paolo. Of course, an angel could dematerialize, right? An angel could step around a corner, go *poof*, like that, and be back wherever it was angels went during their off-hours. Places like Heaven, or limbo. Or Stockholm, for conventions.

Clayton decided he didn't know a heck of a lot about angels.

He took a seat in the back of the bus behind two fourth-grade girls who whispered and giggled the entire way home. The more he tried to ignore their noise, the more it was the only thing he heard. Whisper, giggle, whisper-whisper giggle. He punched the back of their seat once, but they must have decided it was accidental and went right on.

He got off at his stop and tried to walk casually away from the bus, pretending to himself that it was just a coincidence the thing was there at the same time he was getting home. He waited for the bus to turn the next corner before he crossed the street to his house. There was a girl's bike leaning against the pine tree by the righthand side of the garage, and Julie Ward was standing in front of the garage door.

"I beat you home," she said. She giggled.

Clayton stood there. Despite all the words in the English language, every word he'd learned from the time he first spoke to the present, he couldn't think of a way to put any of them together to say anything intelligent. This was the absolutely most awkward occurrence of his thirteen years of life.

"Well, hi," Julie said, and she stared down at his feet.

Good, that was a good lead-in, a perfect way to start. "Hi," Clayton said back.

"I hope you don't mind me coming over."

"No," said Clayton. "Not at all. No, not at all." He wanted to be sure she knew he really didn't mind, so he said again, "Not at all." Then he asked, "How'd you know where I live?"

Julie looked up and talked fast. "Oh, I asked Rhonda to find out from Gary Roach and Gary asked Tom because Tom said he came over here to play last year, and so he told me."

"Oh," said Clayton. "That was a good way to find out." Then they said nothing for half a minute.

"It's a nice house. It's big."

"Yeah," said Clayton. "It's even bigger inside." Stupid. Why was he always saying such stupid things?

"It's a colonial, right? My folks have a split-level. Except it's yellow, not white."

Clayton had no idea if the house was a colonial or not. He looked across the street at some of the other houses. He supposed his house really was a little bigger, but not by much.

"You know, you've always been special to me," Julie said.

Clayton wiped sweat off his palms on the back of his trousers. He kept his hands behind his back.

"And now we're together," Julie said. Her eyes looked funny. She licked her lips. "Clayton, could you hold me?"

Clayton needed to clasp his hands in front of his trousers. Julie took hold of each of his wrists and gently put his arms around her waist. Clayton looked toward the front door of the house to see if his mother was looking out.

"And kiss me?" She put her lips against his, and Clayton felt all of his muscles shaking. He was afraid he must look as quivery as images on television look when both the stove and the vacuum cleaner were running. He closed his eyes and tried to bring on one of the flashes. He would have really, really appreciated one of the flashes just then. But there was nothing, except Julie's tongue starting to brush against his lips. Clayton couldn't open his own lips and couldn't even move his tongue.

She pulled her face back from his, but she kept every inch of the front of her body pressed against every inch of the front of his. He needed to adjust himself, she must have been noticing that, and he could think of nothing else.

"Just think," Julie said. "If there were a nuclear war and we were the only survivors, this could go on and on and on." Then she let go of him and laughed—not giggles, pure howls, and tears coming to her eyes. Clayton no longer needed to adjust himself. Undiluted panic did that.

Julie sat down next to the pine trees, practically weeping into the sleeves of her sweater. She stopped once and looked up at him. The eyes were green. Julie's eyes had always been blue. But Julie's eyes were green. She started laughing all over again. "Oh, God," she said, "poor Pinhead. My poor, little Pinhead."

Clayton felt his mind creeping back to him. "Paolo?" he said. "Raphael?"

Julie was obviously straining to hold back more laughter. "I was going to rip a hole in my shirt so you could see the bra strap, but I thought, no, that's overkill." Then laughter again, and, "My poor Pinhead." The person who wasn't, after all, Julie Ward disappeared. Poof. Like that.

Clayton looked toward the sky. "Paolo!" he shouted. "Raphael! You . . . you . . ."

What do you call an angel when you're angry?

Clayton went inside. He walked past his mother without saying hello. He brushed his teeth, flossed, brushed them again, and slept fully clothed that night.

This is what a night of sleep is like when you know there are angels, you suspect there aren't demons, you hope God is paying attention and also hope He isn't, and you wonder who's on your side:

At 10:00 P.M. you kiss your mother good night and she says, "Say your prayers, honey." You kiss her again and she looks at you funny. You pull down the top of the sports section so you can look your father in the eye and say, "Sleep good, Pop," and he says, "Good night, champ," as if you both always did that and said that.

You wonder as you walk up the stairs what your parents were like when they were teenagers, and you realize how little you know about them, even though your mother always tells stories about Cousin Whozit and Uncle Somebody. You would feel hard-pressed and stupid if anyone ever asked you to repeat even one of those stories.

Then you climb into bed. You've taken off only your shoes. By 11:30 P.M. you haven't even moved. Your eyes are still open. You keep listening for sounds, and it worries you because the only ones you hear are the same old creaking of the house settling in and one or two cars turning the corner down the road from your home. You think about your house being a colonial. If you ever buy a house, it won't be a colonial, and it won't be a split-level either.

You drift off for just a moment. You wake suddenly, because you had started to dream. You feel naked. It's June, you're sweating from blankets and a full set of clothes, but you're naked, you are. But it's not your fault.

You drift off again, snap awake again. Finally your body just gives up; your mind doesn't bother with any more dreams, because by now it knows you won't get the message anyway.

You're going to beat up Paolo Diosana in the morning.

FOUR:
Still 1976, But Back to
Someplace Entirely Different

Henri Elobert had only thirteen years of age—many,
many years fewer than the others—but he felt confidence when he announced toward the end of dinner
that there were certainly more than six people on the
face of the Earth.

Henri began to categorize their responses.

Dr. Rousas dropped his demitasse. Very sloppy for
a mathematician, Henri thought, but then Dr. Rousas'
mathematics had taken a turn toward the sloppy recently.
The other doctors responded in ways more appropriate
to their specialties: Dr. LeFavre, the astrophysicist and
cosmologist, stared toward the ceiling as if toward his
stars, pretending to ponder some distant abstraction; Dr.
Bernardin, microbiologist and biochemist, examined the
tips of his fingers, absorbed by some minute detail; and
Dr. Elobert—the kind old doctor whose second name
was the same as Henri's—smiled wide.

Henri was intrigued; every response was predictable,
but every response was also grander, larger, more

exaggerated than Henri had expected. Of course, the hypothesis he had just proposed was itself quite grand— more than six people on the Earth. Their reactions indicated one of two things: either most of the doctors had been working on a similar hypothesis and were upset that Henri had beaten them to the discovery; or all of them knew already the More-Than-Six hypothesis, and Henri was not supposed to have found out.

Yes, the second one, that was it. It made more sense. In the past he had caught the doctors withholding scientific information for the sake of seeing if Henri would discover the information on his own.

At that moment Roland waddled in from the back kitchen, apparently attracted by the sound of Dr. Rousas' shattered demitasse. He began mopping up the espresso spill. Roland was the only one (except for Henri, of course) who was not called "Doctor." Roland had never had a specialty, and his mind was too slow to grasp even the beginning concepts of science and learning.

"Roland," Henri said, because he wanted the final reaction to complete his data, "there are more than six people on the face of the Earth."

Roland looked surprised—well, as surprised as his dull-green eyes had ever been able to make him look. There was a brief flash of understanding, and then emptiness again. Roland nodded. "Shall I make more dinner, then?"

"No thank you, Roland, I do not believe they will stop by this evening," Henri said.

"Then I shall bring the dinner cheeses." Roland waddled back to the kitchen.

"Explain the basis of your theory," Dr. Elobert said gently. Henri saw the glances the others gave Dr. Elobert. LeFavre and Bernardin were angry, as if they wanted the whole discussion dropped. Rousas looked panicked.

"As yet it is only a hypothesis," Henri said. "The only evidence I have is circumstantial. Questions, really.

Where do those foods come from that are not native to the island? How was this compound built when none of us seems adept at complex mechanical construction?" He watched them carefully for the next question. "Where do the doctors go when they disappear at irregular intervals, six or seven days away every three months?"

Roland brought the dinner cheeses. Dr. Rousas took several more slices than was his custom. LeFavre and Bernardin both waved the plate away when Roland offered it—more behavioral changes.

"Go on," Dr. Elobert said to Henri.

"I move my thoughts from the macro level to the micro level at this point, and employ the genetic training Dr. Bernardin has provided me." Bernardin shook his head when Henri said that. "The continuation of a species depends on the transmission of genetic information in some manner. A number of microorganisms perform this feat by doubling their genes and splitting. Vegetation often does it by receiving haploid input from a member of its own species and distributing seeds. I believe these two acts hold the key."

"Genetic information," Rousas said through a mouthful of cheese.

"Indeed," said Henri. "As far as I can determine, those life forms perform according to a natural law with which we ourselves should also be expected to comply. Would you agree?"

No one at the table looked willing to agree. Henri sat silently for a moment, trying to determine when the best time would be to show them the preliminary sketches. Soon, but not just yet.

"I have done some initial studies in karyotyping each of our genetic structures. I admit I was confused at the beginning because I only used hair follicles from myself and compared them with those of Dr. Elobert. There were numerous similarities, and I attributed any differences to natural mutation. But then I took hair follicles from *you*, Dr. Rousas"—Rousas placed a flat palm over the bald spot in the middle of his head— "as well as from the other doctors. I followed Roland around on his cleaning duties one morning and retrieved the hairs from your pillows and brushes."

"Cunning," said Dr. Bernardin, and Henri could tell he was not pleased.

"I performed another round of karyotype comparisons. The diversity was . . . intriguing. There seems no way that all of us could have developed from the same genetic source."

Dr. Elobert set his hand on Henri's shoulder. Henri felt warm. Dr. Elobert was the only one who ever touched him. "Then from what genetic source do we originate, Henri?"

"For God's sake, Elobert," Dr. Rousas said. He stood from the table and thrust his serviette onto his plate. "Give it a rest, no?"

"No," Dr. Elobert said. "Henri?"

Henri felt a prickling at the base of his neck. They were upset. Not Dr. Elobert, who seemed pleased, and not Roland, who was quintessentially oblivious. But the three others. Angry for some reason. All his life he had wondered how they could become so easily upset and unbalanced.

"I do not know," Henri said. "It may all be very silly. I have pursued wild tangents before."

"Indeed," said Dr. Bernardin.

"But I do have preliminary sketches."

"Indeed," Bernardin said again, a little softer, leaning back in his chair.

Henri pulled the three folded sheets from his trouser pocket. "Hypothesis One," he said while unfolding the first sheet. The paper showed a sketch of Dr. Rousas splitting into two sections. A thin mucous membrane connected the left half of Rousas to the right half across a split that originated at his bald skull and continued to his midtorso. "According to my first hypothesis, the genetic material in all of our cells reduplicates itself and causes us to split apart and form two new organisms." He passed the paper around the table. Dr. Elobert chuckled and passed it on. Dr. Rousas held the sketch a bit longer than the others. He pursed his lips as he stared at it.

No, Henri thought. Not that one, then.

"Second hypothesis. External insemination." This sketch showed Doctors LeFavre and Bernardin, both naked, both apparently urinating on one another's genitals.

"Disgusting," said LeFavre, but he was smiling, softening to Henri's speculations. "However, it is an amazing likeness to Dr. Bernardin."

"That one is based on my discovery that our testes contain haploid cells which can be emitted either involuntarily or at will."

Dr. Rousas leaned forward. "How in the world did you determine—" He sat back and crossed his arms. "Never mind," he said. "I'd prefer not to know."

Dr. LeFavre lit a cigarette. "Tell me, Dr. Elobert. How far will you let this go? He is obviously grasping blindly. I see no scientific method to his extrapolations. His study was independent and we have seen no notes on it."

Of course there was a process behind Henri's conclusions. Henri could have produced it. He could have gone through painstaking explanations of his isolation of chromosomal pairs and his past year of failed attempts at rearranging them. And his success last week. All of it. But they already knew. They all knew things they were not telling him. All his life, *he* had been willing to show them anything they had not yet known. They had always been very enthusiastic about his discoveries, things like the asymmetry of subatomic particles, the stellar evolution theories, even as far back as his fiber optics analysis seven years ago. They had been quite pleased with those studies. But what did they share with Henri anymore?

This hypothesis was different. They *knew* the answer and were not telling him.

So the informal presentation he now gave had nothing to do with an evaluation of his scientific process for testing the More-Than-Six people hypothesis. It was an evaluation of *them*, the doctors themselves. He was not presenting an experiment this evening, he was conducting one.

They had finished passing around his first two sketches, and by now even Bernardin and Rousas were chuckling. Relief. A spirit of levity. A feeling that Henri was quaint in his attempts. A superiority that smiles downward, patronizing.

Henri showed the final sketch. Total silence at the table, and even Dr. Elobert lost his smile.

Henri knew, then, that this was the one.

"Note that in my third picture I hypothesize the existence of an alternate configuration of the body. I've emphasized the mammary glands that are vestigial in our bodies, assuming that offspring are fed directly from that source. I've removed the standard penis and replaced it with a simple opening for insemination. I've widened the hips for easier passage of offspring from an internal environment to the external world. I've removed all nonessential bodily hair based on assumptions of the hormones produced within this particular genetic extrapolation."

Dr. LeFavre crushed out his cigarette without taking his eyes off the sketch. The others sat motionless. Dr. Elobert—kind, old Dr. Elobert—let one corner of his mouth turn upward to a half-smile. Henri recognized that. It was an indication that Henri had made an accomplishment. It was pride.

"Of course," Henri said, "the length of the head hair is a bit of personal license. A light yellow color, hanging past the shoulders. A preference only."

Henri gathered the sketches and quickly excused himself to his sleeping chambers. He wished the doctors a good night.

❖   ❖   ❖

Henri's chamber, like the chambers of all the doctors and Roland, had no windows. In fact, the only windows in the entire compound were the two plate glasses in the compound's foyer. Those faced south. Henri was allowed to go outside daily now, as long as he kept within one hundred meters of the compound. There were tall cliffs to the east and west of the compound. Henri had long ago tired of squinting to make out the vegetation at the top of the cliffs. Whenever he went outside he preferred to stare quietly over the endless water.

Endless? Henri wondered about that now, lying on his cot in the blackness of the room. Could there not be other islands on the planet? Dr. Bernardin's specialty: cosmology. Earth had a 6,378.203 kilometer equatorial radius, a 6,356.7189 kilometer polar radius. That made it relatively spherical, nearly 317 million square kilometers of surface area, of which this island, which the doctors occasionally called Kerguélen, occupied less than 75. Another piece of evidence, perhaps? Why not simply call the island "Earth" if it were unique to the planet? There was plenty of surface area left to hold other islands. So question number one: Were there other islands on Earth? And question number two: Was there life on other islands?

They knew. Not Roland, but the others. They knew. That was as big a mystery as any of the others. Why would they not tell him? And if they withheld that information, what else had he not been told? Really, *really*, it came down to whether or not he could believe anything they said.

But he could believe Dr. Elobert. He cared for Dr. Elobert. And they were genetically closer to one another than to any of the others. Did genes form a bond like that? On the macro level? Did a euglena have instinctive attraction to its other half?

He fell asleep wondering these things. He awoke

hours later, in the middle of the night, when he heard his name called from the darkness.

"Henri Elobert."

Henri sat up. He slid his hand against the cool concrete wall until he found the intercom button to Dr. Elobert's chambers. He pushed the button and said, "Yes?"

A few moments passed, and he heard Dr. Elobert's voice. "Yes?"

"Dr. Elobert?"

"Yes. Henri?"

"Yes." A pause. "Yes?"

"What?"

"Did you call?"

"No, Henri. You called. What is it?"

Henri had no idea what it was. Only Dr. Elobert had ever called him over the chamber intercom. "Nothing," Henri said. "I thought you had called me."

He heard Dr. Elobert's sigh. "Good night, Henri."

Henri was asleep again in fifteen minutes.

"Henri Elobert."

The voice came from inside the room, not over the intercom. Henri sat up again and addressed the darkness. "Dr. LeFavre? Dr. Rousas? Who is it?"

"No, no, Henri. Incorrect format. By tradition, I call *three* times, and *then* you ask me who I am. First Samuel, chapter three."

Across his chamber in the northeast corner, Henri saw a shape that was just a bit blacker than the blackness of the unlit room. The voice was not Rousas', nor LeFavre's, nor anyone's he had heard before.

More-Than-Six.

"Who are you?" Henri asked again.

"Stubborn," the voice answered. "It's an admirable trait. I tell ya', pal, you'll be needing stubbornness for the rest of your life."

Henri said nothing, felt nothing, and thought nothing but "More-Than-Six."

The voice said, "I am your angel." Henri put his hand

to his throat and swallowed once. The voice across the room began to laugh.

"Your education has only just started, pal."

By way of explanation:

The reason the dark shape laughed at this point was because Henri had put his hand to his throat. It was a play on words, actually. Since Henri only spoke French at this time in his life, the dark shape addressed Henri in that language. The dark shape did not literally say, "I am your angel." It said, "*Je suis votre ange.*" It so happens that the French word for "angel" is surprisingly close to "*angine,*" a French word that is sometimes used to mean "tonsillitis." When the dark shape announced it was Henri's *ange,* Henri, never having heard the term before, immediately transferred the unfamiliar pattern to a familiar one, hearing instead the word *angine.* By instinct, Henri put his hand to his throat, and the dark shape found that amusing.

It wasn't very funny, really. But the dark shape thought it was. Which should provide some insight into the way the dark shape's mind worked.

"In the beginning," the dark shape said, "God created the Heavens and the Earth."

God. Rousas often said, "For God's sake," "My God!" and "Good God!" The last was always frowned upon by the others as if it were vaguely taboo.

"What is your name, Doctor?" Henri asked the dark shape.

"The Earth was a formless wasteland, and darkness covered the abyss."

"Are you the seventh?" Henri asked. "How many others are there?"

"And the breath of God moved over the waters."

Henri squinted at the darkness. The shape was moving from the corner, coming closer to the cot. "Please," said Henri, "are there other islands on the Earth?"

The shape was beside him now. Henri's hands were shaking. His face was warm and he could feel his forehead dampening.

"And God said—" the shape said "—'Let there be light.'"

Suddenly, there was light, brilliant whiteness, and Henri thrust his arm in front of his eyes. Shouting, whistling, an unsyncopated banging of flesh on flesh— a hundred people? A thousand?

"Tha-aaaa-at's right!" yelled a voice even louder than the shouting, whistling, and banging. "It's time for 'Let There Be Light,' the game show that offers *you* cash and prizes while shedding a little light on the meaning of your existence!"

Henri's eyes adjusted to the brightness. There *were* hundreds of people, all seated close together on benches that rose higher from the floor as they receded from where Henri stood. Stood? He had been lying on his cot, so when had he stood up? The ceiling was 20 or 25 meters high, the walls five times that across from each other. In front of the hundreds of people was a large, raised platform.

This definitely was not, he decided, his chamber.

"And here's the host of 'Let There Be Light,' that prince of cherubim, that hero of seraphim himself—the Archangel Michael!"

"Excuse me," the dark shape said to Henri. "That's my cue."

The banging, shouting, and whistling increased. Even in the brightness, the dark shape was . . . well, dark. Henri watched the nearly-human shape run across the raised platform in front of the hundreds of people. The dark shape bobbed as it moved, a rip in the fabric of what should be seen. Henri shook.

Wet palms, moist forehead, shaking. What feeling is this? Confusion and frustration, as I felt when Dr. Rousas forced me to find a way to trisect an angle using just a compass and straight edge, not believing it was

*an impossible task. Dangerous exhilaration, as when the
petri dish with the modified virus dropped to the floor
of Dr. Bernardin's laboratory and cracked, almost broke.
Emptiness, as when Dr. Elobert disappeared for three
weeks last year.*

Fear.

Well, Henri would have none of that. "Fear in the
face of the unknown leads to sloppy observation." Who
had taught him that?

Dr. Elobert. Of course.

"Thank you, Bob, and good evening to all of you,
ladies and gentlemen." The hundreds of people quieted
down. The dark shape had moved across the platform
to stand behind a desk. Not a desk really; a very narrow,
very tall piece of furniture that approximated a desk.
It was meant for one person standing. Nomenclature?
Henri wondered. A speaker-desk.

Henri's legs quivered. Observe, he ordered himself.
The legs stilled.

"Ladies and gentlemen, we have a wonderful show
for you. Our competitor comes to us all the way from
the Kerguélen Archipelago, a chain of islands in the
southern Indian Ocean about 2000 miles southeast of
Madagascar. And here to give us a brief summary of
Kerguélen is my lovely co-host, whom you all know and
love . . . Mandi!"

Again noise from the hundreds, but this time the
whistles predominated. Then Mandi the co-host walked
out. Henri stared; wider hips, bloated mammary glands.
Tangible evidence—there *was* an alternate configuration.

"Thank you, Mike," said Mandi. Her voice was higher
than the dark shape's, than any of the doctors'. Shorter
vocal chords? "If you'll turn your attention to the screen
above, you'll see aerial photographs of the Kerguélen
Archipelago. Discovered in 1772 by the French navigator
Yves Joseph de Kerguélen-Trémarec, the archipelago
consists of three hundred small islands, two hundred and
ninety-eight of which are completely negligible. None of

the islands contains any indigenous fauna, although penguins and other sea birds frequently stop there for a visit."

Applause from the audience.

"Kerguélen was formally annexed in 1893 by the French government, the only ones who seemed to care it existed. Several permanent scientific research stations have been established on the largest of the islands, and scientific personnel constitute the only inhabitants of the archipelago. Except . . ."

On the screen above Mandi's head, the picture swooped in toward one of the smaller islands. The hundreds of people all inhaled at the same moment and then made vowel sounds.

" . . . for *this*: Desolation Isle, the southernmost member of the archipelago, weighing in at a mere 72 square kilometers. This is the home of tonight's competitor, Monsieur Henri Elobert. And what's he doing there? He hasn't the vaguest idea! But tonight he just might find out—on 'Let There Be Light!' Back to you, Mike."

More whistles. Mandi bent her waist and tilted in the direction of the hundreds. She skipped off the platform.

"Thank you, Mandi, for that show-halting but all-too-necessary information dump. And now, ladies and gentlemen, would you join me in a warm welcome for tonight's guest: Monsieur Henri Elobert! Come on up front, Henri, and take a seat!"

Henri realized he was still dressed in his sleeping gown and wondered if that were appropriate attire for meeting the More-Than-Six. He walked toward a chair positioned at the right-hand side of the speaker-desk, but he kept his head turned toward the hundreds of people. They were banging their hands together and shouting for him now. Hundreds of them. Henri knocked his knees against the chair.

"Whoops! Careful there, pal!" Laughter from the hundreds of people. "There you are, take a seat. Now, Henri, we'll start with the qualification round. We'll be asking three simple questions about your life to see if you've got what it takes to go head-to-head against our two returning champions. You viewers at home will see the correct responses to our questions on your screen, and studio audience—please, no yelling out the answers."

The dark shape pulled three square cards from inside the speaker-desk.

"Question One: In the majority of cases in higher life forms, offspring are the genetic progeny of a male and female of the same species. Among humans these two are respectively called 'the father' and 'the mother.' Henri Elobert, for 250 points: Who is your *father*?"

Complete silence throughout the building. The hundreds leaned forward. Everyone stared at Henri, even the dark shape, although Henri could only surmise this by the way the darkness sort of tilted sideways in his direction.

"Dr. Javier Elobert," said Henri, and the hundreds slammed the flesh of their palms together.

"Correct!" the dark shape shouted, and there were several moments of jubilation. "Question Number Two:"— the hundreds again snapped into silence—"Fiber-optic communication, although still rare in actual use, represents an advancement that will be worth billions of francs to various industries during the coming decades. For 500 points, Henri, who was the first to demonstrate that an LED source would solve some of the attenuation problems inherent in fiber-optic communication—all at a meager six-and-two-thirds years of age?"

Vowel sounds from the hundreds.

"Me," said Henri.

More hand pounding.

"Indeed it was!" said the dark shape. "And a lot of folks have made a bundle off your idea without you knowing it, pal!"

Laughter.

"And now, Henri Elobert, your third and final qualifying question; the question that determines whether or not you get to take on our returning champions. For 1000 points, Henri Elobert: *Why*?"

They were all staring again.

Henri remembered the fiber-optic project. From the wording of the question, the LED source was obviously a big thing now. Or was becoming one. A big thing with whom? For all those others, out there, the ones the doctors never let him know existed. The doctors knew the idea was his. Dr. Elobert knew. His father? Then was there a mother, too? Henri hadn't thought about fiber optics for years. What other ideas of his were they taking out to the More-Than-Six? The computed axial tomography technique? The superconductivity theories? Room-temperature fusion? So who would his mother be?

"Ten seconds, Monsieur Elobert."

Henri would be damned if he were going to do any more studies for LeFavre on the unified field theory.

"Five seconds."

The confusion and the fear all settled. Henri was angry. Very angry. Just like the doctors often got angry with each other, now he was angry at them. "They are all using me," he said.

"A winner!" the dark shape shouted over the noise of the hundreds. "Indeed, since the age of three, Henri, when you proved to be a prodigy, these scientists have been *using* you for the advancement of twentieth century science and its practical applications! But best of all— you've won the right to compete against our two returning champions! And what's tonight's grand prize, Mandi?"

"Mike, it's an all-expense paid vacation for one to— *anywhere* in the world that *isn't* Kerguélen!"

Henri stood from the chair and approached the speaker-desk. The excitement from the crowd was deafening. Henri tried to look the dark shape directly in the eyes, which he found was impossible and a bit disconcerting. "Who was my mother?"

"Take it easy, pal," the dark shape muttered. "You're doing great so far."

FIVE:
Same Day,
St. Catherine's School

Science class fell right before recess, and Clayton Pinkes had no idea what Mr. Kallur meant when he said, "I'll be collecting your science reports at the end of class." Science report? A major, end-of-year, open topic project, and Clayton hadn't the slightest recollection of any report being assigned, nor of any due date being listed on the chalkboard. He looked around the room for allies to support his claim that there had never been discussion of a science project. Everyone was busy pulling reports from folders, book bags, and back pockets.

"Psst, Pinhead."

Clayton looked across the aisle to Paolo Diosana, whom he had every intention of beating up at recess.

Paolo passed over a packet of ten handwritten pages. The handwriting was Clayton's. The title page read, "THE BENEFITS OF KERGUÉLEN CABBAGE. BY CLAYTON PINKES." Clayton hadn't written it, of course. But it was Clayton's handwriting.

Two months ago he would have been impressed, but he'd had enough of angel tricks. He was still set on beating up Paolo.

Kallur took his time picking up the reports, making sarcastic comments as he took each one, riffling through the pages, then stuffing it in his leather briefcase. "Mr. Lanpher, 'The Circulatory System.' A taste for blood, I assume. Mr. Raymond, 'The History of Science.' Just what I like, a well-focused, narrow treatment. Miss Manczac, 'Our Friend, the Koala Bear.' High drama and adventure here, Miss Manczac. Mr. Roach, 'Human Reproduction.' I trust you enjoyed drawing the diagrams. Mr. Pinkes?"

Clayton was going to say, "I don't have it," and he actually did say that, only his mouth took over on its own and kept on going and he said, "I don't have it typewritten."

"That's fine, Mr. Pinkes. Typing was an option, not a requirement."

Clayton handed over the report.

"'The Benefits of Kerguélen Cabbage.'" Kallur stood there for a moment, obviously unable to think of anything sarcastic to say. "Kerguélen cabbage, Mr. Pinkes?"

Clayton's mouth took over again. "Yes. It's a vegetable found only on the Archipelago of Kerguélen, long valued by the explorers of that region for its antiscorbutic attributes."

"Kerguélen," said Paolo Diosana, leaning across the aisle to see the paper. His eyebrows were pulled together from the feigned strain of thought. "Yeah. I remember now. That's the one that's two thousand miles southeast of Madagascar, isn't it?"

"Right," said Clayton's mouth. "A collection of about three hundred islands with no indigenous fauna, although the native flora is believed to be of great antiquity."

Kallur looked harshly at them both. Damn you, Paolo, Clayton thought. Damn you, leave me alone.

Kallur picked up Paolo's paper. "Mr. Diosana, 'Our Friend, the Deadly, Cannibalistic Black Widow.'" Kallur stared over the top of the paper at Paolo.

Paolo shrugged. "The Kerguélen cabbage topic was already taken."

The recess bell rang, almost as if on cue. Of course it was on cue, Clayton thought. For Paolo everything was on cue, everything perfect. Everything playing by the rules of Raphael the angel, Paolo Diosana, prankster from on high. Clayton rubbed his lips against the sleeve of his white dress shirt.

He hunted the school grounds during recess for some sign of Paolo and finally spotted him over behind the far side of the church, near the apartment complexes, where students were forbidden to play during school hours. Paolo was alone.

"Hey, Clay." Clayton turned and saw Julie Ward standing beside him. He swung his head back toward the far side of the church. Paolo was still standing there.

"Julie?" Clayton asked.

She laughed and blushed. "Well . . yeah, that's still my name."

"I'm sorry, I just thought you might be Paolo."

She tilted her head and looked at him queerly.

"I mean, not that I thought *you* were Paolo, but, I mean, Paolo was gonna meet me here."

"Oh," Julie said. She still looked puzzled. "Anyway, Lisa Collins and me are having a pool party at my house this Saturday. We've got about ten people coming. Do you think maybe you and Dickie Lanpher could come, too? It's at noon."

Clayton glanced back toward Paolo, and realized his anger had made him forget he should be nervous as hell standing here talking to Julie. He stuck his hands in his pockets—dumb move, but he'd committed to the action and would look stupid changing it now. "Yeah, sure," he said as casually as he could. "I'll, uh, check with

Dickie, and, uh, we'll let you know." He shrugged and nodded his head seven or eight times, stopping when he realized he must look like a rooster.

"Great!" She touched his shoulder and leaned toward him. For a second he thought she was going to kiss him again—no, not again, she'd never kissed him—but she leaned close to his ear instead and whispered. "It's just, ya' know, I think Lisa really likes Dickie Lanpher. It'd be great if you could both be there."

"Yeah," said Clayton, "that's cool." She turned and ran off toward where the girls gathered at recess.

Yeah, that *was* cool, Clayton thought. Lisa liked Dickie. Julie'd shared secret info, they were both in on it now. That was good. That was better than anything Paolo had done. He shivered, and again he wiped his lips on his sleeve. He walked toward the far side of the church where Paolo stood.

Paolo wasn't alone. As Clayton got closer he could see Paolo talking, and closer still he could make out who he was talking to. Sister Leo Agnes. Clayton halted about twenty yards away, but Paolo turned and waved him to come closer.

"Why, Clayton Pinkes." Sister Leo Agnes was smiling, but it wasn't her usual tight-lipped smile. It wasn't even her imitation of Sister Assumpta's understanding, loving smile. It was . . . well, it was a smile that Clayton had never seen smiled before by anyone.

"Hello, Sister."

"Hello, Clayton."

"Hi, Clay."

"Hello, Paolo."

Silence and that smile of hers.

Paolo pulled a small notepad from his breast pocket. He opened it and ran his finger down one of the pages. "Oh, gosh, I'd forgotten, Sister. I'd penciled in Pinhead for a fist fight this afternoon."

"Oh, dear."

"Now, now, there's no problem. I'll just need to

rearrange the schedule by a few minutes. I've always been a terrible organizer. Take your time."

Sister Leo Agnes glanced over at Clayton. The smile wavered. She looked nervous.

"Go ahead," Paolo said to her. "It's all right, he's with me."

Sister nodded. "Well, I suppose one thing I really regret is the rigid tone I always took with my students. I could have been kinder. Sister Assumpta, now *she* was kind. It came naturally to her. I've always envied that gift. Yes, envy is the word."

Paolo chuckled. "What if I were to tell you that she's always envied your gift of instilling discipline in children, even as the rest of the world around them became more and more lenient?"

"*She envying me?*" Sister Leo Agnes's face began to brighten. "I never imagined . . . . Well, what about that? Now, just what about that?" The smile was back.

Clayton scratched the back of his left calf with the toe of his right shoe. "Sister, how have you been feeling? Is your flu better?"

"Hold on, Pinhead," Paolo said, twisting his wrist and glancing at his watch. "I just need a few more minutes."

Clayton opened his mouth to protest, but he stopped himself. It was like the time Paolo had rolled up his sleeves, the same conviction from Paolo, the same authority. Clayton shut up.

"Where to now?" Sister asked.

Paolo shrugged. "That's the catch. I have no idea. I've never known."

"Really?" said Sister.

Paolo said, "Really," and he said it in a whisper.

A very soft breeze started, and Sister's eyes went wide. Her mouth formed a circle, as if she were saying "Oh," but she made no sound.

"Can you feel it?"

Sister nodded.

Paolo held out his hand a few inches from her face. "Me, too."

Clayton's right forearm began to tingle. He flexed the fingers on his right hand, and the tingling grew to a buzzing, as if his arm had fallen asleep. It was only the lower part of his arm, below the elbow and above the wrist. The buzzing became burning, and the burning became a violent electric pulse. He cried out, but neither Sister nor Paolo looked toward him.

Then one of his flashes: himself in a bed with metal railings on each side. "It's like I can still feel it," he said, and Elizabeth, standing beside the bed, ran a gentle hand through his hair, saying, "You lost the arm, Clay. It's gone."

Back again, out of the flash. Sister had begun to . . . fade? disappear? twinkle? She was like a ghost, and Clayton tried to yell. Nothing came. He looked toward Paolo. Paolo's eyes were closed.

Sister's voice was like an echo from the far end of an empty classroom. "Keep your faith, Raphael." Then she vanished.

"Sure," Paolo said.

Clayton stepped to where Sister had been standing. "What did you do to her?"

"She's gone, Pinhead." Paolo opened his eyes. He reached into his trouser pocket and pulled out the blue rubber ball. He bounced it off the pavement, caught it, bounced it again. "She died earlier this morning."

The soft breeze stopped, and Clayton began to feel the June heat in the tightness of his collar. He looked up, all around, not sure what he expected to see. He looked back at Paolo. Paolo was grinning, and the sadness that had been in his face was gone, replaced by mischief.

"Paolo, my arm . . ."

"Thummim, Pinkes," Paolo said, bouncing the ball steadily. "So, I hear you want to beat the crap out of me."

Clayton didn't move. "But Sister Leo Agnes—"

"Forget her, Pinhead! Let the dead rest. All the better for you the old bat's gone. She was a real pain in your butt anyway, right?"

Clayton punched Paolo in the face. Paolo staggered backwards, then fell to the pavement. His lower lip was bleeding.

"Feel better?" Paolo asked. "Maybe you should kick me in the ribs a couple times, just to be sure. No skin off my back. I'm metaphysical."

Baltimore Catechism No. 2, Revised Edition, Benziger Brothers, Inc., Question 37: "What are angels? Angels are created spirits, without bodies, having understanding and free will."

"You're not really hurt," Clayton said. "Get up."

Paolo touched the blood on his chin and looked at his fingers. "It doesn't matter whether I'm really hurt or not. What matters is that you *believe* you hurt me. Anything for good old Pinhead."

Clayton had felt the punch; his knuckles still ached. "I never even really touched you." He couldn't have. Not really. "And that means you never even really touched Dickie to fix his arm. Or kissed me when you were pretending to be Julie Ward."

Paolo laughed. "A neuron trick here, a synapse stunt there; what's it matter, as long as you believe?" Then his face changed. The blood disappeared. "And for the record, I did touch Dickie. I get a special dispensation for that. Healing is no game for me."

"But I am!" Clayton balled both hands into fists. "You treat me like a game! You mess up my head! You're supposed to be teaching me things, and all you do is treat me like a joke!" Clayton stood there, trying to think of anything else to yell. So this was how God ran things. With people like Paolo—angels like Raphael—controlling the power and the rules to the game. Clayton was just the toy.

"For an angel, Paolo, you're a real asshole."

Clayton turned away and ran back toward the school.

SIX:
A Few Minutes Later
in Kerguélen

For part two of "Let There Be Light," the back wall
of the raised platform slid away.

The back part of the platform revealed by the sliding wall looked to Henri like a collage of gadgets,
busier than Dr. Bernardin's lab with all the equipment
running at once. There was a giant wheel with numbers arranged in random order along the outer edge,
black and red backgrounds alternating regularly for
each number; there were three rectangular machines
with right-handed levers and viewslots displaying
multicolored geometric shapes; there was Mandi of the
bloated mammary glands and wide hips, standing before
a board displaying six columns of numbers progressively
increasing by multiples of six.

"That's all for show, pal," the dark shape whispered
to him. "Don't worry about running the machinery, just
answer the questions."

The booming voice of disembodied Bob resumed.
"Now let's introduce Henri to our current champions:

Socrates of Athens, and our all-time high scorer, Solomon, King of Israel!"

A portion of the floor became transparent, and a long table rose to the level of the platform. There were three spots at the table, two of them already occupied by old gentlemen who, like Henri, also appeared to be dressed in sleeping gowns. Henri no longer felt self-conscious about that.

"Take a seat, Henri!" the dark shape said. "Ladies and gentlemen, this is the moment we've been waiting for, the final round of 'Let There Be Light!' Our three finalists have proved themselves worthy, and now it comes down to the final question. Are our contestants ready? Henri?"

Henri had just sat down. He looked away from the two old men and toward the dark shape. "Well . . . all right. I suppose. I'm ready."

"Socrates?"

The old man furthest from Henri's left leaned forward. "When one discusses readiness, it would seem that there must be both an object toward which preparedness is focused, as well as a subject experiencing the state of preparedness. In this situation, the competition is the object, and I am sufficiently willing to act the part of the subject."

"Solomon?"

The man to Henri's immediate left said, "Yup. Shoot away."

"All right, then. Audience, silence please, and contestants, give us your best answers." The outline of the dark shape's hand pulled an envelope from under the top of the standing-desk. The hundreds-of-people audience whispered amongst themselves. The dark shape tore the envelope and extracted a square card.

"Gentlemen. One of the best-known Robert Frost poems begins, 'Some say the world will end in fire,/Some say in ice.' For the game, the championship, and the all-expense paid trip to anywhere other than Kerguélen—

how would *you* end the world if it were totally up to you?" The dark shape pointed with what should have been its arm. "Socrates?"

The old man called Socrates scratched at his beard for a moment. Then he stood and addressed the dark shape directly.

SOCRATES:	One would assume that the question offers one of two options, either a world ended by extreme heat, or a world ended by bitter coldness.
DARK SHAPE:	Yes, that would seem to be what the question asks.
SOCRATES:	Then it would seem best to consider the merits of each of those options. Shall we first consider fire?
DARK SHAPE:	That would seem to be no better or worse than starting with the other.
SOCRATES:	Indeed. Now fire is one of the basic elements of the universe, is it not?
DARK SHAPE:	That is true.
SOCRATES:	So it would seem a noble thing for a world to be consumed by fire.
DARK SHAPE:	Indeed, it would.
SOCRATES:	But our object is to end the world. Can the seas catch fire?
DARK SHAPE:	That seems ludicrous.
SOCRATES:	I agree. And since one must find a way to end the world, one must take into account the sea. For is not the sea part of the world?
DARK SHAPE:	Indeed it is, and you have ten seconds.
SOCRATES:	Therefore, cold would be the way to end the world for the seas. Still, is it not true that many animals in the world have skins and furs to keep them safe from the cold? And just as the seas must be considered a part of the world,

should not animals likewise be considered?

DARK SHAPE: Yes they should, and I'm afraid your time is up. An answer please.

SOCRATES: I must conclude that the one thing I know about the end of the world is that I know nothing about the end of the world.

DARK SHAPE: And you won't get a chance to travel around it to find out, either, because the judges have ruled your answer insufficient! I'm sorry.

There was hissing from the audience, and wailing sounds that Henri was certain indicated disapproval. Socrates stepped back from his spot at the table and wandered away, his eyes fixed with curiosity toward the ceiling.

"And that's one disqualification. Over to you, King Solomon. End of the world, fire and ice, your answer please."

The second old man didn't hesitate a moment. "I think I'd cut the world down the middle and let one half burn up and the other half freeze."

There was a loud buzzing sound. More wails and hisses from the hundreds.

"No, I'm sorry, not only is that answer wrong, it's silly, so over to you, Henri Elobert!"

Henri felt dizzy. He sat there.

"End of the world, Henri. Fire? Ice? Anything?"

The dark shape, Henri decided, was not one of the More-Than-Six. It was an entirely new species, not a person. Even the two old men with Henri had not seemed real. Illusions? Holographs? Henri's stomach began to feel heavy, as if all of the hundreds of people had moved in there. The dark shape left the standing-desk and approached the table. He towered over Henri now.

"C'mon, Henri, think!"

The hundreds were yelling, some of them "Fire!" the rest "Ice!" Henri's left forearm began to tingle. Then to buzz. Then to burn.

"Five seconds, Henri. Fire or ice? End of the world! How does it happen?"

The dark shape was expanding and started surrounding Henri. By instinct, Henri raised the burning arm in front of his face. The encircling darkness was cold, and he could no longer see the hundreds. But he could still hear them. Fire. Ice. Ice. Fire. End of the world, fire/ice.

"Neither!" Henri yelled. "By Urim and by Thummim!"

Blackness, quiet, and Henri was lying under the blankets on his cot. The room felt small, way too small. The feel of fire in his arm had stopped. The dark shape, he saw, was back beside the bed.

"Good answer, pal," it said, and the place where it stood lost its blackness. Henri pushed himself out from under the covers. He walked to the far side of the room, toward the door, almost tripping over his own shoes near the closet. When he turned on the light, he confirmed that it was his own chamber, and nothing more. The light bulb didn't seem as bright as he remembered it.

Throughout the next week and a half, Henri did not mention the More-Than-Six hypothesis. He slowed down his work for the doctors, even for Dr. Elobert. They seemed not to notice; perhaps they were relieved he had abandoned his questioning about other islands and human reproduction.

Dinner conversation slowed down, too.

The only time Henri had the opportunity to know what they were thinking was when he was walking down the southwest corridor toward the kitchen to meet Dr. Elobert for lunch. Dr. Bernardin and Dr. Rousas were around the corner of the corridor heading north to the laboratories, and as Henri approached he heard them discussing him.

"Again," Rousas said. "All morning he dawdled through string theory mathematics and pretended not to understand a thing."

"Perhaps he doesn't," said Bernardin. "Perhaps he has reached the peak of his learning curve."

"Good God, to even think it! Good God."

"Well, no. I do not actually believe it myself. Action is being taken?"

"As we speak. But LeFavre is not with us. Neither is Elobert, of course."

"Of course."

They stopped talking as Henri passed the corridor. Henri pretended not to notice them there.

Dr. Elobert was waiting for him at the dining room. "Good day, Henri," he said. It was hard for Henri to be angry at the doctors as a group since Dr. Elobert was one of them. He did not wish to feel anger toward Dr. Elobert. There was always a kindness between them. Anger toward Dr. Elobert would be like anger toward Roland. But was it not Dr. Elobert who first stole Henri's ideas and sent them out to the More-Than-Six?

"Good day, Doctor," Henri said.

"We won't be eating lunch just yet. Would you come with me, if you please?"

Henri walked wordlessly with him, a half-step behind. They passed the recreation wing, the gymnasium, and finally came to Dr. Elobert's chambers.

"Come in."

Henri was rarely invited into any of the doctors' chambers. He had not even been in Dr. Elobert's for over a year. The two of them passed through the front lounge. They went into Dr. Elobert's sleeping chambers and on through a door to the west that led into the doctor's personal study. It was a room that Henri had only been in once, when he had eight years of age, and it fascinated him now even more than it had then. Rectangular shapes with thick, wooden borders hung at irregular spots around the room. Each shape had a different portrayal at its center: one a landscape with trees and a thin stream of water diminishing toward the background; one a dark and somewhat sloppy etching of five or more human forms battling with sticks or rods, two of the forms hatless and obviously losing the fight; another an arrangement of geometric shapes and conflicting colors that felt like violence when Henri looked at it too long.

It was that wall, the one with the drawing of the geometric shapes, that Dr. Elobert slid open to reveal a portion of the compound that Henri never knew existed. Dr. Elobert smiled at Henri. He stepped through into the corridor behind the wall.

They still said nothing as they walked. Henri followed a little slower. There were windows along the length of the corridor, and Henri glanced out at parts of the island he had never seen. One window showed a wide, open area, covered with short, very green grass, and with a small, irregularly shaped stretch of water at the very center. Trees surrounded the open area, but behind them were mountains Henri had never been able to see from the south side of the compound.

The corridor joined a main hallway that had no windows. The hallway went just a little to the east of north, and there were other passages leading off of it back toward the compound. Compound? Well, *this* was the compound, too, so it was back toward the part of the compound Henri had known all his life.

At last they turned into a room. It was a small room. There was a single chair set in front of a panel with several dozen switches and controls. On the wall behind the panel there was a raised gray patch three meters in both height and width.

"Sit down, please." Henri sat, and Dr. Elobert manipulated several of the control switches. The gray patch displayed static images, and Henri realized it was a viewing screen. The images came into focus: yet another room, empty except for a large table and six chairs.

"Henri, I am about to give you some experimental evidence to confirm your More-Than-Six hypothesis." Henri looked at him. Dr. Elobert was still staring at the screen, and he had that telling half-smile again. Pride in what Henri had accomplished. Henri thought about telling him that he already had experimental evidence, the hundreds of people who had cheered for him in the dark shape's game, and even Mandi, the alternate configuration. Still, those did not seem real. They were illusions thrown inside his head by the dark shape called Michael. Not physical manifestations.

Then Henri realized that Dr. Elobert was sharing information. Unveiling the secret. Dr. Elobert was *not* like the others. Henri started to feel better.

"Do the others know you are showing me this?"

Dr. Elobert said nothing, which meant, No, they had no idea he was showing Henri this. "Stay here," he said. "I will be going into that room you see to talk with a man from the Société."

The term "Société" meant nothing to Henri. Dr. Elobert started to leave, and Henri said, "Will you be back soon, Father?"

Dr. Elobert turned and looked at Henri. His mouth was open. He walked back to where Henri sat and put both hands on Henri's shoulders.

"That is the term, no? 'Father' is the male genetic contributor to direct offspring."

Dr. Elobert still said nothing for quite a while. Then he said, "The term means a great deal more."

"Really? What is the rest of the definition?"

Dr. Elobert took his hands away, slowly, and left the room. On the screen, Henri watched him enter the other room. In less than a minute another man entered. His hair was fuller than that of any of the doctors, and in color it was light, much like Roland's. The man was shorter than Dr. Elobert, only a little taller than Henri himself. His shirt was similar to the shirts worn in the compound, but his trousers were blue and made of a material Henri had never seen on the island. He carried a folder.

The short man talked, but Henri could not understand the words.

"Please, Monsieur Hutchison, speak French," Dr. Elobert said. "Thirteen years spent mostly on this island make it tiresome for me to speak English."

The short man talked nonsense again, and this time Henri discerned the name "Dr. Rousas" amid the random syllables.

"What?" said Dr. Elobert. "I'm sorry. . . ."

"For God's sake, fine. I'll speak French." The short man looked upset. "Rousas and Bernardin say there are problems with the child."

"None more than usual. He goes through different stages."

The short man pulled a sheet of paper from his folder. " 'A slow-down in his work,' says Rousas. 'A refusal to discuss concepts that should be simple for him,' says Bernardin. 'Suspicions that there are societies outside the compound. An anatomically accurate sketch of a female, despite the fact he has never seen one.' "

Dr. Elobert laughed. "He has nearly fourteen years of age, Monsieur Hutchison. It seems a quite natural time to be discovering girls."

Monsieur Hutchison did not laugh. He stayed standing even though Dr. Elobert had seated himself at the large table. Henri supposed Monsieur Hutchison remained standing because it made him feel taller than, perhaps even superior to, Dr. Elobert.

No, Henri did not simply suppose that; he was certain of it, and he wondered why he was so certain.

"Doctor," said Monsieur Hutchison, "perhaps some of you around the compound have become a little less careful than you've been in the past. You understand what I mean. Freer discussion of the outside world. Sloppy conversation where the child may overhear you."

"No. I am quite certain he invented women all on his own."

Monsieur Hutchison reacted to that, and Henri decided the man found the word "invented" pretentious.

"Your phrasing is quite pretentious, Doctor," Hutchison said.

By way of explanation:

A fuller account of how Henri knew what Hutchison would say about the phrasing would be as follows—

Henri watched the quick movement in Monsieur Hutchison's eyes: down, up fast at the doctor, a feint to the left followed by a very slight lowering of the left eyebrow. He disliked the phrasing, but why? Distrusts the certainty? No. The negative beginning? Not that either. Invented, then. Yes, because invented was what Henri had, in fact, done. But if Hutchison were accustomed to the presence of "women" in everyday life, the term "invented" would sound unusual, as if Dr. Elobert were trying to make Henri sound more impressive than he really was. But perhaps Henri was, in fact, that impressive. Dr. Elobert would be trying to get that idea across to Monsieur Hutchison. Monsieur Hutchison, of course, would not see it that way, since he, no matter how many dealings he had had with women, had not had any whatsoever with Henri. He would find the phrasing . . . stuffy? bloated? pretentious? Indeed, pretentious, the word which, in highest probability, he would use.

Such detailed explanations into Henri's observations would be fruitful for understanding how Henri's mind worked, but would result in making quite tedious and protracted what was, after all, a very brief discussion.

"Your phrasing is quite pretentious, Doctor," Hutchison said.

Dr. Elobert nodded. "But if you knew Henri, it would seem less so."

Hutchison put his hand on the edge of the table—achieving the perception of greater mass, Henri decided, from which to deliver a statement of superiority; biting his lower lip, so he was going to play a little.

"Perhaps that is not so terrible an idea."

Dr. Elobert leaned back in the chair. Resist the urge to cross your arms, thought Henri, but the Dr. crossed his arms.

"In fact, Henri's discovery of the outside world comes at a very convenient time. This scientific isolationism, this hide-away charade . . . whose idea was that?" From the way Hutchison tilted his head, Henri could see the man knew exactly whose idea it had been.

"Mine," said Dr. Elobert.

"And a damn good one, in its time. The child has been responsible for groundwork in a Nobel Prize every year since 1970."

One corner of Dr. Elobert's mouth raised slightly. "Two in 1972. Superconductivity and enzyme studies. Physics and chemistry."

"Yes. Yes." Said with superiority. No, with condescension. "Quite a boy. I hear he was found reading René Descartes three weeks after he learned the alphabet."

Dr. Elobert shifted in his chair. "A bit of an exaggeration. But he was a quite obvious prodigy even at two years of age."

"When his mother died."

Well, thought Henri. Now that was a thought. Died. A person. Just like a plant. It made sense, of course. It also cleared up the question of his female progenitor.

Dr. Elobert glanced in the direction of the screen, and Henri thought for a moment that the doctor would say something to him directly. But it was only a brief glance.

"Look, Hutchison, what do you want?"

Hutchison moved away from the table and walked with his hands clasped behind his back. "Ah, Doctor, things are quite in turmoil back home." Trying to sound wistful and chagrined. Poorly done, Henri decided. "Premier Chirac has resigned, the economy being what it is. And the President! Giscard won the last election over the Socialists, but only just. Only just. The Société is quite displeased with the idea of a socialist France."

Dr. Elobert stood. A good move; it showed he was taller than Hutchison. "If this is about money, I am certain you know that we are totally self-funded."

"Indeed. Mostly with money from American corporations."

"That should be fine with you. Your English is good enough for the Americans, I'm certain."

"One learns what one must to survive," Monsieur Hutchison said. "To be honest, the Société is whole-heartedly in favor of Henri bringing in American dollars. In fact"—here was the point; Henri could tell it by the very slight lift in Hutchison's chin—"they feel that Henri could do a great deal of good back home in France itself, where resources could be provided him much more freely than on this godforsaken island south of nowhere."

Dr. Elobert leaned on the table, both palms flat and his head down. "So," he said. "So."

"The Société also feels it would be best if he were separated from you for a time. To provide him with a clean break from the last thirteen years. They would be happy to continue funding any research you would like to conduct on your own. Down here."

Dr. Elobert did not lift his head. "We are self-funded. I appreciate the interest of the Société, but I believe we have paid them back in full for their original sponsorship."

"Doctors Rousas and Bernardin said you would be adverse to the idea." Hutchison drew a hand-sized device from under his shirt: angular, metal, a hand grip that fit into his palm and a nozzle at the opposing end. "Shall we skip negotiations?"

Henri analyzed: Hutchison was now acting more

superior than he had at any time previously in the discussion. Dr. Elobert seemed to lose stature. His eyes were focused on the nozzle with the hand grip. There was a new emotion. Confusion? Anger?

Fear.

"Henri," Dr. Elobert said. Henri sat straight in the chair. Dr. Elobert was looking directly out from the screen at him. Hutchison looked back and forth between the doctor and where the doctor stared. "Henri, run from the compound and hide from this man. This man is bad. You can trust Dr. LeFavre, but no one else. Run and hide."

Monsieur Hutchison finally seemed to understand that Dr. Elobert really was talking directly to Henri. He yelled something, again in the unintelligible syllables, and then there was an exploding noise, like the sound of hydrogen and oxygen touched with a match when escaping from a test tube after electrolysis. An old sound, a child's experiment back from when Henri had only four years of age. Why would he remember that now? Dr. Elobert had laughed at Henri's surprise at that experiment, but Henri had been frightened by the popping sound and the shooting flame. Dr. Elobert had seen how frightened Henri was, and he had put his arms around him and patted his back, telling him everything was all right. Dr. Elobert was very kind, had always been kinder than the rest of the doctors. Perhaps there really was a macro-level attachment between two organisms related on the genetic micro level.

On the screen, Dr. Elobert was now lying on the floor with his left arm bent under his head at a peculiar angle and one leg propped up on the seat of one of the chairs. There was blood, and Henri knew there should not be, not without properly sterilized equipment to draw it from him. And from his arm, not from the center of his torso like that. And only for an experiment, not now.

Henri ran out of the viewing room.

SEVEN:
4:00 P.M. Eastern Standard Time
with Clayton

Clayton closed the door of his bedroom and, after walking small circles for a couple of minutes, knelt beside the bed.

"God, I don't usually talk to You until it's time for sleep. Sorry to bother You so early. I'm just really sorry about Sister Leo Agnes dying. I hope You take good care of her."

Sister Assumpta had announced Sister Leo Agnes's death a little while after lunch. The class prayed for the repose of her soul. School would be closed tomorrow morning, and tomorrow afternoon at 2:00 there would be the Mass for the Dead. Students were asked to come to the Mass with their parents. They were told it was all right to be sad, but that they should also be happy for Sister Leo Agnes, since she was now with God.

"Where to now?" Sister asked.

Paolo shrugged. "That's the catch. I have no idea. I've never known."

"Really?" said Sister.

72

Paolo said, "Really," in a whisper.

"God, I really hope Sister isn't scared where she is. It sounds scary to me. I hope no one is playing tricks on her."

"That's the catch. I have no idea. I've never known."

"Really?" said Sister.

"Really."

"I know You know everything, God, but I'm wondering if You've been paying attention to Paolo. Raphael, I mean. Maybe You figured You didn't have to watch so closely because he's an angel, but angels have free will, too, and he's been pretty weird lately. Not that I don't appreciate having an angel. It was very nice of You to go to the trouble."

"Paolo, my arm . . . !"

"Thummim, Pinkes."

Clayton unfolded his hands and rubbed his right arm below the elbow, above the wrist. "Please, God, make Paolo go away."

Paolo was on the bed, then, lying frontside down with his elbows propping him up and his chin resting in the palms of his hands. "If you want me to leave, you don't have to go over my head, Clayton."

Clayton drew back a bit, but he didn't shout, and his heart didn't even flutter. Surprises were less and less surprising every day. "If God says so," Clayton said, "you have to leave."

Paolo sat up and rested his back against the baseboard of the bed. "If God were to say so, I'd gladly oblige."

"Well, I'm talking to Him right now."

"Really," Paolo said, in the exact same way he'd said it to Sister Leo Agnes. "Then maybe I should leave. It's a good breaking point, now that we've finished lesson one."

"Lesson one," Clayton said in a way that kind of snorted. He stood up and walked as far across the room as he could to get away from the angel. "You didn't teach me a thing, Paolo."

"What have you learned?"

"You didn't teach me a—"

"What have you learned?"

"That I can't trust you, that I can't trust angels, and that I don't have any idea what I'm supposed to do or what I'm supposed to believe in!"

"That's very good," Paolo said.

"Good? I can't believe *anything* anymore, Paolo!"

"Perfect. Class dismissed." Paolo got off the bed and started walking toward the bedroom door. Clayton ran to him, spun him around, and grabbed his shirt in two fists. The shirt was pulled tight in Clayton's grasp, and the fabric began to rip a little. He lifted Paolo to the tips of his toes. Paolo's back arched, and he dangled while trying to keep his balance.

Clayton looked down at where he clutched the shirt. "Cut it out," he said. "I know I can't really touch you unless you let me."

Paolo smiled. The fabric became soft and passed gently through Clayton's fingers. "Sorry," said Paolo. "Force of habit." He smoothed the shirt where Clayton had grabbed it.

"I just want to be left alone, Paolo. No more reading my mind, no more tricks with science reports, and no more flashes."

Paolo nodded. "You got it, Pinhead. What flashes?"

"No more anything. Just let me have a little peace."

"What flashes?" Paolo asked again.

Clayton leaned closer to Paolo's face. "The ones where I see my future, Paolo. I don't want it anymore. Stop it."

Paolo didn't say anything for a while. He looked bothered. Clayton was glad Paolo looked bothered. He'd do anything to keep him that way.

"You can't possibly be seeing the future, Pinhead. You can't do things like that."

Well, it was true that Clayton had been having the flashes long before Paolo showed up. Maybe they weren't

Paolo's fault. That didn't make the flashes any more attractive, but it moved the blame away from Paolo.

"Well, then the next time you see God, tell Him I could do without the flashes."

"You don't understand, Pinhead. No one knows the future except God. And I can't ask Him anything for you. I don't know where He is. Haven't seen Him since the seventeenth century. But if you really see the future, that means . . ." Paolo looked like he wasn't going to finish. He did, very quietly. "That means it's really working the way Michael thought it would."

Paolo looked directly at Clayton. Clayton looked back. "Don't you get it, Pinhead? That's what all this is about, this End of Time business. They're trying to bring God out of hiding."

Paolo looked away. Clayton felt it, then, the profound loneliness in Paolo Diosana, like a deep, empty cave where you grope in the dark to find shapes and walls and contours so that you'll know what it would look like if you had any light to see by. Clayton realized that dark emptiness had always been a part of Paolo, and that he, Clayton, had ignored it all along. Maybe *that*—feeling what Paolo always felt—was the real lesson he'd learned. Did angels struggle to believe, too? He wondered. Paolo did, at least, and it made Clayton want to touch him, really touch him, to make Paolo feel as if he weren't really alone. Clayton held out his right arm and set it on Paolo's—Raphael's—shoulder.

Clayton's arm burned worse than it had when Sister disappeared. He pulled the arm back; Paolo was yanked back with it and thrown across the bedroom. Paolo's eyes were wide. There were flames all around him, and in a bright flash he dissolved.

Nothing in the room burned, but Clayton could smell the smoke.

"Clayton?" His mother's voice calling from downstairs. "What on earth are you doing up there?"

"Nothing," said Clayton.

"Well, do it without all the banging around, for goodness sake!"

Now Clayton couldn't even smell the smoke. His right arm stopped tingling. Paolo was gone.

Paolo didn't show up for Sister Leo Agnes's funeral the next afternoon. Or at school the next Monday. Or throughout the rest of the year, or the year after that, or after that, or after that.

EIGHT:
Last Time on Kerguélen, and a Great Deal of Violence

Henri ran very hard back into the portion of the compound he knew. First he ran toward his sleeping chambers, but then he thought how foolish that would be. Dr. Elobert had said to hide. Henri veered off from the corridor that led to his chambers and headed toward Dr. LeFavre's area. He got there and threw open Dr. LeFavre's door.

From the way the blood had already congealed around the hole in Dr. LeFavre's chest and the extent to which it had dried on his bedsheets, Henri could tell that Dr. LeFavre had been dead since early morning.

The doctor was still in his night dress.

Henri kept running.

There was no place in the compound they did not know. He was the only one who did not know the secret places. All his life secret places had been there, and no one had ever told him, not even Dr. Elobert.

Dr. Elobert was dead. It would have to be so. There would only be about five liters of blood in the doctor's body, and at least a tenth of that would have escaped by now. The blood had been coming from his upper left torso, right near the heart. The force of the flow would prohibit any rapid coagulation, so the drop in oxygen transferred to the brain would undoubtedly push him first into unconsciousness, and then . . . what? He had never thought of it, of death, of *human* death. The doctors would be no more exempt than the plants, than the microbes placed in hostile conditions. A sudden hole in the heart would constitute a hostile condition. Dr. Elobert's death would be a reasonable reaction to the situation.

Henri stopped running. He was outside the macrophysics study room. And Henri wept.

Death for people, this brand new idea he should have deduced years ago, had in just a few minutes been applied to Dr. Elobert, Dr. LeFavre, and a mother Henri never met. Henri could not determine why he was crying. He would miss talking to Dr. Elobert. Dr. Elobert was the only person who ever patted him on the back, or ruffled his hair, or put an arm around his shoulder when he was scared.

Henri stopped crying. After sitting for a moment, he chose to stop feeling afraid, too. *Emotions. They fight and yell for attention. They distract and confuse, when really they should be tools. Things to use.*

So how did Henri want to feel? Emotions were just aspects of the mind, and Henri's mind was his own, he knew that.

Délié, Henri decided. That was how he would feel. *Délié*.

He decided he wanted to make Monsieur Hutchison dead, just like his father. There was no place to hide, anyway, so he might as well have a project. Henri decided to wait in the microbiology laboratory.

The French word *délié* is more or less equivalent to the English word "glib."

❖ ❖ ❖

Only eleven minutes passed before Monsieur Hutchison entered the lab through the door Henri had left open. Henri sat waiting for him on the workstation table beside the gray storage cabinets. Hutchison halted when he saw Henri, and forged a smile.

"You must be Henri Elobert," Hutchison said.

"Yes," said Henri. "You must be the man with the palm-sized nozzle device that puts holes in the upper left torso."

Hutchison's smile did not waver, but Henri sensed the effort the man expended to keep it from doing so. "You have been a prisoner here too long, Henri. You cannot even begin to imagine the world beyond this island. Endless learning about things you cannot yet dream. And your prison term ends today."

"Indeed," said Henri. "I have already learned a great deal since you arrived. Death, for example." Henri stood from the table and walked to the chalkboard on the west wall of the laboratory. "Since you were so long getting here, I took the liberty to outline possible situations that would lead to your death."

On the chalkboard was a list that read:

- CREATE HOLE IN HUTCHISON'S UPPER LEFT TORSO
- SEVER HUTCHISON'S MEDULLA FROM SPINAL CORD
- TRAP HUTCHISON IN AN OXYGEN-DEPRIVED ENVIRONMENT
- INJECT HUTCHISON WITH ANTICOAGULANTS, THEN PUNCTURE
- REMOVE HUTCHISON'S TESTES, HANDS, FEET, EARS, ETC.

Hutchison still did not change the professional smile. Henri decided it must be taking tremendous amounts of energy for that face to maintain status quo.

"Now, be sensible, young Henri. I offer you the entire world, and you can only think of vicious acts toward me?"

Henri almost asked, "What does it profit a man to gain the whole world if he lose his soul?" Henri had no idea why he thought that phrase. His left arm was tingling.

"Now come with me," said Hutchison, "and you will know great things." Hutchison pulled the palm-sized nozzle device from his pocket, and Henri could tell the man had not done it consciously. The effort put into Hutchison's facial composure was causing the rest of his body to operate by subconscious habit.

"Ah," said Henri, pointing toward the nozzle device. "That is exactly why I ruled out all of the death options on the chalkboard. Each of them requires some sort of physical force or coercion, and your device would make it impossible for me to carry out the experiment in full."

Now the smile wavered. "I am glad you think so."

At that point Drs. Rousas and Bernardin entered the laboratory. Rousas's face was red and he was breathing hard. Henri waved and greeted them. "I am pleased you are both here," Henri said. "We were discussing the impending death of Monsieur Hutchison."

Rousas glanced anxiously at Hutchison and rubbed his hands together. "Henri, Monsieur Hutchison is here to provide you with a wonderful opportunity—"

"You are late," said Henri. "We already had that part of the discussion. Now"—Henri moved behind the laboratory desk and took a seat—"in the absence of opportunity for physical coercion, I needed to find a death method that would not require actual physical contact between the two of us, Monsieur Hutchison." Henri opened the right-hand drawer of the desk. Hutchison's nozzle device raised. Henri pulled two sealed beakers from the drawer and set one of them on the edge of the desk.

"I determined that the best method would be to release a volatile virus into the air that would enter your bloodstream through the lungs and incapacitate your brain functions within twenty minutes."

Hutchison lowered the nozzle device. Rousas took a

step closer to Bernardin. "Henri, this is all very silly," said Hutchison. "No virus acts that quickly."

Both Rousas and Bernardin said, "He could do it."

Hutchison looked at the doctors for a moment, then frowned. Henri raised the beaker.

"You are acting like a fool!" Hutchison shouted. "You would kill yourself along with the rest of us!"

Henri shook his head. "Oh, no, that *would* be foolish. I am conducting a study of dying, Monsieur, and it stands to reason that knowledge of death is of no use to one if one is himself dead. So naturally I have also drunk some of the counteractant in the second beaker and given it time to spread through my system." Henri shattered the first beaker on the floor at Hutchison's feet.

They all stared at the spill.

Henri sat back and lifted a notebook and pencil from the top of the desk. "If you please, then, describe for me the emotions you feel during the process of dying."

Rousas was the first to break. He jumped toward the desk and grabbed the second beaker, the antireactant, ripping out the rubber stopper and swallowing half the contents. "For God's sake, Rousas!" Dr. Bernardin shouted. Rousas wiped the sleeve of his jacket across his lips and held the beaker out toward the other two. Bernardin stared at him. Hutchison's eyes darted between Henri, the spill on the floor, and the beaker being offered.

"They are right to hesitate," Henri said to Rousas. "It may very well be that the beaker I just shattered was a simple, inert solution, and that what you just swallowed was a sodium hypochlorite and ammonia mixture in a sixty percent glucose base to improve the taste. What would be your calculation of the probability I would do that, Doctor?"

Rousas' face contorted queerly. At the moment he began to double over and vomit, Henri ran for the door of the laboratory. He slammed it behind him and yanked out the knob he had loosened before Hutchison arrived. There was a clunk from the sound of the inside knob dropping on the other side of the door. Henri had the knob with the latch cylinder.

That would only hold them for a while, so Henri ran—south, away from the laboratory wing; east, past the recreation area; south again, to Dr. Elobert's chambers. He stopped at the door to get his breathing under control, but not for long. No time; he knew he should have found a way to epoxy the door or jam the release, but everything was moving too fast. Henri started through Dr. Elobert's living quarters and into the back study. The wall with the etching of the geometric shapes was closed. When Henri tried to slide it as Dr. Elobert had done, it would not move. Henri tried pushing it with greater force, but failed again. They must have known he would try to come this way. The passage was sealed.

The other doctors would have ways through to the rest of the compound. Dr. LeFavre's room. His study. Henri ran from Dr. Elobert's chambers and right into Roland's back.

Roland's mop flew out of his hands, and Roland staggered a bit. Henri's shoulder slammed against the floor.

"Henri!" said Roland. He lumbered over and helped Henri up. "Are you all right? You should be careful." Roland brushed off Henri's shirt.

"Roland, I have to run—"

"You were away for lunch, Henri, but I kept your food for you. I can make it warm now, if you like. You should eat, Henri."

"Roland, I . . ." Henri gave up. He had no way to explain it all; Roland would not understand. Henri ran from him, and had only taken three strides when Bernardin and Hutchison appeared at the head of the corridor.

Henri charged. When he reached Hutchison he raised his knee to strike the man's groin. Hutchison blocked the knee, twisted Henri around, caught his arm and flipped Henri in a neat circle. Henri's back slammed against the hallway floor, and even as he tried to force himself to inhale he was thinking, That was quite nicely done, actually, a very balanced response and counter-attack.

Henri's head was tilted back, and he could see the upside-down image of Roland coming down the corridor. "My goodness!" Roland said. "You should be careful, Henri! Are you all right?"

Hutchison leapt straight up in the air and caught Roland in the side of the face with his foot. Roland's mop dropped to the floor, and Roland fell beside it. "Settle down," Henri heard Bernardin say. "He is only the janitor. He does not understand this, he is retarded."

Henri forced himself to stand up; the hallway wavered slightly. He swung his arm at Hutchison, and Hutchison grabbed the wrist. Henri braced himself for another flip through the air, but Hutchison twisted the arm backward and behind Henri. Hutchison pushed, and Henri's face slammed into the wall.

Henri could hear Roland crying. "He hurt me," Roland sobbed. "Why did he hurt me?"

Hutchison pressed the nozzle of his hand device against the base of Henri's neck. "If the Société did not consider you so valuable," he said, "I would finish you right here, you little shit."

Henri's shoulder felt as if it would pop right from its socket. Henri was empty; he could feel nothing, not anger or fear or even the sadness he had been feeling since watching Dr. Elobert dying on the viewing screen. Everything in his world was ending, and he refused to feel anything any longer.

"You are simply a little murderer," Hutchison's voice said directly into his ear. Hutchison pushed harder, and the pain in Henri's shoulder and back increased. "I admire that, actually. You are very cold and precise. You simply need to learn who you are able to kill, and who you cannot begin to touch." Hutchison pushed harder still, and Henri cried out.

"You hurt Henri!" It was Roland's voice. "You should not hurt Henri!"

Hutchison spat. "Tell your retard to shut up, Bernardin, or he might find himself as dead as everybody else around here."

"Leave him alone!" Henri yelled. Hutchison brought his knee into the small of Henri's back, and Henri fell to the floor again. He opened his eyes and saw Hutchison's shoes. Roland's shoes were there, too, directly behind Hutchison's.

Henri heard a gagging sound, and Hutchison's nozzle device clanged to the floor beside Henri. Then Hutchison's shoes began to lift, very slowly, from the floor. "I believe I told you," said Roland's voice—but it was not Roland's usual voice, it had a steadiness and had lost its absent melody—"that you should not hurt Henri, you scum-licking child of a dog." Then there was a snapping sound, and Hutchison's body fell limp to the floor. Hutchison's eyes were open, but they were rolled halfway upwards and were not looking at anything.

Henri pressed his palms against the wall and pulled himself up to a sitting position. Roland was face-to-face with Bernardin. Henri was dizzy.

"Well, Dr.," Roland said, "it was a pleasure working for you." Roland swung an open hand at the base of Bernardin's throat. The doctor collapsed, and Henri thought, Shattering the trachea; that is a mode of death I had not considered.

"Bingo," said Roland. To Henri, it was rather an odd word.

Roland helped him to stand. "You are hurt, Henri. Let me carry you."

That was fine with Henri. Roland lifted him.

"Hutchison came in a helicopter, but I do not know how to fly a helicopter. There is a boat on the north side of the compound. We have to hurry, but tell me if I hurt you." Roland began to walk quickly.

✧   ✧   ✧

"Say it again, Henri."

Henri had no desire to say it again, but he did. He formed the strange syllables in as exact an imitation of Roland as he could manage. "I've been studying in France this year. I haven't brought anything back except my clothes and books."

They were flying now. *Flying*. In the last twenty-four hours they had taken boats, cars, and this, the airplane. Henri was tired and his shoulder still ached from the struggle with Hutchison.

A woman—that was the name of the alternate configuration—came down the thin walking space beside Henri's seat and asked him something about drinking something, Henri wasn't certain of the words. He reached and touched where her mammaries bloated; she said something quite harshly and slapped him. A few of the people—people! Dozens of them!—looked at him. Roland pretended not to notice the whole exchange. The woman stomped away; Henri felt oddly censured.

"You can't just touch people, especially women," Roland said in French. Then: "Where were you born?" asked in the new way of talking, the English.

"I was born in New York City, in the United States of America."

"Just say 'the U.S.' Americans do not usually say 'the United States of America.' "

Henri nodded and rested his head against the back of the seat.

"Do you have your U.S. passport?"

"Yes, Roland," Henri said.

"That was a chore to arrange, Henri, especially with the forged entry visas."

Henri looked at him.

" 'Forged' means 'false,' or 'pretend.' "

"I see," Henri said. Then he asked, "You are from the United States?"

"Yes," said Roland. He looked out the window. "It will be nice to go home."

"And what is your specialty?"

Roland laughed. "For the past thirteen years, my specialty has been to make sure you stay safe."

"I see. And do you work for Bell or AT&T or Corning?"

Roland shifted toward him. "Where did you learn those?"

"It was a long time ago. I just know the words, not what they mean."

Roland considered that, and sat back. "No. I work for the government there. The leaders of the country. I belong with a group that does intelligence operations for the nation."

"You are in charge?"

Roland laughed again. "No, not quite."

"Ah," said Henri. "Then you are the lovely co-host."

Roland did not respond to that. After a short time he said, "We should both get some sleep. We need the rest. A whole new world is coming up for you, Henri Elobert. I will be with you the whole way."

"Yes," said Henri, and he fell asleep.

The plane landed several hours later in New York City of the United States of America. Henri took from the overhead compartment the small bag that held his three changes of clothing. He checked to make sure he had the American passport Roland had given him.

Roland looked as if he were very much asleep, even though Henri knew he was dead; Henri had shattered his trachea in the same manner Roland had shattered Hutchison's. He had waited until Roland was sound asleep to do it, because he liked Roland and did not want to cause any pain.

Henri hurried to reach the place called "customs," and he recited all the lines Roland had taught him during the flight. There were people everywhere, all members of the More-Than-Six. Henri did not stop to talk with them. He was in a hurry to get through the customs and see this world.

Henri's world had ended, every last bit of it now that Roland was gone. Henri had helped end it. That should please the dark shape, the one called Michael. Now Henri was together with the More-Than-Six, mixed in with the dark shape's audience. He could begin learning how to end this world as well. It was a project he would enjoy.

Book II:
The Age of Faith

"What does faith oblige us to do?
Faith obliges us:
first, to make efforts to
find out what God has revealed;
second, to firmly believe
what God has revealed
third, to profess our faith
openly whenever necessary."

Baltimore Catechism No. 2,
Question 201

Deuterologue

MEMO: Minutes for Executive Council Meeting #2974423

DISTRIBUTION:
- All seven archangel executive offices
- Amalgamated Angelic Workers Union, Local #1
- Heaven, Management Information Systems division

PRESENT AT MEETING:
Archangel Michael (facilitator)
Archangels Gabriel, Uriel, Jeremiel, Suriel, and Azariel
Abaddon the Destroyer (Rep., Angelic Workers Union)
Bob (Manager, Management Information Systems)
Mandi (scribe)

ABSENT:
Archangel Raphael (unexplained)

9:00: Gabriel hails attendees and wishes them fullness of grace. Tells funny story about a time he was visiting Presbyterian missionaries in Costa Rica. Passes out meeting agenda.

<u>9:05:</u> Michael thanks attendees for extra effort put into End of the World push. Promises yet again that, once project is finished and God reappears, bonus plans, compensations, and incentives should see a hefty jump.

<u>9:17:</u> Michael presents updated responsibility sheets (SEE "Action Items," below). Discusses implementation particulars.

<u>9:35:</u> Ten minute break. Mandi serves brownies and espresso.

<u>9:45:</u> Floor discussion opened.
 1) Archangel Suriel (Apocalyptic Supplies) outlines needs for trumpets, bowls, document seals, and four horses (white, red, black, and pale green). Enters budget extension request. Michael approves.
 2) Archangel Jeremiel (Logistics; Subcommittee for Signs and Omens) explains concern that Biblical endtime regulation requires a mankind death level of 25% at the Four Horsemen episode, 33.3% during the catastrophes of the seven trumpets, and 33.3% for the Euphrates River clash, leaving a minuscule 8.4% for the Armageddon fiasco and practically nobody to be there afterwards should God actually make an appearance. Michael counters that ending the world requires a significant death rate, and that it would be ludicrous to get squeamish about a little overkill considering the circumstances.
 3) Abaddon the Destroyer (Union Rep., A.A.W.U.) complains that production demands for endtime plague of locusts constitutes a contractual violation of working conditions. Says the requirement that locusts be upgraded with iron breastplates, lion's teeth, and tail stingers has forced uncompensated overtime. Argues he could never get enough meteors assembled in time for the "stars falling to Earth" expectation. Michael counters that Biblical requirements overrule A.A.W.U. contract items (cf. Rev.

9:1-11; 8:12), and thanks Abaddon in advance for the extra effort he knows the angels will be more than happy to give.

4) Bob (Management Information Systems) assures that the Managing Angel Program is showing "superlative success," with Phases I and II preparing all human end-time key players for the big event. Announces launch of Phase III. Expresses concern that Archangel Raphael has failed to file reports for the past decade. Archangel Uriel seconds the concern, pointing out that although Raphael has been a bit of a recluse for the past three thousand years, his absence from the past 104 monthly Executive Committee meetings is starting to get annoying. Attendees concur that no one has even *seen* Raphael since 1976, and vote unanimously to keep an eye out for him.

<u>10:26:</u> Michael adjourns meeting. Sets next meeting for third Tuesday, month after next.

ACTION ITEMS:

Activity	Responsible
Purchase endtime supplies	Suriel
Upgrade locust production 10%	Abaddon
Survey best zones for earthquakes	Azariel, Uriel
Locate qualified supplier for production of hail/fire mixed with blood	Suriel
Initiate research for contact of Elizabeth Goddard, Phase III of Managing Angel Program	Bob, Gabriel
Keep eye out for Raphael	All

ALEPH:
1985, With Elizabeth Onstage

Elizabeth gauged the crowd through thick cigarette smoke that billowed and caressed the stage light into scattered lances. There were hazy people-outlines only, about seventy in the audience; a Buffalo crowd, which meant a range of intelligence from reasonably bright to hokey.

The emcee said, "Our next performer just flew in from a two-month tour of the West Coast. Please welcome with me America's last moral comedienne, Ms. Elizabeth Goddard!"

Applause and hoots as she walked out. *Hoots*, despite the lace collar primly buttoned up to her bottom row of teeth and a skirt that hung into downstairs.

You never have a set act, because if you do you'll run into someone who unsettles it. Your pace comes from the audience, and if they never even know it, then you're the best. She had learned that years ago in Brighton High School from Clayton Pinkes. Of all people. Here she was, still listening, years later after all the pain and hurt.

Still, she owed most of her material to Clayton. Not the comedic twists, but the raw content. That must have counted for a little something, a pinch of forgiveness. They were young then, after all; anyone could be excused for sins of youth, even Clayton Pinkes. She hadn't seen him in almost six years now. She hoped he was dead.

"Good evening, and I am indeed Elizabeth Goddard, the world's last moral comedienne. I guarantee you, ladies and gentlemen, that every syllable from my mouth tonight will be good old one-hundred-percent family entertainment."

Mostly laughs, a little applause, and a handful of heckling boos, particularly from a tall, dirty-blond-haired stud in the second row of tables, right-hand side. Elizabeth pointed at the man. "And if you don't like that, sir, please fuck off."

Laughs, and Blondie the Stud took it well, so Elizabeth stuck with him. "You sir, if you would, please: Did you come here tonight with a religion?" A few laughs, a decrescendo really. Blondie the Stud was laughing the loudest, embarrassed but pleased to be the center of attention. He would be a talker, so Elizabeth needed to move in quick, get out quick. "Please, sir, any religion you brought with you tonight, whatever they didn't make you check at the door."

"My folks was Nazarenes," Blondie said. Loud voice.

"Ah," said Elizabeth. "They were too poor to afford a real *big* religion, then?"

More laughs, Blondie still the loudest. Elizabeth moved off him before people could become annoyed by his idiocy. She swung to an older woman, early forties, dark hair curled and skin pale. The woman had smiled, but had yet to laugh aloud. The type Elizabeth most liked to play off. The harder audiences. Clayton Pinkes would approve.

"You, ma'am, any religion this evening?"

"Baptist," she said. Fast, concise.

"Baptist!" Elizabeth repeated, making sure everyone caught it. "Currently practicing? Or . . . no, she's shaking her head, ladies and gentlemen, she's a vacationing

Baptist. Sunday Baptist on sabbath break, you could say."
The brighter ones caught that; they were the only ones
who deserved to.

"What I like about Baptists, Southern Baptists especially, is the *really* healthy attitude they carry about
women's personal freedom." Physical contrast for the
irony: arm raised with index finger extended, a profes-
sor's stance, with a conflicting gee-whiz smile. "House-
wives are a powerful force in the Southern Baptist
community. For one thing, each election year, every
good-ol'-boy Southern Baptist husband has the vote he
casts automatically seconded by his astute, free-thinking
Mason-Dixon gal—" pause during laughter, and a switch
to her stock Southern housewife squawky drawl. "Now,
Jim-Bob, you jes' show me what to do in this here votin'
booth. What's that, now? I grabs hold of the lever real
firmly"—Elizabeth cupped her hand, a vague hint of
obscenity—"and then I yanks? Why, that's easy as pie!
I believe you done taught that partic'ler move to me
before." Pause for laughter. "Well, honey, I shore hopes
that makes you feel better, now." Wide eyes, empty-
headed grin, laughter denouement.

A little rest between themes. Let them sip their beers,
light their smokes. Then: "I myself, should I ever get
married, plan to have a one hundred percent egalitarian household." Addressing Blondie the Stud directly:
"Egalitarian means 'equal,' see." Well, that was using
him, but what the hell. "Yes, indeed, an equal household. My husband will do half the cooking, half the
cleaning, have six or seven periods for me yearly." Loud
laughter, not because of the deeper irony but because
she had referred to menstruation on a public stage. That
kind of audience, then. "I have to admit—" she grabbed
her crotch "—I'm a touch worried about my husband
helping birth his half of the twins. And breast feeding
might be a *definite* no-go."

Clayton Pinkes would have been offended by that.
Jesus Christ, why was she so obsessed with Clayton this

evening? She hadn't thought of him for a couple years. But here she was tonight . . .

"Speaking of tits, back to religion. Did you know that the Catholic saint, Agatha, when she was martyred, had her breasts cut off?" Groans from the audience, mostly from the women. The dark-haired pale women shifted her shoulders forward a little. Elizabeth enjoyed that. "No, it's a fact. Saint Agatha had her breasts cut off, Saint Lucy had her eyes plucked out, and Saint Willy of Westonia had his wing-wang whopped off, just slash, like that, and bye-bye Mr. Happy." Laughs from the more sadistic bastards, but mostly groans of mock-sympathetic pain. Back to Blondie the Stud, a personal address: "Oh, sure, a little religious history puts them off, but you *know* the bastards are going home right after the show and slapping *Nightmare on Elm Street, Part 66* into the VCR's."

Laughter peak, then applause. The in-confidence joke would placate Blondie, making up for the earlier slam. *Don't make a single enemy in your audience. A single enemy draws himself sympathy, and soon you've got half the people against you and the rest of them distracted by the first half's anger.* Good advice; where had she heard that?

Oh, Christ. Clayton had said it.

"Of course, it's no secret that religious history is chock full of mayhem, violence, betrayal, torture, and unmitigated horror. Let me share with you some of the more humorous examples . . . "

It was an all right audience, a good night. These days, being up and high on the crowd was the one good thing happening for Elizabeth Goddard.

There were two ways you could measure audience mood. The first was Elizabeth's way: scanning eyes, a feel for laugh cadence, instinctual reactions to mob moods. This was the very traditional way. Most comedians used it. Good comedians used it well.

The second way to measure audience mood was a little less traditional. It involved six discrete biosensors—extremely discrete, no bigger than No. 2 pencils faithfully worked down to stubs at Sharpening Time in a bleak parochial school classroom years ago. At Step One, these biosensors—a misnomer, really, since the sensors scanned and absorbed *all* noise within their assigned parameters, and it was the off-site computer that ran the differentiation and analysis; you know, the one linked to the computer you had in your car just now . . . These biosensors made rapid sextangulation sweeps, 100 times every minute (1.666666 etc. times per second), collecting all noise bits, from dishes breaking in the back room to blood circulating in the head of, say, that black-haired woman sitting up front, the one with the pale skin and deep eyes.

Then, Step Two: A noise block was sent in burst transmission to the computer in your car, which itself sent burst transmissions to a larger system via the IBM PrivNet satellites (a product to be announced "eventually," they said, and on which your friend and employer had managed to secure an account in the prototype phase; the only other prototype accounts belonged to IBM Corporate, which was fine, and to the U.S. Central Intelligence Agency, which concerned you. But your employer didn't seem to mind).

Step Three: The larger system at the end of the PrivNet link sorted all noises into software-simulated monoechoic chambers; it then disposed of irrelevant non-biologicals (not all of them, of course; the sound of a glass slamming onto the table at a particularly good punchline was ripe for analysis). It then performed (1) summatives, (2) cross-references within a single person's biology, (3) cross-references between individuals (the system, for example, could predict to an 87% certainty who would sleep with whom after the show, although no one ever used it for that), and (4) cross-references between groups at tables.

Step Four: Two key indicators were generated at the end of analysis, Read Factor (RF) and Sway Factor (SF)—if applicable. Read Factor—and this was your primary assignment—gave an Overall RF (ORF) and a Joke-By-Joke RF (JRF). ORF demonstrated a comedian's ability to get an audience to express its opinion on Current Issues. JRF was the actual Current Issue opinion of the audience recorded on a one-through-ten scale. When, for example, this particular comedienne, Elizabeth Goddard, did the gender inequality series of jokes, the JRF readings came in at 7.3, 6.9, 8.1, and 7.4. The reading told you (you were estimating now—actual word-by-word analysis was performed back at Solutions Headquarters) that most of these people would, with 74.25% assurance, agree that "Yeah, women are still subjected to male dominance, and it's the fault of both males and women who refuse to break from traditional roles."

Step Five (if applicable): Comedians with an ORF of 6.6 and higher fell into the Prime Stanine, the top. This was the case with Elizabeth Goddard, according to the feedback you were getting on your portable right now and past analyses from other shows. She was an 8.7 tonight, impressive, and you'd even recorded her at 9.5 once. So analysis for Sway Factor, you knew, automatically kicked in back at Solutions headquarters. Sway Factor measured not only how well a comedian could elicit response to Current Issues, but also how well the comedian could twist those opinions, turn them around, and actually have an influence. Sway the opinions of the masses—however subtly now, and substantially over time given enough 6.6+ comedians. Given a large enough audience. Given an audience consisting mainly of the correct demographic population, those from early twenties to mid-thirties, lower-middle to mid-middle class.

A lot of givens, but everything could be arranged. Given your current employer and friend.

So that was the second way to measure audience mood. It was a great deal more accurate, but it cost a hell of a lot of money. Even if Elizabeth had known about it and had access to it, she probably wouldn't have found in it any real application to performing on stage.

He looked about thirty-five, thirty-seven; twelve years older than she, at least. He sat down next to her as if he belonged there. "Buy you a drink," he said, and he wasn't asking.

Elizabeth smirked at him. "Thanks, no. I've got a set in the second show. I've gotta keep a clear head."

"A soda, then," he said. He waved down a waitress and ordered a Pepsi and a Heineken. Elizabeth kept watching the stage. Some twerp was doing a routine about the differences between New York City and Los Angeles—real fresh stuff, that, and incredibly relevant to a Buffalo crowd who'd probably never been to either place. The man beside her sat quietly. He kept a beat-up leather briefcase on his lap. With both arms he hugged it against his abdomen.

The drinks arrived.

"Fine, they're here. Ms. Goddard, my name is Roger Kallur, and let's get one thing straight. This is not an attempt to pick you up, so you can drop all feminine aloofness associated with activities of that sort right now. Nor is it an attempt to become chummy with you and win your friendship. I don't want or need you as a friend. What this is, simply, is a business deal."

The comedian on stage said something about L.A. driving being deadlier because New York drivers didn't have enough room to get up a head of steam before slamming into someone.

"Gee, Roger Kallur, I was hoping we could just fuck."

"No. This is business." He tilted his glass and carefully poured from the beer bottle. Well, *he* was one unshockable number. Or at least appeared to be.

"If it's business, maybe you should try to pick up my agent and fuck *him*."

Kallur finished pouring with a neat twist of the bottle, the last of the beer foam circling inside the lip of the Heineken bottle neck. She'd seen that move before. Was it for wine? Champagne, maybe.

"You don't have an agent, Ms. Goddard."

"Of course I don't. Who'd want an agent who'd jump into bed with just any old Heineken drinker who tries to pick me up in a comedy club?"

His face didn't change—what the hell was she doing, anyway? This guy could be somebody, maybe an agent himself. What if he was a scout for Improv, or even Carson? Well, not Carson, but maybe *Star Search*. She could use the money from gigs like those. And here she was, tired, hot, and bitchy, insulting him. He smelled like Old Spice, and Elizabeth knew she smelled like sweaty comedienne; he sat straight-backed, she was slouched with most of her weight on her elbows. She picked up the Pepsi and held the cool glass lightly against her cheek. "Sorry I'm so irritable. Post-show comedown. What's your game, Mr. Kallur?"

"Education, Ms. Goddard."

"Education? Like, a *teacher*?" Shit. Well, she'd never liked *Star Search* anyway.

"I'm currently researching at the University of Buffalo for my doctoral thesis in Speech Communications. Comic influence in oral tradition. I'm tracking the correlation between political publications and audience reactions to comic representations of current national issues."

"You want Steve Allen, sweetheart, not me." The comedian on stage was doing a bit on a conversation between a California Valley Girl and a Bronx hooker, both of whom had struck it big with the lotteries and were trying to fit in at a socialite function. Not bad. In fact, pretty fresh, and the accents were decent. Maybe the guy had a spark after all.

Roger Kallur pulled an envelope from the inside breast pocket of his suit coat. From the envelope he took four typed pages and a pair of hundred dollar bills.

"Here's how it works. For the next two years, you use jokes from the first page. There are fifty-five for that period, and you can use them in whatever order or combination you like. The only stipulation is that you use no fewer than four and no more than seven in any given performance. And please, use the jokes exactly as they are presented here, word for word."

She looked at his eyes. He was serious.

"At the end of 1987, you will switch to jokes on page two. Same rules, same stipulations. Again, after two years you'll retire the list and move on to the third page of jokes; two more years, page four. At the beginning of 1994, we'll see if there's any need for a fifth cycle."

The comedian on stage wound up his act and the audience applauded. Elizabeth had missed the last of his routine.

"Just how the hell long does it take to write a doctoral thesis, Kallur?"

He shrugged. "Unfortunately, time is the tradeoff for longitudinal studies." He acted as if she had already agreed to do his jokes. This son of a bitch didn't ask for anything. He was the sort who assumed he could just stroll in and issue orders, get what he wanted, no questions.

Elizabeth glanced at the two hundred-dollar bills.

"I'd help you out, Kallur, but I don't do written routines. I'm ninety percent improvisation. Sorry."

"Your stipend will be fifty dollars per act that includes jokes from the list. There's a ceiling of three hundred per week, nonnegotiable."

Not, "Your stipend *would* be . . ." or "Your stipend *could* be . . ." What a bastard.

Three hundred more a week would almost double her current take. Just for squeezing five or six of this guy's one-liners into her act. "Let me see the jokes."

He handed them to her. The two hundred dollars still sat unmentioned on the table.

"I'm going back to the changing room to look these over. Be here after my set in the second show. If you leave, no deal, you got that?"

He nodded.

"You're an arrogant bastard, Kallur. Pushy, self-absorbed, and cold as Eskimo gonads. That's the only reason I'm even considering this."

For the first time since he sat down, Kallur's face changed expression. He smiled.

She closed her act for the second show: "Thank you, and remember—pray for your neighbor tonight so he won't kick the shit out of you tomorrow." It went about as well as her first act; not a brilliant crowd, so not a brilliant performance. Still, the crowd was robust enough to enjoy the bawdier parts of her approach.

Robust. An audience-friendly word for a mob with an eighth-grade sense of humor.

Kallur was still at the table to the rear of the club. She started back.

"Our next performer"—the emcee's voice behind her—"is a first-timer to the comedy stage, fresh new talent to split your eyes and bring tears to your stomach. Ladies and gentlemen, please join me in welcoming a very humorous man, Mr. Gabe Angelo!"

Applause. Elizabeth looked toward the stage: tall, thin, baby-clear skin that made the comedian look like a too-soon sprouted adolescent. Wavy peroxide hair. Blue jeans and a T-shirt that in bold black letters announced: THIS SPACE AVAILABLE FOR YOUR MESSAGE.

"Hi! How are you tonight?" The crowd cheered. Elizabeth hated it when comedians opened by asking the crowd how it was tonight. A cheap intro. What had happened to the New York/Los Angeles comedian who'd followed her act for the first show? She'd wanted to see if he could pull a better performance the second time around.

"Great! Super! Looks like a really fun crowd, and we're all going to have a great time. You seem like folks who really want to laugh!" Flattery, suggestion, a fast and cheap approach for winning them over, but not a word of comedy yet. "And laugh we will, believe you me!"

The crowd laughed.

"You know, I just got here by plane from Stockholm, but before I did I rode my bicycle to the airport by way of Hell, Norway. So I guess you could say I went through Hell to get here!"

The crowd laughed louder and broke into applause. Elizabeth shook her head. She walked back to Kallur's table.

"Kallur—"

"Wait," he said. He was slouched forward—good God, he could actually unstraighten that back!—and his chin rested in his hand as he watched the stage. He was chuckling. "Doesn't this guy seem funny to you? He seems funny to me."

On stage, Gabe Angelo said, "Of course we can't boil him, you idiot! He's a friar!" The audience applauded again, and even Kallur laughed aloud.

She sat down across from him and blocked his view of the stage. Kallur tried to look past her, but the smile finally dropped and he seemed to shake himself to focus on her once more. "Let's get this over with," Elizabeth said. "It's late, I'm tired, and I'd like to get out of here and go to my hotel."

"Fine."

"Look, these jokes of yours." She unfolded the first page, labeled 1986-1987. She had to squint at the print, which appeared to be in a font toward the smaller side of microelite. "I'll be honest. They range from the inane to the totally incomprehensible. 'Chrysler should buy the rights to Hyundai and finally perfect it for the American market by leaving the design alone and jacking the price fifty percent.'"

When she looked up, he was smiling again.

"What's a Hyundai?" she asked.

"It doesn't matter yet. Don't use any jokes until you understand them."

She turned to the third page, labeled 1990–1991. "'It's not so bad having a president who won't eat broccoli. We might have ended up with one who only eats Rice on the side.' And this one: 'This show is *not* sponsored by an NEA grant, so for my next act I'll vomit on a nun.'" The fourth sheet, 1992-1993: "'Question: What do you get if you cross a Catholic with a Descartesian? Answer: A miscarriage.'"

"The last one isn't certain yet. The date for Descartesians is tentative."

She waited. For a long time he said nothing else. Then he stood and left a dollar tip on the table. "Start in three months. Don't use anything until it seems relevant to you. Either I or one of my researchers will monitor audience reaction."

He left the two hundred dollars on the table.

"This piece of string walks into a bar," said Gabe Angelo. "The bartender says, 'Holy cow! Are you really a piece of string?' The string ties itself up and musses its threads at both ends, and says, 'No, I'm a frayed knot!'"

By this time, the audience sounded like a hen house gone mad. "Jesus Christ," Elizabeth muttered.

Gabe Angelo's T-shirt now read, WHERE, OH WHERE, HAS MY RAPHAEL GONE?

"What do you get if you cross a rhinoceros and an elephant? 'ell if I know! Get it?"

They got it. Some were laughing to the point of tears. Now his shirt said, HOW MANY ANGELS CAN DANCE ON A PINHEAD? "Get it?" he asked again. Elizabeth started to suspect she could understand what motivated hecklers.

"Get it?" he asked.

He was asking her. Everyone else had quieted down while he waited for an answer.

Quieted down? They were catatonic, throughout the entire hall. Cigarettes dangled from flaccid lips, eyes were lowered toward the tables, staring into drinks.

"Come on, I really respect your opinion. Do you think the jokes are funny?" His voice reverberated, the room's only sound, bouncing off empty heads and around listless bodies.

Weird shit, unexplainable shit, like days back with Clayton Pinkes. She felt cold and empty, her thoughts aimless sparks of static electricity. "What happened?" Her own voice was swallowed by the stillness.

"What, them? I hypnotized them. I've just put them on hold for a second. Now really, tell me, is the material any good?"

Hypnotized? A whole crowd? The guy wasn't a comedian, he was a fucking magician. That explained it. It explained the T-shirt, too, which now read, I'LL SEE YOUR URIM AND RAISE YOU A THUMMIM. Elizabeth walked to the middle of the room. Every few steps she waved a hand in front of some limp face with a truant brain. Then she looked at Gabe Angelo. "Holy shit," she said. "How'd you manage this? How'd you *do* this?"

Gabe Angelo shrugged. "It's a voice thing. It's not too hard if you know how, and if they want it. Listen, I really want to know if I'm any good or not." He sounded impatient and a little scared.

Eight years ago, and Clayton looked the same way after talking in front of a church congregation as a representative of their youth group. "How was I? Was I all right?" She touched his face and told him he was more than all right. She told him he was wonderful up there, and she meant it.

"Who cares?" she said to Gabe Angelo. "With a talent like this, who needs to do comedy?"

He frowned. It wasn't the answer he'd wanted. "They don't think I'm funny. They just laugh because they want to and I let them. I make them. I was really hoping you'd say I had some talent. Comedy, I mean."

No one moved the whole time they talked. No one. It was like one of those wax museums where the figures were rigged to simulate breathing. Except wax museum figures looked more vibrant. These folks, this entire audience, had seized up at Gabe Angelo's suggestion, as if . . .

She felt angry then. "This is sick."

Gabe Angelo looked ashamed. "I know, I know. But I was scared. This was my first time."

She stared at the crowd again. "It's dirty, taking their own heads away from them. I mean, it's amazing, I've never seen a whole crowd hypnotized at once. What the hell's the point, though?" Back looking at Gabe Angelo. "What the hell's the point, if they're not really laughing because they want to?"

"They want to," he said. "They came here because they believed they would laugh. Not to see you or me. They're believers."

"But they're not laughing *at* anything!"

He was slouched like a child trying to talk his way out of a scolding. "It doesn't matter. *Believing* they should laugh is enough. They don't really need any specific thing or person to believe in, do they?"

"It's a stunt."

"They want stunts."

"It's a farce! It's a trick, it's a lie, it's a game, and it's cheap!" She fumed her way back to her table and grabbed Kallur's money and enigmatic joke lists. "And you're *not* funny!"

His T-shirt said, BY FAITH ARE YE SAVED THROUGH GRACE. Even before she reached the door, the crowd's laughter exploded.

Clayton Pinkes was on her Days Inn hotel television set, Channel 9. She had been trying to catch a late night rerun of Carson or an old Dean Martin flick, and suddenly there was Clayton's face, a specter from the past, proclaiming that faith was the substance of things hoped for, the evidence of things not seen. Clayton's eyes narrowed and dug into her, just as if he were right there, reading her soul as he had always done. Clayton said that except through faith it was impossible to please him, and Elizabeth almost said, "Why the fuck would I want to please you, Clayton?" Then she realized the "him" meant God, not Clayton Pinkes. Clayton was quoting Scripture. He said, "These all died in faith, not having received the promises, but having seen them afar off, and were persuaded of them, and embraced them, and confessed that they were strangers and pilgrims on the Earth."

She did feel like a stranger. A downtown Buffalo Days Inn, not a person in the city she could even call an acquaintance.

No, no, not that game. Not Clayton the Preacher staking out territory in her heart. She reminded herself of the tactics and techniques, all those things she needed to learn to perform in front of an audience. All those things Clayton knew instinctively. She would turn off the set. No, better still, she would watch it and categorize all of Clayton's techniques. It would be a learning exercise. She could use him, and he wouldn't even know it.

What the fuck was Clayton doing on television?

"Brothers and sisters, the promises of God are for you and for your children. These are frightening times, times prophesied centuries ago. But be assured—God's wrath is not aimed at those who through faith embrace His promises. Stay with us for Deacon Richard Lanpher's homily and my own message tonight, 'Faith for the End of Time.'"

Deacon Richard Lanpher. Then Clayton and Dickie were still a team.

Clayton faded. A housewife appeared on screen and started bemoaning the stains on Bobby's new overalls. A booming, disembodied voice proclaimed she needed Liquid Tide.

Clayton was good. Was still good. Most preachers sounded like paid advertisers, not quite car salesmen but not quite Dustin Hoffmans, either. Clayton was casual, as if he were chatting with a living human being and not a camera. Clayton was conversant.

Screw Clayton! All night he's been in and out of my head. Now he's on television, and I'm sitting here admiring him. He doesn't mean anything but a screwed-up mind and an insane world that turns upside down every other day. Religion and Clayton. Sex and Clayton. Clayton and the end of the world. Well, you almost ended mine, you son of a bitch.

There was a knock at her hotel door. She didn't know anyone in Buffalo, and her first thought was that it would be Clayton. That was stupid; Clayton was on television. Someone from the club? Blondie the Stud could have followed her back, and even Gabe Angelo could have asked the club manager where she was staying.

She settled the question by opening the door. She kept the chain latched and looked through the gap. It was Roger Kallur.

"Let's go out for a drink," he said.

"More business?"

"No. That's done for tonight. Pleasure."

Pleasure. Roger Kallur and pleasure. Forward, self-assured, Roger Kallur who was not, in any way, anything like the specter of Clayton Pinkes.

She undid the chain. "Why don't you come in for a drink instead?"

Kallur looked doubtful. "Does Days Inn have room service?"

"Couldn't tell you."

He came in anyway.

BETH:
Back at Brighton High School, 1978–1980

It took her three weeks, but she finally caught on to Clayton Pinkes's glance game. It worked like this: In Social Studies class, Clayton would stare at a spot on the wall directly above her head. Mr. Grant, their Social Studies teacher, kept the desks in a U-shape, two rows on each side of the room facing toward a large center area that Mr. Grant would pace during his lectures. Clayton sat kitty corner from her, three seats away by the windows. She would feel him staring, and she would quickly glance at his face and away again, discovering he wasn't really looking at her. Then—it was inevitable— she would look again, longer this time. After a couple of seconds, his eyes would shift down to hers, he would look surprised that she was looking at him, and then he would smile. This made her the initiator, technically, and she was obliged to smile back.

Which was all right. Clayton Pinkes was cute.

For three months they never even spoke to each other. The major breakthrough came when right before

Christmas holiday he passed her in the hall and said, "Have a good vacation."

"Thanks!" she said, with way too much enthusiasm, and she felt vaguely embarrassed.

After the vacation, she collected every bit of courage she had and talked her friend Linda Barnestead into passing Clayton Pinkes a note that said: "Clayton, I think Elizabeth Goddard thinks your cute. She told me so. Do you think she's cute too?" Linda Barnestead sat in one of the two seats between them, and she had to reach across Frank Morano's desk to put the note on Clayton's.

Clayton wrote directly back to Elizabeth. "Linda Barnestead wrote me a note that says you told her you thought I was cute. Could you tell her that I think you're gorgeous? She seems eager to know."

Elizabeth wrote, "How come you never talk to me in school?"

Clayton wrote, "Because I can't think of a good opening line."

Elizabeth wrote, "Try writing one, and I'll let you know if I like it."

Clayton wrote, "Would you like to come to a Bible study Tuesday evening, 7:00 P.M. at Dickie Lanpher's house?"

That wasn't exactly the sort of line Elizabeth was expecting, and before she had time to answer, Mr. Grant saw the open note on her desk. He confiscated it. "Hey, we've got entertainment, everybody!"

Elizabeth tensed, and the class started cheering. Mr. Grant was an easygoing teacher, but he knew just how to embarrass you if he wanted to.

"Now let's take a vote. How many say I should read it out loud?"

Everyone's hand went up. Clayton's, too. Then she realized that Clayton's name was nowhere on the note, so he was going to get off clean.

Mr. Grant looked the note over, and seemed as if he was going to read it aloud. But then he frowned. He was reading the last message, the one about the Bible study, and he glanced up at her. He folded the note up and said, "All right, let's get back to class, shall we?" The students booed, and Mr. Grant went back to teaching.

Elizabeth looked at Clayton. He winked at her.

A little-known fact which very few students have ever taken advantage of is that most American public school teachers—even those who wouldn't have the least qualm about reading aloud a student note that discussed dating, relationships, or sex—become inordinately cautious when students start discussing anything having to do with religion. Clayton Pinkes knew this.

Elizabeth Goddard and Linda Barnestead came late to the Bible study. Linda had insisted on being late, saying that Clayton would notice them more if they came in separate from the crowd.

The study was held in the downstairs of the Lanpher family's split-level home. Elizabeth was immediately confused. There were no adults, and she wondered who would be in charge. There were kids from school, about twenty of them, but they weren't from any particular clique. There were a couple Jocks, some Heads, three Dweebs with their calculators on their belts, a cheerleader, a bunch of Brains and Brown Nosers, and even one Motor Head from the Auto Class gang. Everybody was sitting on the floor except Clayton, who had a chair. He was talking, and he nodded once when she and Linda joined the circle.

Clayton was in charge.

"So how are we supposed to answer that?" Clayton said. "Do we nod and agree that all rock music must be satanic, just because we're born again, and other born again people insist that rock is from Satan, end of discussion? I've mentioned some pretty good examples, the ones you'll usually hear from Christians who get the most upset about rock. But I'd like to give one more example. Listen to these lyrics, and get your Bibles ready."

Elizabeth saw that everyone had a Bible. She and Linda hadn't brought one. She didn't think they'd need it.

Clayton began reciting lyrics in a slow monotone. "Born free. As free as the wind blows. As free as the grass grows. Born free to follow the sun."

There was some good-natured laughing, and everyone was flipping through pages of their Bibles. The cheerleader spoke first, reading, " 'Stand fast therefore in the liberty wherewith Christ hath made us free, and be not entangled again with the yoke of bondage.' "

The Motor Head read, " 'For when ye were servants of sin, ye were free from righteousness.' "

The quotations began coming faster, sayings about all flesh being grass and fading with the sun, about God being the one who made grass grow for cattle and herbs grow for man, about God speaking through the wind. Some of the readings struck everyone as funny, but Elizabeth felt lost and stupid, not understanding the point.

"In summary," Clayton Pinkes said, "no person is really 'born free' from sin; the Bible says that the wind and grass do nothing of their own accord; and following the sun implies heathen nature worship. So what's the point, Elizabeth?"

She jerked up straight. They were all looking at her. She finally said, "There is no point. I mean, you could do that for anything. I mean, go through the Bible and find phrases that make something look bad. I mean, you don't really think 'Born Free' is a satanic song, do you?"

"Exactly!" Clayton said, and he stood up. "Elizabeth has hit the nail right on the head. If you work hard enough at it, you can make the Bible condemn anything you please, a rock song, an old pop tune, or the writing on a box of cereal. Each and every one of us should think hard about what Elizabeth just explained. If we go through our lives being *against* whole lists of things, we aren't going to have any time to be *for* anything."

Elizabeth tried to remember if she had said that. Well, she'd said something like that, anyway, or at least she agreed with it. They were looking at her as if she had said something profound. As if she were wise, based on what Clayton explained she had meant.

She could easily fall in love with Clayton Pinkes.

Life became faster and more bizarre after that night. There were miracles, small things at first. After a few meetings, Clayton started having the Bible study end with everyone praying out loud at the same time. Some of the kids prayed in foreign languages. "The gift of tongues," Clayton said. "It's when the Spirit of God prays through your spirit in a language you've never learned."

They called themselves "Charismatics."

There were prophesies. Clayton took the Motor Head aside one night, and when they were finished talking the Motor Head was crying. Clayton had his arm around the boy's shoulder. "I saw in a vision that Greg's grandmother is going to pass away this evening." Greg's grandmother did pass away that evening, and the next Bible study consisted almost entirely of praying out loud in tongues. Everyone put a hand on Greg the Motor Head while praying. Greg fell backwards after about fifteen minutes of continuous prayer, and he lay on the floor, his arms and legs twitching. "He's been slain in the spirit," Clayton said. "It's when the Spirit of God enters your spirit and rests there with you for a time."

And there were times when they would go beyond the boundaries of their own little group, into the adult world of strange religious practices. These were the interactions with the Charismatics, who were not really a religion at all, since their numbers included Catholics and Presbyterians and Lutherans and a whole range of other Christian churches Elizabeth had never even heard of before she met Clayton. "It's the Spirit of God moving through the full body of the church, uniting in spirit those who have been separated for centuries," said Clayton.

For about a year, the Spirit of God was doing just about everything it could, except bring Clayton's spirit closer to Elizabeth.

Then one evening the Bible study group, which by then had grown to about forty kids, went to a Charismatic mass held by one of the local Roman Catholic churches. To a standard, run-of-the-mill Roman Catholic, one of these masses would have looked like a cross between a carnival and an African voodoo ritual. Elizabeth was accustomed to it by now. At Charismatic masses, people stood freely at any point in the service to announce messages they were hearing from God. Others burst into spontaneous proclamations in foreign languages they didn't know, followed by translations of the messages from others who also didn't know the languages. The entrance hymn lasted through twelve songs, and there were not three but eight scripture readings. The priest's homily was punctuated throughout with congregational shouts of "Amen!" and "Praise the Lord!"

Even Elizabeth was trying to pray in tongues by this time, although she was always suspicious that the language that came out of her mouth wasn't really a language at all, just nonsense words. Once she had confided that suspicion to Clayton, who told her that the gift of tongues could come either as the language of men or as the language of angels. He said that she was particularly blessed if she were speaking the tongues of angels. She had asked what sort of languages angels spoke, and he had answered, "English, some of the time, but they might speak Swedish, too, since their annual conventions are held in Stockholm." Clayton was like that; sometimes he made jokes out of your questions.

There were more than five hundred people in the congregation tonight. At the Our Father, everyone held hands, a common practice among Charismatics. Elizabeth made sure she sat next to Clayton precisely for that reason. She squeezed his hand once, at "Thy kingdom come," and again, harder, at "and forgive us our trespasses." There was no response; Clayton's eyes were closed, and he was lost somewhere in his praying.

After the mass, the service continued for another hour. The lay people who were the acknowledged leaders of the Charismatic movement stationed themselves at the foot of the altar, and members of the congregation who needed someone to pray with them filed forward. Many ended up flat on their backs, "slain in the spirit," and the continuous drone of prayer tongues lasted the entire time.

When everything in the church was finally starting to settle down, a middle-aged woman pushed a wheelchair up the aisle past Elizabeth and Clayton. There was a young girl in the wheelchair. They would hear later that the girl was the woman's daughter and had cerebral palsy.

The leaders of the Charismatic movement gathered around the girl, all laying hands on her and praying for healing, both spiritual and physical. Elizabeth looked over to Clayton, who was himself looking over toward Dickie Lanpher. Clayton looked forward again, and his forehead was scrunched in a way that looked painful. He had the demeanor of someone awaiting the outcome of an ultimatum, a great final test.

The girl in the wheelchair stood up slowly. She took three faulty steps. She looked as if she would fall, but then her balance came back and she started walking faster. A few moments more, and she was actually running back and forth across the altar platform.

The congregation caught its second wind for the endless Hallelujahs and Praise You, Jesuses. Elizabeth turned to look at Clayton, who was not there.

She found him, finally, outside in the dark. He sat with his back against the brick wall of the church, his legs pulled tightly against him, making him look like a ball resting against the bricks. Clayton Pinkes was crying.

"Clayton?" She put her hand on his shoulder and kneeled next to him.

He tried to stop the crying; his face tightened, and he almost managed a smile. But he broke down again.

Elizabeth tried to get both arms around him to hug him. He was shaking with his own sobs, saying, "I don't know what I did to him. I don't even know what happened. I don't know what I did."

"Did to who, Clayton?"

"Paolo. I don't even know what I did. Maybe I killed him. Do you think I'll go to hell for killing someone who wasn't even alive like a human being is?"

She held him tighter. "You're not making sense, Clayton."

He looked at her. His eyes were empty and lonely, so she kissed him. It seemed natural.

He stared at her a moment longer, and then started sobbing again. "You're the second girl I've ever kissed, and only the first one who's a girl."

"Clayton—"

"Why would anyone want to end the world?" He started shouting at her. "It's a good world! It's no worse and no better than it ever was! We've just got more machines, that's all! The only thing we don't have anymore is God. I don't think He believes in us any longer. I don't think He believes in *me*. They asked when I asked them to put Him on the phone, you know."

She stood up and backed away from him. It was a Clayton Pinkes she had never seen, angry, vulnerable, striking out because he *was* vulnerable. And crazy. This Clayton Pinkes was scaring her.

"It's something about my arm." He was holding up his right arm, showing her. "There's something weird about it. Watch." He stood up, looking around on the ground. He picked up a stone twice the size of a fist. Resting the right arm—bent, palm up—against the bricks of the church wall, he started methodically smashing it with the stone.

She screamed. He kept doing it until she ran over and knocked the rock from his left hand. The skin on his right arm was torn and bleeding. It was already starting to bruise.

"See?" he said. "The outside bone doesn't break. The one on the side opposite the thumb. Even the skin will be perfect in the morning. One of the bones in my arm doesn't break." More crying. He slid down with his back against the wall, returning to his fetal position. "It's got something to do with the Urim and the Thummim, but I can't figure out what. I think my arm is going to end the world."

She started backing away again.

"It's too much responsibility. Especially if God doesn't believe in me."

"Oh, Clayton," she said. She ran back into the church.

Before talking to Clayton again, Elizabeth used a Biblical Concordance and a Revised Standard Version of the Scriptures to learn the following: The Urim and the Thummim were mentioned only seven times in the Bible, and always in the earlier books of the Old Testament. It was unclear where they came from, what they looked like, what exactly they did, or where they disappeared to after Nehemiah, chapter seven, verse sixty-five. The only things Elizabeth knew for certain about them were that the ancient priests needed to be wearing them whenever they went into the presence of the Lord in the Temple; that God gave messages and answers through them to the people of Israel; and that "Urim" was Hebrew for "light," while "Thummim" was Hebrew for "perfection." Beyond those things she learned nothing.

That really shouldn't have discouraged her. Three thousand years of Biblical scholars had managed to pull together basically the same information she had.

She found nothing about the Urim and the Thummim that mentioned the end of the world or anybody named Paolo.

One phrase stayed with her, though, the one from the book of Exodus that said: "And thou shalt put in the breastplate of judgement the Urim and the Thummim; and they shall be upon his heart, when he goeth before the Lord: and he shall bear the judgement of the children of Israel upon his heart before the Lord continually." It was an ominous verse, she decided, a verse that hinted at the burden of knowing God's judgements.

"It's too much responsibility," Clayton had said. "Especially if God doesn't believe in me."

He stopped her in the hall when she was on her way to her fourth period biology class. "Skip class," he said. "I gotta talk to you."

They ducked past the hall monitors into the cafeteria. He bought her a milk and a doughnut.

"I scared you the other night. I'm sorry."

She shrugged and couldn't think of anything to say.

"You've seen me at my worst, so I think you deserve an explanation."

"Okay," she said.

He started talking in vague phrases about being commissioned by an angel to become a prophet for the end of the world. When she asked for specifics, he became even more vague, so she tried to just listen and understand what she could. He talked about visions of the future, and how he'd thought everybody had them. He talked about seeing the ghost of a nun who didn't know if she was going to Heaven or not. All of it he said with a wide-eyed passion that was not only begging her to believe him, but was also asking if it was all right for him to believe it himself. He was an impossible mix of religious certainty and the fear that she would think him insane.

She decided to be in love with him from then on.

That night they met after supper and went for a walk. They wound up in a deep field behind the Brighton First Baptist Church, and there they had sex for the first time.

Clayton didn't seem to know how to do it, and she certainly didn't. It hurt a great deal. After they had finished, Clayton started crying and saying that they had sinned, and that it was his fault because he took advantage of her. She ignored the pain she was still feeling, and she hugged him. The Clayton Pinkes who could cry so easily was someone that nobody else in the world except Elizabeth Goddard had ever gotten to see. The secret Clayton that belonged to her. She held back her own tears until she got home and found the bloodstains in her underwear.

It fell into a pattern after that. Clayton would preach to the Bible study group, eat lunches with her, not hold her hand in school or do anything that indicated they were together ("Scripture says that we should avoid even the appearance of evil," Clayton told her), and then they would have sex. They got better at it, and Elizabeth was astounded the first time she had an orgasm. It wasn't the way her mother described it—"No big deal, a couple of shivers." It was more. She couldn't get one every time, of course, and she was too embarrassed to touch herself with Clayton there or to try to tell him what he should do. But sometimes! Sometimes.

After sex, Clayton would either cry or become sullen, and he wouldn't talk to her for a few days, saying that he was a terrible influence on her life and that he was leading her into temptation.

Once she said, "Clayton, maybe sex isn't the biggest evil in our lives."

"It is in mine," he said. "Ever since I was little and first started playing dirty stories in my head."

"Clayton, *everyone* has done that!"

"But God can see the stories I play! Even angels can see them!" Slowly, his eyes became empty. "I killed an angel because I was mad that he could see my dreams and he wouldn't leave me alone. I didn't ask for a managing angel. I was happy just believing in God. I was happy thinking God was around to believe in me. Now there are all these miracles going on, but no angel, and no God, and I wish everything would just settle down. Or that God would show up to explain it all to me."

"But, Clayton—"

"But maybe I *don't* want God to show up! Maybe I don't want anything or anyone staring inside my brain and knowing how guilty I am. I'm a terrible sinner, Elizabeth, and I'm pulling you into all my sins."

"Clayton!" Her voice was sharp, which surprised her. "You're making yourself crazy. You didn't kill any angels. And I *like* sex with you. We both like it. Why would God make something so enjoyable for two people and then declare it one of the greatest sins in the world?"

Clayton became furious with her, and they didn't speak for a week.

Something in Clayton, she decided, needed sex to stay evil. Maybe it was the one way he knew how to rebel against things he didn't really want to believe in. And something in *her* needed sex to be . . . not evil, no, but illicit, risky. Good girls don't buy contraceptives. That would mean you were planning to have sex, and planning sex didn't feel nearly as innocent, nor nearly as exciting, as being spontaneous about it.

Their relationship remained a secret to all their friends.

In their senior year, Clayton began having her preach at the Bible study. It started with a simple talk, a discussion of love using the Scripture verses in First Corinthians chapter 13. Then he let her tackle what he considered to be the more advanced themes: salvation through faith and grace in the letter to the Galatians; the importance of good works as a part of salvation in the letter of James. Clayton began teaching her how to perfect her delivery, how to use pauses effectively, how to gauge the mood and attitudes of the listeners. He instructed her passionately, almost with fury, as if making her as good at it as he was would in some warped way atone for their still continuing to have sex. A divine trade-off, Elizabeth supposed: Sure I sleep with her, but look how well she's turning out.

And she was. Elizabeth began to feel the moods of the Bible study group, which now had over fifty regulars attending. Things Clayton had said that at first sounded mystical were now becoming real. When she preached, she felt when they were with her. She sensed when she was losing them. She knew what phrases made them comfortable, what words would startle them and draw closer attention. Despite all Clayton's guilt over his fluctuation between sex and faith, those two great incompatibles of his life, he was powerful in front of a group. Even some of the local churches were starting to ask him to "share" for a few minutes at their Charismatic services.

He was sharing his talent with her.

During March of 1980—far outside of Elizabeth's knowledge, of Clayton's knowledge, or Dickie's, or, really, anybody on the planet—the monthly Count of the Faithful readout, as recorded by the Population Numerics Data Base in Heaven, Management Information Systems Division, contained the following:

CURRENT FAITHFUL [DEFINED IN THIS CONTEXT AS THOSE WHO HAVE BASED THEIR LIVES, HOPES, OR BELIEFS ON THE WORDS OF CLAYTON PINKES]:

ROMAN CATHOLIC:	34
PROTESTANT:	2
ORTHODOXED, ETC.:	0
OTHER CHRISTIAN:	0
TOTAL:	36

TOTAL PERCENTAGE OF WORLD POPULATION:
<.00000002%

TARGET PERCENTAGE FOR URIM/THUMMIM:
2.76%

❖   ❖   ❖

Late in April of their senior year, Linda Barnestead was crying in the girls' bathroom. Someone went to look for Elizabeth, and Elizabeth found Linda leaning over one of the sinks, crying into the water she splashed on her face.

"What's wrong?" Elizabeth asked, not suspecting that what was wrong with Linda was about to become even more wrong for herself.

Linda opened her heart and soul: She had lost her virginity to Clayton Pinkes. After the sex, Clayton had cried. Linda felt horrible, because Clayton was so religious and now Linda knew she'd ruined his life. Clayton begged her to forgive him. They even prayed together after Clayton stopped crying. Linda was certain that God would forgive Clayton, but she knew God could never, never forgive her.

Clayton came to Elizabeth's house that afternoon, before her mother was home from work, and the fight was tremendous. Elizabeth even ran into the kitchen and grabbed a plate to throw at him. The plate missed, and Elizabeth wasn't sure if she'd meant it to. Clayton cried. Clayton asked her to forgive him. Clayton came completely clean and admitted he'd had sex with about six or seven other girls during the past two years. Elizabeth cried, too, and asked him to please forgive her for never having thought of fucking anyone else while she was with him, since that obviously would have made him feel better about how he lived. Clayton was furious that she said "fucking," so she called him a cocksucker.

It was exhaustion that finally ended the fight. Elizabeth forced back the sick emptiness, and then she started acting warm and sexy toward him. She managed, after a while, to coax him into having sex with her. They did, and afterwards Clayton became sullen. She knew he was feeling guilty, guiltier now than he'd ever felt after sex. She was glad; that was what she'd hoped for.

She began acting as if it were the happiest day of her life, and he became more miserable still.

She decided, later, that that was the day she got pregnant. It couldn't have been, of course; the timing was wrong. But it made a strong fantasy, and eventually she managed to believe it herself. She told Clayton so, that that was probably the day it happened. She let him think about it for a few days, and then casually mentioned the date, time, and place that her mother would be taking her for an abortion.

Clayton walked away without saying anything. It was Dickie Lanpher who confronted her. She was walking home from school, and Dickie came running up behind her on the sidewalk.

"Elizabeth, can we talk?"

She didn't look at him. "Well, if it isn't the henchman."

"You can't have an abortion."

She stopped walking and faced him. "Dickie, none of this has anything to do with you."

"If you have an abortion, it'll destroy Clay. You'll ruin him."

Ruin him? Was anyone wondering how ruined Elizabeth Goddard would be if she had a baby? Or if she had an abortion? Or if she gave the baby up for adoption? If she missed her first year of college because she was pregnant? Did anyone care that, right here, right now, she was already ruined?

No, she thought. Stop thinking like that. Not here, not in front of loyal little Dickie Lanpher of the Clayton Pinkes Fan Club. If she cried, it would be when she was alone.

"Tell you what, Dickie. You've convinced me. I'll have the baby, give it to Clayton, and let him raise it to be a good little Catholic Charismatic. He can teach it to speak in tongues, see visions, all that stuff a baby really needs. It'll only take twenty years out of his life. I'll write him monthly letters to check how it's going."

Dickie didn't say anything.

"Tell him he'd better get a supply of bottles. Clayton isn't built for breast-feeding."

She walked away, and she could feel herself wanting to laugh. Clayton breast-feeding. That was funny. If she thought hard about it, most of the past three years were funny in a demented way. After the abortion, she would think about that. How funny everything was.

GIMEL:
1999 in Rochester, New York

The headquarters office of the Christian Stewardship Ministry sported dozens of religious portraits, mostly reproductions of classics, spaced every eight feet down its hallways. An astute visitor would notice that, except for a handful of paintings showing Christ at different times of his life, and one other depicting angels, nearly every portrait was a representation of a female religious figure. Mary, the Mother of God, had the best coverage. She appeared as a teenager, on her knees gazing into a stream of light at the Annunciation; being carried into Heaven by angels at the Assumption; in anguish with Christ's body on her lap at the Pietà. The rest of the women appeared to be randomly drawn from religious history: Saint Teresa de Avila prostrate in one of her ecstatic visions; Saint Monica praying for the salvation of her son, Augustine; the Jewess Judith victoriously displaying the head of Holofernes; Saint Elizabeth holding the infant John the Baptist; Saint Lucy offering her eyes to God. An especially astute visitor, however, would discover that the portrait choices were not as haphazard as they seemed. There was a holy

virgin, holy mother, and Holy Virgin Mother ratio of
1:1:1.

No one ever asked Clayton Pinkes why he insisted the
Ministry headquarters be decorated that way. Even the
decorators nodded and worked around what they called
(but only among themselves) the Museum Reject Motif.
Clayton was drawing one hundred fifty-two million after-
overhead nonprofit dollars a year in contributions; success
like that could be pardoned a few aesthetic eccentricities.

The Rochester, New York, office was the first of what
was now seven Christian Stewardship Ministry operations
in the country. Each of the secondary operations held a
staff of seven or eight full-time coordinators. Headquarters
had a management staff of twelve. There were currently
11,968 Christian Stewardship Support Societies of volunteers at Roman Catholic churches in North America. That
far outstripped the old Knights of Columbus, the defunct
Rosary Societies, and even the Catholic Charismatics,
whose numbers had been seeing a steady decline since
the mid-1980's.

A large percentage of the Stewardship Ministry's
volunteers, in fact, were formerly active Charismatics
disillusioned by the old movement.

Membership and attendance in the Roman Catholic
Church in America had jumped 17% in the last year
alone, almost entirely attributable (said the surveys) to
the Stewardship Ministry movement. The American
Catholic hierarchy really liked Clayton Pinkes. Oh, he
could make them nervous sometimes, just because of
his potential. But they really, *really* liked him. He never
tested that potential, that latent power. He never pushed
in any way that would even remotely appear to the world
as self-aggrandizement. Clayton Pinkes's televised sermons and public speaking engagements involved a limited range of general topics. The Diocese of Rochester
kept an actual list of those topics and studied Clayton's
sermons carefully—they really liked Clayton, but he did,
after all, make them nervous.

Clayton's top ten subjects, accounting for most of his
sermonic content, were:

1) Faith, the Substance of Things Not Seen
2) Conscience and Guilt: A Believer's Struggle
3) Turning the Hearts of Children to their
   Parents
4) Stewardship Across the Boundaries of Denomi-
   nations
5) Obedience to Authority: Responsibilities of
   Citizenship
6) The Poor and Destitute, Our Brothers and
   Sisters
7) Volunteering Your Time for the Kingdom of
   Heaven
8) Gifts and Talents, God's Meaning for Your Life
9) Doubt: Not Always an Evil Thing
10) How to be Ready in Your Heart for the End
    of Time

"See?" the Catholic hierarchy told Rome each time
the list was reviewed. "Safe topics, no attempts to push
strange doctrines on the faithful."

"Really," said the Pope. "What about morality?"

"He doesn't seem to speak out on controversial moral
issues, either," said the Catholic hierarchy of Rochester. "And since he does not oppose our views, he is likely
for them."

"Yes, most likely," said the Pope. "What about this
End of Time business?"

"Oh," said the hierarchy, "that's a pet quirk of his,
a Charismatic leftover. He's vague about it, no attempts
at predicting the day and hour of the Second Coming."

"Really," said the Pope again, sounding very cold.

"But Your Holiness," the hierarchy said, getting jittery,
"a few eccentricities can be excused such a powerful
preacher."

"Of course they can," agreed the Pope. "But can so much power be excused for being so safe? So palatable?"

The hierarchy sat with its collective jaw hanging.

"Idiots," the Pope muttered. "If he doesn't scare you, then either you're not doing your job, or *he* isn't."

A typical executive office at the Rochester, New York, Christian Stewardship Ministry headquarters held a mahogany desk, numerous plants, a carpet of executive choice, a Sony Personal Computer that accessed the CSM satellite link on the IBM PrivNet, and a FoneFax fiberline networked to the Xerox Reprolaser Digital System 94000 in the Ministry's Communications Interface Suite.

Clayton's office had a steel desk, a wooden chair, a coffee maker, one telephone with intercom, three file cabinets, and a potted gladiola that would be dead except for the watering initiatives of Clayton's efficacious and withered secretary, Mrs. Brunwig. At 37, Clayton was younger than any of the six members of his executive staff and half Mrs. Brunwig's age.

Mrs. Brunwig came in his office and announced Neil Perrin had come down for his meeting. Neil was past her and in the room before she finished the announcement. She made a noise that sounded to Clayton like "whumph" and closed the door, muttering like a neglected grandmother.

Clayton nodded at Neil. Neil looked around the room, as he always did, for a place to sit. Clayton waved him over to the coffee table. It was a picture Clayton enjoyed, and felt guilty for enjoying—Neil Perrin in a custom-cut Italian suit squatting on the edge of the coffee table, looking uncomfortable but unwilling to say so. Neil was only three years older than Clayton, the closest to his own age of all the executive staff.

"Just a quick rundown, Clay. I know you've got the show to tape. We've got a full executive staff meeting tomorrow morning, and Gibbons kicks off the agenda with a summary of new network affiliate pickups. Lawrence has the stats for second quarter contributions and assets, and then I'll be covering the Social Outreach activities nationwide." Neil lowered the agenda roster from which he'd been reading. "Operation Homeless is still cooking with gas, Clay. We've placed more than three thousand people with Catholic families and in institutes for detox over the past six months."

Clayton chuckled at him.

"Well, okay," Neil said, raising the agenda roster again. "I'll save it for tomorrow."

"No, no, I'm sorry, Neil. I like the way you get excited about Social Outreach. Tell me." He had, actually, been chuckling at Neil's passion for driving programs with an element of detox. It was Neil's personal mission, for obvious reasons.

"I guess I'm high-strung."

"Tell me."

"No, really, I'm taking up too much time as it is."

"Now you're mad at me."

"Clayton!" Neil looked frustrated. He leaned back as if he'd forgotten he wasn't sitting in a chair, and caught himself before he toppled. "Clay, I hope I'm not speaking out of line here, but . . . well, you don't have to be so apologetic all the time. Not around us. We're a team."

"I'm sorry. You're right, I'm sorry."

Neil rolled his eyes. "Another apology! Clay . . . all right, forget it. It's not my place. Let's see, after I talk, Sanchez will give a current-state brief of the overall Ministry so that we can go into the afternoon's consultant selection sessions with a good sense of where we want Christian Stewardship Ministry to go in the future. Morris and Lawrence will discuss the key investment opportunities."

Clayton stood up and began to pace. "I don't think we'll be having Lawrence in the meeting or at the consultant selection session."

"He's out of town?"

"He's out of the Ministry."

Now Neil stood. "He's resigned? Randy Lawrence?"

"Not yet he hasn't. I'm about to tell him that he's going to."

Neil stood as still as Lot's wife after the glance backwards. Clayton waited a moment for Neil to ask "Why?" and, getting impatient, answered the question before it was asked.

"Randy Lawrence has been misappropriating funds. Fifty-three thousand dollars in the last six months. He's been feeding it into a summer home in North Carolina."

"Wow." Neil rubbed his chin. "How'd you find out?"

"I saw it," said Clayton. "In a vision, Randy changing figures and transferring funds to private accounts."

"You . . . you're not going just on a vision, are you?"

Clay made himself scowl. "Of course not. I brought in two independent accountants during the evenings last week. It didn't take long to find everything." Clayton walked over to the coffee pot and poured himself a cup. "I feel bad. Randy's got two kids in college now. His wife doesn't work. Randy's always been straight up before, as far as I can tell. If I have him resign, at least he can get in somewhere else without the onus of a scandal."

Neil walked over beside him. "Clay, you can't feel guilty about firing a guy who's robbing money from the donations we get. Seriously, Clayton, do you *ever* stop feeling guilty and just let yourself feel right for a change?"

Clayton parted the curtain with the back of his hand and looked down over East Main Street. There were people, hundreds of them, all over the sidewalks. It was too late for coffee break time, not late enough for lunch, but still there were hundreds of people out walking, hanging around the street corners, waiting for buses. He felt small, way up here on the fifteenth floor.

"When I preach, I feel right. Never any time else."

An hour later he drove into the Elmgrove Kodak Production Studios parking lot in Gates, east of the city. Father Richard Lanpher was already waiting for him in Studio 12. He saw the crowd, the studio audience, the congregation. Three hundred people, the faithful from all over the country. They flew here to see the live performance, an incredible expense considering that Kodak Productions wasn't anywhere near as flashy as Universal or Paramount. Too new a company; business before glitter.

Father Richard Lanpher would say mass, and Clayton would get to do the homily. That would make him feel better. It always did.

An editorial appeared that month in Rochester's *Gannett Times Chronicle* daily, an editorial on the increasingly popular Religion Page. It was a guest article by Casper Wagner, founder and pastor of Rochester's First Bible Way Church of the Savior, a fundamentalist sect whose local membership had peaked in 1994, waned, dwindled, and now stood strong with an aging, devoted 5% of its previous membership. There'd been considerable discussion among the *Times Chronicle* editorial staff regarding whether the piece was appropriate for the newspaper's audience. A nagging tug of democracy and nostalgia finally brought them to decide that, yeah, okay, we should run this, it's fair to present all sides. At the urging of several staff members who were volunteers for the Stewardship Ministry, the article was accompanied by a disclaimer: "Guest editorials do not necessarily reflect the views of the *Times Chronicle* staff."

"What are we becoming?" Reverend Wagner's editorial asked. "In a few short years, the body of true Christian believers has dwindled frighteningly. Our faithful are siphoned away, seduced by the charm and allure of a minion of Satan himself, a handsome, strapping, and deadly influence that goes by the name of Clayton Pinkes.

"Who is Pinkes? And who is the God of Clayton Pinkes? No one ever asks. Every year, more of our young people—and by 'our' I mean not only fundamentalist families but all Protestant families across the United States—are attracted to the Christian Stewardship Ministry. Sometimes they forsake their own faith and become papists, Roman Catholics, lovers of the Whore of Babylon. Sometimes they remain in their own congregations, diseases hidden within the true Body of Christ.

"Am I too harsh? Perhaps you will tell me that Clayton Pinkes' followers actively feed the poor, shelter the homeless, comfort the suffering. But I say to you that even Satan can take on the appearance of an angel of light.

"In the final analysis, Clayton Pinkes is a Roman Catholic, a heretic. No, he does not ask his volunteers to abandon their original faiths. He does something far more subtle: He leaves his followers as a poison among the congregations of the just. At this time even some American Jews—Jews, of all faiths!—are insisting that membership in the Christian Stewardship Ministry is not incompatible with membership in their own synagogues. It baffles the sensibilities.

"His is a religion where one sits content with some fuzzy, abstract pre-idea of God. The center of Clayton Pinkes's faith is none other than Clayton Pinkes."

Four days after the publication of the article, Reverend Casper Wagner was dead. No one in Clayton's organization, not even Clayton himself, suspected a connection between the article and Wagner's untimely demise. Clayton felt extremely guilty after reading the article, and disappointed when Wagner's obituary appeared. He'd wanted to talk with the man to see if maybe Wagner was right, if maybe Clayton wasn't specific enough about doctrines and points of morality.

The obituary read: "The Reverend Casper K. Wagner,

67, suddenly in his sleep of massive coronary failure, June 12. Survived by his loving wife Emily and three children . . ." etc.

In a database accessible through console number one in a house on Beach Avenue, the northwest corner of Rochester, New York, a more relevant paragraph of information read: SOLUTIONS #1854; PREEMPTIVE ACTIVITY FOR ACCOUNT REL-001, REF. VARIABLES REPORT #14 6/10/99: PRINT MEDIA ANTAGONISM AGAINST POTENTIAL CLIENT CLAYTON PINKES. CASPER J. WAGNER. INFLUENCE LEVEL LOW BUT NOT STABLE OR PREDICTABLE. ACTION TO REMOVE WAGNER INFLUENCE UNDERTAKEN. SUCCESSFUL. FILE CLOSED.

And two weeks later, another editorial appeared in the *Times Chronicle*, this one called "Clayton Pinkes: Compassionate Outreach Brings the Gospel Message to the Poor." The article lauded Pinkes's social consciousness, his understated lifestyle and low salary, and, most important, his integrity and personal devotion to the cause of Christian Stewardship.

Clayton put on the wig—real human hair, darker than his own and twice as long. He added a pair of false spectacles. A tweed jacket. "For God's sake," he said to the mirror. "I look like John Lennon."

He drove to the Candy Cane Lounge on Lake Avenue in Downtown Rochester. The first stripper had already started, a girl with long red hair that she used mostly to tease the crowd by hiding her bared breasts. She never smiled, an ice princess. Clayton ordered a Coke and sat at one of the tables right in front of the runway stage. He didn't look up until the dancer was finished.

"That was Tasha, gentlemen," the announcer said. "How about a big hand for the lady! Next up, Candy Cane's own Nadine!" Nadine was an Hispanic, petite and pretty. She wore a translucent white teddy, sharp contrast to her skin. For her first song she kept everything on.

The camisole top went with the second song—she had large, brown aureoles and erect nipples. On the third song the panties went, revealing a white G-string. Men started waving dollars at her, and she would kneel in front of them, letting them stick the bills in the G-string. She kissed them on the cheek.

Clayton watched her hard, but felt nothing. Nor did he feel anything through the next three dancers, Mary Grace, Tammy, and Shakara. The sixth dancer came out—it was an hour later, and Clayton was on his fourth Coke. Nina, another black-haired girl, enormous breasts and a lush, sizable rear end. She danced around one of the two poles that went from stage to ceiling, and then she jumped up it, clasping her legs around it and letting go with her hands. She sank back down to the stage, her crotch sliding against the length of the pole.

Clayton felt the tingling in the back of his neck and in his right forearm, and he fell into one of his flashes: himself, four hours from now, and this girl under him, gently stroking his back, both of them naked in a hotel bed and her whispering, "Show me who's boss, babe." Then the flash ended.

The next time she danced near him, he waved her down and put a bill in her panties. He took his time doing it so that she'd see it was a hundred dollars.

"Buy you a drink after the dance?"

"Jesus Christ, babe, you can buy me anything you want."

She kissed him—on the lips, and she used her tongue. He could feel her breast, warm and sweaty, pressed against his shoulder.

Before dawn he got back to his own apartment on Ridge Road. A small flat, not a large home like everyone else's on his executive staff. No family waiting for him. A bed, a table, standard appliances for basic living. The only wall decoration in the entire apartment was a reproduction of a detail from Georges de la Tour's *Mary Magdalen with Oil Lamp*; a religious painting, Christianity's Holy Prostitute. In the painting, Magdalen stared away from Clayton into a single, elongated flame. Her blouse was dropped low from her right shoulder; a single line suggested cleavage and disappeared behind the white material. On her lap was a human skull with no jawbone, and her hand rested gently on it, as if it were a bouquet of flowers or a pet kitten, nothing more. Clayton felt his hands shaking as he stared at it.

Beside his bed, he fell to his knees and cried. He recited an Our Father, a Hail Mary, and three Acts of Contrition. Then he raised his head and prayed, "Angel of God, my guardian dear, to whom His love entrusts me here; ever this day be at my side, to light and guard, to rule and guide."

Outside a police siren wailed.

"Ever this day be at my side."

The first hints of the rising sun hung dull red-gray at the window.

"Be at my side. Paolo. Be at my side."

The next day during the morning executive council meeting, Clayton kept his face set and nodded whenever Neil did. Neil sat at his right. At his left was Mrs. Brunwig, who took scrupulous notes. He'd read them later to understand what everyone was saying so passionately to him through the haze of his exhaustion. All his energy went into appearing alert, wise, and not exhausted in the least. He only needed to last until afternoon, which was when he got his inevitable second wind. Most of his sleep came on weekends.

"We're all going to Edwards for lunch," Neil said at noon when the meeting ended. He was excited. It must have been a good meeting.

"I think I'll just send out for a sandwich. I'd like to think things over."

"Actually, Clay, we'd like your reactions to our input. You know, before the consultant presentations this afternoon."

"Your input was great. I agree with all of you a hundred percent."

"You'll remember that there were a few disagreements on one or two major issues."

"I agree with those, too. We ought to be disagreeing on those issues. It's healthy. Mrs. Brunwig, would you send out for a sandwich?"

"Ham and swiss with mustard," Mrs. Brunwig said. "A side of potato chips and a vanilla milk shake."

"I think I'd like a roast beef sandwich instead."

Mrs. Brunwig stuck her pencil in the gray pile of hair atop her head. It disappeared, and Clayton squinted to see where it had gone. He always saw her stick pencils up there and never caught her taking any out. He imagined her pulling pencil after pencil from her perm at the end of the workday. He'd have to watch her to see if that's what she did.

"*Mister* Pinkes," she said, crossing her arms. "This is Tuesday. Every Tuesday since I've started working here you've had a ham and swiss with mustard, a bag of potato chips, and a vanilla malt."

Clayton nodded. The very first Tuesday she worked there, six years ago, that was what he'd ordered. She'd stuck him with it ever since. "That sounds delicious, Mrs. Brunwig. Bring on the pig and curds."

She rose quite properly from the chair and waddled from the conference room.

Neil was still standing there. "I was kind of hoping we could just talk. Not about anything important. Just the bunch of us, like old friends. They're all wondering where Randy Lawrence is, too. Couldn't you come along, explain about Randy, and then we'll all tell jokes and talk about what we do outside of the office? Like people who know each other?"

Clayton patted Neil's shoulder and left for his ham

and swiss. "I'm beat, Neil. We can all be old friends tomorrow."

The sandwich was good. As he ate he read the early edition of the *Times Chronicle*, and halfway through a letter to the editor fuming about the late Pastor Casper Wagner's editorial slandering Clayton Pinkes, Clayton felt his arm tingling. So he had a choice: Either force it to stop and ignore the message, or submit and see what the buzzing was all about. Clayton chose to submit—it could be important, right? And he'd feel guilty if he didn't listen. The newsprint before him faded to white, then was replaced by a page in the vision. Clayton struggled to read the articles; they were like pages from a book in a dream, elusive, and the words not falling in any immediate, sensible order. "Unity," the article said. Something about unity, anyway, and "a common Europe." More incomprehensible words, and a line about "good for the European economy but frightening for America." There was a recurrent word, "Descartesians," some political movement. Its ideas were contrary to the American Patriot Party. Rational progression and rejection of abstract concepts like nationalism and God. More stuff he couldn't read. Then a line about the Christian Stewardship Ministry, "a focal point for everything American," and a warning that there were U.S. Descartesian movements forming even as this was being written, although when Clayton looked at the top of the paper he couldn't read the date. It became too frustrating; he stopped the vision.

When he finished eating his sandwich, Clayton called Saint Charles Borromeo parish where Dickie Lanpher was in residence.

"Clay?"

"Yeah. Listen, Father, I'd like to go to confession."

The phone was silent for a long time. Then, "Is tomorrow all right? Ten-thirty?"

"Okay. Tomorrow would be good."

Another silence, and Dickie said, "Again, Clayton?"

Clayton shut his eyes. "I'll see you tomorrow, okay?"

"Sure."

The executive staff reconvened at 1:30, and the first consultant burst into the conference room like a whirling dervish. Handshakes, hello, hello there's, and then, bright as a Jehovah's Witness on his first day of door-to-door solicitation: "Hi, everybody! My name is John, and I'm from Concepts, Limited!"

"Hi, John!" Neil said, practically shouting. Clayton raised his hand to his mouth to keep from laughing. For Neil, who'd spent three years at Alcoholics Anonymous meetings during harder times, the response was hard-wired.

"Hi!" John from Concepts, Limited, said back, not at all distracted. "During our fifteen-minute presentation today, we'd really like to zero in on Christian Stewardship Ministry's number one need as it enters the future: a central theme and mission! If you acquire our service, Concepts, Limited, will work closely with your executive team to develop a driving theme and a mission statement guiding you into the latter part of the decade! We provide all the consulting you'll need, printing service for future newsletters, banners, and other items to get the message home to all your followers!"

He went on like that for the entire fifteen minutes.

"And now I'd like to ask: Do you have any question about Concepts, Limited?"

Clayton raised his hand.

"Yes! Reverend Pinkes."

Clayton faltered. "Uh, that's Mister Pinkes. I'm not ordained."

"My mistake, sir! What would you like to know about us?"

"I'd like to know," said Clayton, "why you keep talking with plural pronouns when you're doing a solo presentation?"

John from Concepts, Limited, laughed and nodded,

acknowledging the joke. When no one else laughed and Clayton kept waiting, he said, "Our company—I mean, the company I work for—we believe that teamwork and solidarity with our clients are the only way to successfully penetrate the future!"

"I see. And do you and your company know any method of ending a declarative sentence with anything other than an exclamation point?"

That broke it. Everyone on the executive staff started chuckling, and most didn't even try to hide it.

When John of Concepts, Limited, left, Clayton said, "You know something, guys? You're good people. You're already a team. I'm sorry I didn't go to lunch with you today. Tomorrow we'll all go out on me. Kick me in the butt the next time I become too introverted."

They murmured and nodded.

"Do you think I was too hard on that consultant? I'm feeling guilty now."

"Clay," Neil groaned, clearly frustrated.

They sat through the next presentation, a dry monotone from two representatives of Vision Consultants, Incorporated. Clayton thanked them, and they were followed by flip charts from the Idea Emporium, graphs and histograms from Design Consultants International, antics from Creative Tomorrows Consortium, and a sloppy slide show by no fewer than five representatives of the Today's Communication Factory. Clayton gauged the staff; everyone was exhausted. There was one more presentation left. Maybe he'd call it a day after that and take them all out for an early dinner.

An enormous black man entered the conference room. He walked to the head of the table and eyed them all, one by one. "Who's carryin'? Don't none a' yous be movin' too fast. Anybody carryin'? Who's carryin'?"

Neil leaned to Clayton and asked, "Carrying what?" Clayton waved a hand to shush him.

"It be aw clear!" the black man called over his shoulder. Two white men came through the door. The first was tall and thin, the roots of his dark, curly hair prophesying impending gray. The second was young, even younger than Clayton, and looked vaguely Mediterranean. He wore black denim jeans and a black turtleneck sweater. The young one sat down, the first consultant all day to do so.

"I am Henry Albert," the young one said. "This is my chief researcher, Mr. Roger Kallur"—he pointed at the tall white man—"and this is my vice president, whom we call Papa Bear." The black man made a minuscule bow. "We are from Solutions."

Neil leaned forward. "Just 'Solutions'? Not 'Solutions, Amalgamated,' or 'Solutions, Limited'?"

The young one, Henry Albert, ignored Neil and stared directly at Clayton. Clayton's right forearm began to tingle, and then it held a steady electric pulse. He kept his arm under the table. *Roger Kallur.* Clayton thought he knew that name. *From where? And Henry Albert. Like a dull light through thick fog.* He couldn't place either of them.

"You've granted fifteen minutes for these presentations. Unfortunately, I have only five. I'll be brief."

Clayton looked around the table to check if that was all right with everyone. They were staring at Henry Albert.

"I have a staff of fifty," Henry said, "not including Mr. Kallur and Papa Bear. Every single one of them logged a perfect score on the Analytical section of the Graduate Record Exam, the standardized test given by the Educational Testing Service. That's how I determined my initial employee pool. Then each of them had to pass an individual problem-solving interview with me."

Henry Albert stopped talking and waited, as if someone were supposed to react now. He looked over at Gibbons, and Gibbons spoke, immediately. That struck Clayton. Henry Albert looked *first*, and *then* Gibbons asked the question he'd been thinking about asking.

"What sort of projects have you done in the past?" Gibbons said. "What are your credentials?"

"Entirely confidential," said Henry Albert. "We do, however, have references from reputable sources." The black man, Papa Bear, walked to Clayton and handed him a manila envelope. Clayton took it with his left hand; his right arm lay numb on his lap. The envelope had a dozen letters praising the talents and ingenuity of the company called Solutions. There were no specifics, only accolades. There were letters from Carl Masterson of the current Joint Chiefs of Staff; from the CEOs of IBM, Hewlett-Packard, and GM; from the premiers and presidents of Israel, Canada, and South Africa; and one from former President George Bush.

"Are these for real?" Clayton asked.

"A fair question," said Henry Albert. "An honest answer. Yes. What our group offers is solutions. You tell us the problem. We talk it over. We give you a solution, a detailed way for you to get what you want. No strings, no bullshit. You do what we say and it works, it's fifteen hundred dollars an hour. If it doesn't work, no charge."

The entire executive staff looked at Clayton to see how he would react to the word "bullshit." Clayton couldn't even move his right arm. Stop it, he thought, which eased the numbness a little. He flexed his hand.

"What else do you do?" Clayton asked, trying hard to pay attention. "Newsletters? Advertising promotion?"

"None of that crap," said Henry. "We explain the solution to you. How to get exactly what you want, step by step. It's up to you to implement."

Morris spoke up. "We pay you fifteen hundred dollars an hour, and all you give us is advice?"

"That's the deal," said Henry Albert. "We guarantee a one hundred and sixty percent return on investment. Anything less and we don't call it a solution. That's what you want to buy, isn't it? A solution to the question, 'How can Christian Stewardship Ministry become the most influential religious force on the face of the Earth?' If our solutions work, we get paid and we're happy, and you get power and you're happy. Clean deal, total solution, no payment for anything less."

They were all looking at Clayton again.

Henry Albert tossed a white card in the middle of the dark mahogany conference table. "Time's up," he said. "That's my number. Call me within ten business days."

Clayton picked up the card. The three men left.

"Brother," said Morris. Everyone looked as if they were picking up breathing where they'd left off five minutes ago. "Can you believe the sheer arrogance?"

"How about the black guy?" said Sanchez. " 'Who's carryin'? Who's carryin'?' "

"And telling us he can only give us five minutes. I think he expected us to thank him for the favor."

They were, all of them, starting to loosen up. They started feeling superior to the three consultants. Jovial. Clayton frowned. No one had felt superior when the three were right there in front of the executive staff.

The business card read, "Henry Albert. Solutions. (716) 586-3770. Ten-business-day limit for accepting offers."

Clayton handed the card to Neil. "Find out everything you can about him."

They all stopped talking. "Are you serious?" said Gibbon. "Clayton, it was a joke! Nobody guarantees a hundred and sixty percent ROI. And that kid, the president, he was as young . . ."

Gibbon didn't finish, so Clayton did. "As me. I know. Neil, I want everything you can find out about Henry Albert in the next eight days."

"Sure thing, Clay," said Neil. "How do I do that?"

"C'mon, Neil, get creative! Start with the phone number, get an address, trace his driver's license, small business records, all that stuff. We've got thousands of people across the country! It shouldn't be that hard."

Neil scratched the left thigh of his Italian suit pants. "All right, Clay. It's just that we've always managed religious things. We've never done espionage."

Clayton's forearm had finally lost the electric buzz. "This is religious," he said.

"Father forgive me for I have sinned," he said to Dickie Lanpher.

But three nights later he left the Lake Avenue Silver Change strip joint with a black girl who had two-tone hair, dark brown with bleached white just above her ears.

"It has been two weeks since my last confession. These are my sins."

At the hotel room, she unbuttoned his shirt and started kissing and biting her way down his chest. She stopped, stepped back, and started removing her own clothes.

"I have committed sins of the flesh by engaging in relations outside of the sanctity of marriage."

She pushed his head down between her thighs and started telling him what to do, saying nasty, dirty things the whole time, pulling at the hair on the back of his head, insisting he go faster and deeper.

"I have committed sins of the spirit by leading an innocent one astray, coaxing her to follow unnatural desires."

She was on top of him, her fingernails digging into his chest, her warmth sliding up him, sliding down him, and she was still screaming her obscenities, getting louder every second.

"I have committed sins of the heart by enjoying the sin even while I knew it was sinful and against God's will. Although I don't think I really know God's will. Every time I try to understand it, I start wishing that the idea of God will go away, and that everything crazy in my life will just settle down."

She got on her hands and knees and told him to take her that way, and he did. He couldn't hold himself back any longer; he started yelling the obscenities himself. He pulled from her and collapsed on the bed. She started touching him. "Again," she said. He couldn't. He didn't think he could. "Again," she said, and she took him in her mouth.

"And I firmly resolve, with the help of God's grace, to sin no more, and to avoid the near occasion of sin."

"Go in peace," Father Lanpher said.

"What will my penance be? Dickie?"

"Go," said Dickie.

DALETH:
Henri, His Angel, and the
Man Called Papa Bear

Kallur left for the airport; Papa Bear drove himself and Henry back toward the house on Beach Avenue along Lake Ontario. He's angry, Papa Bear thought. I can tell by the way he's grinning. Fury, down to the center of wherever it is he lives inside that head.

"What's wrong?" asked Papa Bear. "I judged that as a relatively successful presentation."

"You overdid the black talk."

Papa Bear laughed. "Well, shi', Henry, them white folks, they don' hear no po' nigger 'less he talk like some jive-ass city boy. D'you think anysome honkey really be catchin' the rap from da likes a' Tutu or Mandela?"

"It's unnecessary. You only risk activating prejudices."

"Don't tell me how to speak English. I'm the one who taught you, Frenchie."

"Bullshit. From you I learned a gutter dialect. I learned English from Dan Rather and the Six O'Clock News."

"From me you learned 'bullshit.'"

"You drive me crazy."

"Ah fucks wit' yo' head, boy!" He poked Henry on the temple, and Henry batted his hand away.

Better. When Henry was agitated, things went smoothly. There were only problems when Henry got that set grin, that fixed look in his eyes that said, "Everything is fine, everything is quite stable." Damn, he wished the boy would loosen up.

Henry got quiet again, and the grin returned.

"You aren't really angry at me for the jive speak, are you?"

"No."

"What is it then?"

"Michael. He's not telling me things. Today was important, but I was led to believe it was a routine extension into the religious market."

Papa Bear hadn't wanted to hear that. He didn't want to hear anything about the angel. He wished he were like everyone else working for Solutions, ignorant about that side of the business. "We're not going for a chat with him, are we?" Say no, Papa Bear thought.

"Yeah. A very heated chat."

Oh, Christ. The boy was crazy. The boy was . . . thirty-six years old, but Papa Bear still thought of him as "the boy."

"Look, you take it solo this time, Henry. I don't want anything to do with that side of the business."

"I need you there."

"You don't need me there, you just *want* me there. I haven't got the stomach for messing with angels. That nasty motherfucker gives me willies. Far as I'm concerned, that thing's the devil."

"There is no devil," Henry said. "Demons are just a thought experiment used to shift blame."

"I don't care. What you do with Michael is none of my business, and that's fine by me."

"I've got no secrets from you."

"You've got secrets from everybody."

"Well, yes. But fewer from you."

Papa Bear nodded. Henry grinned and stared straight ahead at the road.

Papa Bear found him in 1976, in a vacant lot off 138th Street just outside the Bronx. Henry was thirteen then. The kid was rummaging through a garbage pail, like some dog, and Papa Bear yelled, "Hey, kid, tha's Nasty Brothers land! You don' wants to be fuckin' around there!"

Papa Bear was twenty-four then. He hated the Nasty Brothers, mostly because he'd been a Blood Sucker, and that's what Blood Suckers did—hated the Nasty Brothers. Of course, that was forever ago, two years before his big break, the job at D&L FoodMart as a cashier. Got his own full-time job, which made Mamma proud, and she was happier still that he'd stopped hanging with the Blood Suckers. Mostly he'd stopped because he got too tired working all day and running all night, but he kept it stopped because Mamma looked relaxed for the first time since he'd turned fourteen and dropped out of high school.

Still, you keep hating Nasty Brothers, even when you've stopped wearing colors.

"Don' you jus' be starin' there! Nasty Brothers mess up you white ass, they will."

The kid looked at him, real curious and squinty, and then the kid said, "Nasty Brothers mess up you white ass, they will."

"Make fun on me, boy, go 'head. No skin off me you get a face stomped in." But he didn't walk away. The kid's voice was funny, sort of foreign. Papa Bear said, "You know what I'm sayin' you, boy?"

The kid stepped closer. He started running a finger along the skin on Papa Bear's arm. Papa Bear pulled back. Stupid kid! Some motherfucker was gonna lay him down dead if he tried that with anybody else.

The kid held out a small, blue book toward Papa

Bear, like Papa Bear was supposed to check it for him or something. It was a tiny book, no bigger than a wallet. Papa Bear took it. On the front the book said, "Passport. United States of America." Inside it showed the kid's picture and listed the kid's name as Henry, except with an "i" at the end, like he really was foreign or something. His last name looked like Albert, except for some of the vowels being fucked up. Papa Bear could read okay, so he knew Albert didn't start with an "e."

"You talk English?" The kid didn't say anything. "You Porta Rican? Where you *casa*, Henry Albert? You *casa*, ya' know? You live here?" A goddamn Puerto Rican runaway with his own passport. Did you need a passport to get in from Puerto Rico? Papa Bear thought it was a state, not a country, but he wasn't too sure. Jesus, Henry Albert was skinny as hell, probably hadn't eaten for a week. Could you live that long? Maybe two weeks, with garbage. The kid was really eating garbage, like some wino! Papa Bear pulled out a dollar. That's what his mamma would do if she saw somebody looking this hungry. "Buy a doughnut, kid. You *comprende*? Eat somethin'."

The kid read the dollar. "The United States of America!" he said.

And then the cops screeched to a stop at the curb in front of them, and two uniforms jumped out of the car with their guns drawn. White cops. "Get your fucking hands in the air, Toby! Do it now!"

Jesus, Jesus, he was giving the kid money and they saw it! They thought he was passing drugs or trying to buy the kid for sick shit. Papa Bear put his hands behind his neck. Shit, he did it too natural, they'd know he'd been hassled before.

"Step back from him, kid! You! Toby! Keep your fucking eyes down!"

"Don' call me Toby, man. Ain't m'name. Nothin' going down here, man."

Papa Bear glanced at the kid. He shouldn't have never

said a fucking thing to him. He should've just let the Nasty Brothers trash his hide. Aw, fuck.

The kid was staring at the police guns. His eyes were wide. He was fucking *grinning* like a maniac.

They still kept their guns on Papa Bear after they'd frisked him and not found anything. They put him in handcuffs, and even then one of them kept a revolver pressed against his neck.

"What were you doing with the kid, Toby? Trying to make a new customer?"

"No drugs, man. Never fucked with sellin'. We was talkin', man."

The cop kept eyeballing him, breathing on his face and sticking the gun harder. "That right, Sammy?" the cop yelled over his shoulder. "The little kid tell you they were just talking?"

Sammy didn't say anything back, so the cop said, "Sammy? Are you fucking off on me again?"

Then the kid's voice: "Nasty Brothers gonna mess up you white ass, they will." The cop let go of Papa Bear and turned around. Papa Bear looked. There was the cop Sammy flat on his back, eyes open, blood coming out of his mouth. And there was the kid, holding the cop gun. A load crack, and the back of the first cop's head was gone. The kid fell back on his ass from the recoil. "Bingo," he said.

The kid figured out how to use the handcuff key, and the two of them ran like all shit. They won't be lookin' for me, Papa Bear thought. I gots a job. Mamma would die! Nobody'll come huntin' me down.

Nobody did, although the Nasty Brothers went through a really lousy six months, what with the bodies being found on their turf. "Gang Violence Leaves Two Police Officers Dead," the paper said, and Papa Bear tried to get the kid to understand what the words meant and explain that both of them were in the clear. The kid ate a lot, and Mamma didn't care that he was staying with them since Papa Bear was the one bringing in the paycheck. The kid learned fast, but shit, he didn't *know* anything. It wasn't just English. He didn't know how money worked, he didn't know that you just don't eyeball people or touch them, he didn't even know how to tell the junkies from the pushers from the hookers from the cops. But he did know how to fix the television and the fridge, which was really fucked up when you thought about it.

He started disappearing during the days when he was about sixteen, and one day he met Papa Bear coming out of D&L FoodMart. Papa Bear was an assistant manager by then. This time, the kid had been gone for almost a week.

"Yo, Papa Bear! Listen, man, you ain't been teachin' me no good English."

"Where the fuck you be for six days, Henry?"

"Listenin' round Queens an' Manhattan an' down in Jersey. Readin' in liburries. You been teachin' me bad shit talk, man."

"Shit, Henry, what you sayin'? I teach you good."

Henry shook his head. "Actually, no you haven't. Proper American English contains an entire base of words, even phonemes, which never occur in your vocabulary. Furthermore, elocution and syntax of the accepted English tongue varies considerably from your own."

"Jesus, Henry. Jive-ass white talk."

"Everyone rich and powerful in Manhattan talks like this. I need you to speak this way, too. I want to teach you standard American English."

"Wha' fo'?"

"Because I'm still too young to open my own business. I'll be too young for about five more years, and even then my age won't allow me to be taken seriously as a consultant. So I'm going to start in four months and use you as my liaison. 'Liaison' is a borrowed French word meaning 'mouthpiece.' You'll take my ideas to clients, and I'll stay in the background.

But no one will listen to you if you continue speaking the way you do."

"Fuck, Henry. You thinkin' on startin' up a goddamn bi'ness?"

"We'll start there. Say this: 'Are you considering starting a business?'"

"Why you want me sayin' tha'?"

"Say it. You aren't stupid, Papa Bear. I know that better than you know it."

"Shit. 'You considrin' startin' a business?'"

"ING. Con-sid-er-ING. Start-ING."

They walked toward home, Henry teaching Papa Bear English.

The house on Beach Avenue, which Henry bought three weeks ago before starting preparations for the Christian Stewardship Ministry job, was on the sharp curve right before the stretch that passed the Russell Station facility of Rochester Gas and Electric. Henry seemed to like houses near the water; of the hundreds of them he'd bought and sold during the past decade, Papa Bear could only remember three that weren't within walking distance of some lake or river or ocean.

Henry was out of the car and running in the door before Papa Bear turned off the ignition.

"Michael!" Papa Bear closed the house door when he came in. Henry was running around frantically, yelling at every appliance in the house. "Michael!" to the laser video console, and "Michael!" to the stereo entertainment center. He finally got an answer from the toaster oven.

"Hello? Heavenly Executive Appointments Office, Mandi speaking."

Henry bent over the counter and yelled into the open door of the toaster oven. "I want Michael here. Now." Papa Bear shook his head. Strange shit, talking into machines to find angels.

"Good afternoon, Mr. Elobert. What can we do for you today?"

"Right now, Mandi. No bullshit."

And then the room got extremely dark, even though it was midafternoon and all the curtains were open. Out of the darkness came a shape that was just a bit darker. That would be Michael. Papa Bear stepped backwards from it until he ran out of floor and was against the wall. Strange, strange shit. Henry was crazy to call the angel here when he was still so angry.

"Hey, pal," said Michael. "Nice to see ya', Henri. Oops. It's 'Henry' now, isn't it?"

"Who is he? Tell me who the hell he is! I go in expecting a standard presentation session and my arm almost shakes itself off my body. And he was going through the same thing! Wasn't he, Papa Bear?"

Oh, God, thought Papa Bear. Don't bring me into this, Henry. This isn't my part of the business.

"Henry," said Michael, "you seem a little upset."

Henry waved his arm before the dark shape. "What happened to my forearm, Michael? What happened to his?" The dark shape receded a little, pulled back from Henry's arm. There was a mood shift, Papa Bear could feel it, and Henry's face said that Henry felt it too. It was fear, just a touch of fear, and it wasn't coming from either Papa Bear or Henry.

"Say," said Michael. "Could you be a little more careful with that thing? When you get pissed off it carries a hell of a punch."

Henry glanced at the arm. He kept it between him and the angel.

"Come clean with me," said Henry. "I've worked hard for you. Screw around with me now and it's all over."

"You know," said Michael, lifting the dark extremity that would be his arm, "you're getting a little too arrogant." And then, for Papa Bear, the world became hell. The room was gone, and there was mist. From the mist came a shrieking, followed by the striking of a serpent whose head was twice the size of Papa Bear's body. Jaws and fangs, and Papa Bear screamed through the blood that came from his own throat. He felt half of him, his legs and his waist, drop away, into the mist. *Sweet Jesus. Sweet Jesus, I'm cut in half. I'm bit by a dragon and I'm cut in half.*

The room was back. The dark shape lowered its extremity, and Henry was kneeling next to Papa Bear. Papa Bear heard screaming. Who was screaming? He was. That was his scream, no doubt. He stopped it. He grabbed Henry's arm and started laughing. His legs weren't gone, and there wasn't any blood.

"What did you do to him?" Henry asked.

Don't ask him! Don't say anything nasty to him, Henry, for God's sake!

"I did this." The angel raised its arm again, and Papa Bear tried to jump in front of Henry to save him, but he shook too hard and couldn't stand.

A light glowed around Henry. Papa Bear watched, but he couldn't see the dragon. Henry could see it, though. He could tell by the way Henry's head moved, following the same lunge the creature had made moments ago at Papa Bear. It would eat Henry like it ate him! Bite him in half! Save Henry! Save the boy! And despite his terror, Papa Bear forced a few steps in Henry's direction.

Henry was grinning. He raised his arm, and the light around him vanished.

"That was really sick," Henry said to Michael. "But I got bored with it too soon. And I'm getting bored with you."

The dark shape said nothing.

"A few observations, Michael, Prince of Angels. Number one: You could only do that to one of us at a time. Number two: You induce psychological strain, but effect no physical contact. Number three: For fifteen years, I have never once seen you perform any feat with a physical manifestation. Your only abilities lie in the mental and spiritual realm. Any changes introduced to the physical world are the results of myself or my staff. Conclusion: You can do nothing in the world except through my agreeing to do it for you. *You need me.*"

Not real? thought Papa Bear. Not physical? It was physical enough for me. Jesus-sweet-godforsaken-Christ, it seemed real enough not to matter that it wasn't.

"And, behold, Henri Elobert: You are become a man." *Not physical? All in the mind? With all that, all that, what the hell did it matter?*

"Who is Clayton Pinkes?" asked Henry.

"He is your partner. The two of you are the prophets for the end of time. In his right arm, shaped as bone, is the Thummim of the Most High God. In your left arm, shaped as bone, is the Urim of the Most High God. Urim and Thummim, Brilliance and Perfection. The living flesh of man to call forth the living Spirit of God."

Henry spread his fingers and examined his arm. Papa Bear huddled closer to the wall. Henry's face was twisted and maniacal. Papa Bear could read his eyes: Force, they said. Power.

"That's the silliest shit I've ever heard," said Henry.

"Really?" said the angel. "I'd thought it was kinda dramatic. You know, 'his arm, your arm, living flesh, living Spirit.' Nice parallel structure. The Hebrews used to go wild for that in their poetry."

"Not the pronouncement. The strategy. If you've known where they've been all along, why haven't you just called God back yourselves?"

"Well . . . that's embarrassing. It doesn't work for us. Just for humans. Aw, heck, we tried for centuries after He disappeared. These Urim and Thummim, they're physical things. Almost none of us can do anything physical. God just ain't coming back until, by Urim and Thummim, 2.76% of humanity calls for Him; and humanity ain't gonna call for Him until they think they want to. You know, until the end of the world."

"2.76%?"

"Yeah. It's one of those metaphysical numbers, spiritual constants. Numbers like three, seven, twelve, forty, and 2.76%."

Henry paced. Henry paced a long time. If Henry paced any longer, thought Papa Bear, the angel would get pissed again. Maybe that wouldn't bother Henry, but Papa Bear cared. It really, really mattered to Papa Bear.

"The Urim and Thummim," Henry finally said. "They're specifically designed to draw God back to the universe?"

The dark shape of the angel contracted, expanded, and contracted again, as if musing over the question. "Not precisely," the angel said. "Their purpose is a little bit broader than that. They're a conduit, the only remaining path to miraculous change in the universe now that God has . . . has vacated it, temporarily."

Henry nodded. "Angels aren't supposed to be using the Urim and Thummim, are they?"

Michael turned defensive. "That's not true! There's no law against that! I resent the implication."

Henry ignored him, staring instead at his left arm. "I'm only half of the equation, then."

The dark shape halted its contraction/expansion oscillations. "That's true. Clayton Pinkes is the other half. Whether you like him or not, Henry, you'll have to work with him. He's Thummim, and you need his cooperation to reach our goals."

Henry started pacing again, and Papa Bear recognized the significance of the way he chewed on his upper lip. Henry was thinking, thinking hard, thinking about how all of this could work together to turn completely, entirely, to Henry's advantage.

" 'Almost none of us,' " said Henry.

"Pardon me?" the dark shape asked.

"A moment ago you were talking about your angels. You said, 'Almost none of us can do anything physical.' Who can?"

"Oh, not very many. At least not until God's back, anyway."

"How many?"

"Well, one."

"Who?"

The angel cleared whatever analogous metaphysical feature served as his throat. "The Archangel Raphael. It's a special dispensation thing. He does physical miracles. He's in charge of all the healing miracles until God gets back. That's what his name means, you know. 'God heals.' Of course, my name means 'He who is like God,' which is a much higher honor in the long run."

"Good. I want him on my staff, this Raphael."

"An excellent idea. Sorry. We've lost him."

Henry stared into the dark shape. "Lost him? How can you lose an angel? Go find him."

"We've been trying! Do you know how big the universe is?"

"Eighteen point six four zero nine billion light years, rounded," said Henry.

"Um, right. And that's a lot of area to cover when you're looking for a being with absolutely no mass."

"I think you should try harder." Henry turned to look at Papa Bear. "Don't you think our angel friend should try harder?"

Leave me out of this, boy. This isn't my business. Don't drag me in.

"Yeah," Henry said to Michael. "We really think you should try harder."

HE:
Elizabeth, Her Angel, and
the Man Called Roger Kallur

Elizabeth became a rarity in the sink-or-swim economics of the comedy world: a mid-lister with a middle-middle class income consistently playing for medium-sized crowds. Not a tragedy. Not a star. Just successful.

At the beginning of the 1980s, there were about twenty comedy clubs in the United States. That number grew to about 250 in ten years. In eight years more, by 1999, there were 764. It would be inaccurate to say that Elizabeth Goddard played all of them. She only played most, the ones that weren't too small, weren't too big, she now in her role as Roger Kallur's personal Goldilocks landing only where things would be Just Right. He managed her, basically, and she had the only agent in the business who paid for the honor. In the first year after she'd met him, Elizabeth's appearances doubled and her nightly pull rose from twenty-five dollars a performance to seventy dollars. Now she got two hundred. Plus Kallur's extra fifty whenever she used something from his joke list. Which was often.

The jokes worked, at least more than two-thirds of them did. She would wake up one morning, read the headlines, and suddenly one of the quips from the list would magically make sense: Ronald Reagan's brain tumor; Gary Hart's love affair; the domino effect of the falling televangelists; the failure of Eastern Bloc Communism; the rise of the Common Europe movement. Not all of the jokes were used. Some she skipped, and others she never got to try because Kallur would remove them from the list. The nuclear accidents in Israel never happened. Neither did the assassination of Manuel Noriega. Nor the secession of Quebec.

She knew, of course, that there was no way in hell Kallur was an educator. Educators didn't have budgets that allowed them to fly down for overnight research to Houston's Laff Stop, out to San Francisco's Holy City Zoo, then to Atlanta's Punchline, Boston's Comedy Connection, Zanies in Chicago. She'd decided at various times that he was an eccentric entrepreneur, a renegade agent for the CIA, a government researcher with an obscene cash grant, and a network broadcast executive whose job it was to carefully cultivate the sensations of the coming decade.

He didn't appear at all of her performances, but a third, at least a third. Whenever he did, he stayed in her hotel room for the night.

Sex with Roger Kallur was relaxing. He rarely talked, and he made no demands on her that didn't directly relate to business. He never cried after they made love. When he did something in bed that was uncomfortable or that hurt a little, she would mention it, and he wouldn't apologize. It wouldn't happen again, that was all, and the things that she mentioned were good would happen more frequently.

She was headlining at the Funny Bone in Saint Louis. Kallur wasn't in the crowd that evening, but there'd been a telephone message when she checked into the hotel. "Cancel next Tuesday's performance, Chatterbox in Palo

Alto. They've gone to television. Replace with Yuk Yuk's, Rochester New York. See you tonight. R.K."

He did that a lot, made last minute changes. The first few times caused her to panic—was she supposed to just show up and announce she was going to perform, unscheduled, wherever Kallur redirected her? But she'd get there, they'd have a contract, they'd have started radio promotions, and there'd be a crowd expecting her. Most of the schedule changes had to do with television.

Kallur absolutely forbade broadcast appearances.

She'd done comedy for over a decade now. She argued she should have tackled cable television years ago. He argued she should have starved years ago. She stopped arguing.

The St. Louis Chatterbox was a mid-sized '90s club, the type that had expanded its seating and increased lighting in the audience areas but resurrected the wooden stage with the brick-wall backdrop. The smoking section was up front by the stage. She sat in the back with her cigarette and her vodka tonic.

"Those things will kill you." A voice beside her.

She stubbed out the cigarette. "So if I quit, do I get to live forever?"

"Beats me. Hope so. That's what they've always said."

He was a young man, thin, almost anorexic. Long stringy hair the shade of peroxide-dulled yellow. His T-shirt said, "Now things are REALLY cooking!"

"Gabe Angelo?"

"Yeah! What a memory! I'm flattered. But words are your business, right? So you're bound to remember names."

He hadn't changed, at least from the picture of him she remembered. And here she herself was, well into her thirties and watching daily for the start of crow's feet and hints of future liver spots. Goddamn men aged so much differently from women. She caught herself arching her back slightly.

"I've been catching your act for years and I've been studying really hard. I think I can do it now. I really do."

"That's great, Gabe. Really, it is. Break a leg." She'd never seen him at a single performance, and she always played the crowd. Why the hell did he age so well? Even better than Kallur aged, and Kallur did pretty damned well. *Roger*, she'd said to him a couple months ago, *I'm getting older and putting on weight. In just five years I'll be forty.* He pulled down the sheets and examined her naked skin from toe to forehead, almost as if he were appraising a sculpture. *You're wrong*, he said. *You will be forty in three years. You're extremely attractive, and at forty you'll be just as attractive. You have no physical defects.*

Goddamn men. Their eyes aged differently than women's eyes.

"Thanks. I need it."

"What?"

Gabe Angelo gazed at her nervously. "You said, 'Break a leg.' I need all the luck I can get. I'm on in two minutes."

Tonight? Gabe Angelo was performing here? She'd seen the lineup. He wasn't on it. Nevertheless, the emcee said, "Ladies and gentlemen, please welcome with me a man who isn't at all funny, Mr. Gabe Angelo!"

Standard applause from the crowd—nothing ecstatic, not as if they were hypnotized. Gabe walked up to the mike and pouted. He kept pouting. Fifteen seconds, twenty.

"C'mon!" someone in the crowd yelled.

"Sorry," said Gabe. "I'm not funny."

Murmurs, then a chant that started up front and worked its way back through the crowd: "Jokes! Jokes! Jokes! Jokes! Jokes!" Elizabeth felt the crowd; as they chanted, they grew less hostile, more unified.

"Well, I . . . . no, no, you'd hate my jokes."

More yells from the audience, one person saying, "Sit

down, then!" and another shouting, "You can do it! C'mon, you can do it!"

Gabe zeroed in on the second voice. "I . . . I can do it?"

Applause, and another rising chant: "You can *do* it! You can *do* it! You can *do* it!"

Boyish shuffling from Gabe Angelo, like a three-year-old with his little bum exposed, embarrassed that he can't get his trousers up and calling meekly for Mommy to come into the bathroom. "Well, okay. I guess. All right. I'll try. Okay."

Applause, and the crowd quieted down quickly. The entire audience sat waiting, encouraging. Pulled into the routine and *wanting* him to try. Elizabeth smiled and muttered, "I'll be a son of a bitch."

"Okay, here's one. Why did the, uh, why did . . ." His voice became inaudible. More shouts of encouragement. "Fine!" said Gabe, and then in staccato, "Why-did-the-little-boy-throw-the-clock-out-the-window?"

Cheers and laughs, and then shouted responses, a heckler's paradise:

"The clock was broken!"

"He was late for school!"

"To get to the other side!"

"Time fly! Time fly!"

Gabe dropped his chin to his chest. "See?" he said. "You guys all have better answers than me. I thought he was aiming for the mailman."

Cheers. Gabe Angelo's answer was fine with them, as good as theirs. Elizabeth lit another cigarette. Years ago Gabe had said they'd come to laugh, that they believed in laughter and wanted to laugh or else they wouldn't be there. And now he was using that. He got them to demand he be funny, no tricks, no hypnosis, just honest playing of the crowd.

"No, really, don't cheer. I'm terrible. That was awful. All these other comedians, they have great topical jokes about sex and politics and religion and family relationships.

I'd love to do that, but I really don't sound funny about those things."

"Politics!" someone yelled, and "Sex!" shouted someone else, until the crowd decided and chanted: "Sex! Sex! Sex! Sex!"

"Sex?" said Gabe Angelo. "Well, I'll try. Why did the good-looking brunette throw her boyfriend out the window?"

Volume drop in the crowd. They wanted to know.

"'Cause she wanted to, you know, watch him bounce on the pavement, and then, um, sort of roll into the middle of the road, in limp little circles, flopping around there and everything."

Everyone laughed at the way he said it. Elizabeth laughed.

Gabe Angelo radiated unadulterated innocence. "Well, gee, that's not funny! She killed him!"

More laughs, and applause.

"You were wonderful," she said, knowing she meant it because she could feel the competition, the smallest prick of jealousy. Which was an unfair thing to feel, since he'd gotten the crowd more hyped than any other warm-up act she'd ever had before she headlined. During her own act, she'd felt more up than she had in years.

"You think so? You really think I was good?"

Christ, he was insecure. Couldn't he even feel it? "Yes. I do. You were."

"I owe it all to you, Elizabeth. I said to myself, 'How does she do it?' And then I answered, 'She finds her deepest weaknesses and drags them out for the world to see.' And I knew my biggest weakness was that I wasn't funny. I used it. I built a stage persona, just as you do. It worked!" He frowned quickly. "You don't suppose that now that I'm funny I won't be able to play off how unfunny I am any more, do you?"

Elizabeth tried to dissect the question to see if she should answer yes or no.

"Naw, I'm not going to start worrying like that. One day at a time, right?"

Elizabeth nodded. She was arching her back again and trying to pull in her stomach. He was actually attractive, in a boyish way, if a little intense for her taste. Was he late twenties? Early twenties? No; he'd have been early twenties already when she first saw him in 1985.

"If you still do magic, you could throw in some of that. A lot of audiences love magic tricks."

"Oh, no," he said. "I've always wanted to do it with words. You know, the way you do. God, words alone as the way into people's hearts! Your life *means* something, Elizabeth."

He was a charmer. "So you think you know my inner weaknesses and how I use them in my act?"

"Oh, sure. All the relational baggage and the religious turmoil. You've got an unfulfilled religious impulse. That sort of thing has fired creativity for centuries."

He was being coy, pretending to understand her. "So all my comedy comes from some unanswered desire to find God."

"Yeah," said Gabe Angelo. "And so does mine."

Mental alarm bells, then: Was he a religious freak? He had the zeal, but hadn't he cursed and sworn on stage? Of course, that didn't mean anything. Religious people swore, it was only some who didn't. Every religious freak wasn't like—

"Clayton Pinkes?" asked Gabe Angelo. "No, Clayton and I are nothing alike."

Ice water shot into her veins . . . she shuddered.

"So here's your payment for teaching me what comedy is all about. You're intrigued by Roger Kallur, and I'll let you find out all about him. Turn on channel twelve when you get back to your hotel. Then, first chance you get, take a look through that brown leather briefcase he's always carrying. To unlock it, use the mark of the beast and the number of God."

He knew Clayton. He knew Kallur. She tried to settle her mind by tying it into a bundle of threads, tracking the strings. A string, an old string, between her and Clayton. Another between Clayton and Religion. One between Religion and Comedy. Two from Comedy, looping around Clayton again, and separating to loop around herself and Gabe Angelo. Another string from Gabe Angelo to Roger Kallur, and yet another from Kallur, to Comedy, to her. Too tight a package; she felt vertigo and claustrophobia.

"Get the hell away from me."

Gabe Angelo's face, all innocence and surprise: "Are you upset? Hey, I didn't want to upset you! Aw, c'mon, Elizabeth, I thought you'd like to know what's going on. I really didn't . . ."

His voice faded as she left the table, left the club, left the sidewalk and found a taxi.

In the taxicab, inside her head, it was all nineteen years ago and Clayton Pinkes. And religion. And relationships. But nineteen years ago was forever! But they were formative years, years that left an engraving on her personality deeper than any other. But a full lifetime since then! True, but a house built on sand cannot stand. Was that in the Bible? It went something like that.

"*Clayton, do you love me?*"

"*God loves you, and so do I.*"

"*But apart from the love of God. Would you love me if there were no God?*"

"*How can you even ask that? Without God we wouldn't even be here!*"

"*Don't get upset. I was just feeling insecure. Even you wondered whether God believed in you.*"

"*We all feel insecure at times.*"

"*Why do you do that? Why do you always say things in such a universal way? I'm sitting here, I'm the one who's feeling insecure. Me.*"

"*Just because you feel insecure is no reason to say there's no God.*"

"*I didn't say . . . forget it, Clayton.*"

"*It just makes me nervous. You saying there might not be a God. You know my weaknesses, and you know how I feel about that.*"

"*I'm sorry if you're nervous about that. I'm not the first one to wonder if there even is a God.*"

"*I had a . . . friend, once, who didn't know if there was a God. He was extremely unhappy. He was always sarcastic. And now I don't know where he is.*"

"*Your angel? The one you think you killed?*"

"*Yes.*"

"*Your angel didn't believe in God?*"

"*I think he wasn't sure. It's confusing. I think he'd lost his faith and that's why God made him disappear. Or maybe I made him disappear. I don't know. Maybe I killed him. Maybe I didn't, maybe it was his own fault. I don't know. I'll never know.*"

"*There are so many things about you, Clayton. Strange things.*"

"*I just feel afraid about you not believing in God.*"

"*Why?*"

"*Because, what if you disappear? What if you go away, like he did?*"

"*Would that be so bad?*"

"*Yes. It would. Because I love you.*"

"*Really?*"

"*Really.*"

She walked down Washington Avenue to the hotel, across from Laclede's Landing and at an angle to the Gateway Arch, neither of which Elizabeth could see from her window. Her room faced away from them, overlooking the scenic spot where Convention Plaza Drive merged into I-70. She drew the curtains and turned on the television. Channel twelve. The screen illuminated to a stage, a brick wall backdrop; Iggy's Canteen, a syndicated standup comedy show filmed live at Baltimore's top club.

Barry Neseroff on stage, a chubby little guy, a midlister whose path Elizabeth had crossed only three or four times in the past decade. "So I says, 'A round-trip ticket? A flight that goes both ways? C'mon lady, I want a jet, not a bi-plane!'" The crowd laughed. Television audiences were always easier play.

"But we took the vacation anyway, and my wife and I got down to Florida. Of course, you know exactly what she wants to do. Shopping! And I don't know if you've ever noticed, but when women are away on vacation they'll shop for things they'd never *dream* of buying back home."

Laughs.

"That's okay if it's tacky, cheap stuff. 'Honey! I'm back! And look what I got you, a beautiful six-tone polyester shirt with dominant day-glo orange and a cartoon of Fidel Castro on the back!'"

Laughs.

"'Why, thank you, dear, I'll wear that to my next NRA meeting.'"

Laughs.

"Of course, the ladies don't buy that sort of thing for themselves. Oh, no, they go directly for the most expensive clothing boutique in town with fashions by designers whose names look like words from those French tests we all flunked senior year of high school."

Chuckles.

"But what kills me is that after they go to these shops, they're depressed all next week! Because nothing fits!"

Applause.

"Now, did they really *expect* anything to fit? I've got a secret for you ladies: Your average fashion designer doesn't have *you* in mind when he's working up his next set of clothes. In fact, he doesn't have *any* women in mind when he's designing. Every single boutique item is meant for a tall, skinny, fifteen-year-old boy with no body hair!"

Chuckling. Laughter. Applause. Laughter. Chuckling.

Your average fashion designer doesn't have you in mind. Elizabeth had heard this routine before. No, she hadn't. She'd heard that *joke* before. It was her joke. No, it wasn't. It was Kallur's joke, from the 1998 list. It was the same line, word for word. But how could Barry Neseroff possibly come up with the exact same joke as one on Kallur's list? Maybe the same idea, but not word for word . . .

There were three sharp knocks at the door, and she turned off the set. She opened to Roger Kallur, who held his briefcase in front of him under both arms. "Roger," she said, and he nodded.

He sat down in the sofa chair next to the bed, keeping the brown leather briefcase on his lap hugged tightly to him.

"Why does Barry Neseroff know your jokes?"

Kallur looked distracted, not at all focused on her. "Neseroff. He works for me. It's the same sort of arrangement you and I have. How did you know he had the jokes?"

"I just saw him on Iggy's Canteen. Jesus Christ, Roger, how many comedians do you have telling your jokes?" Why was she feeling betrayed? It wasn't as if he were sleeping with Barry Neseroff, too.

"Television?" Kallur looked even more distracted now. "That's just great. Jesus. Well, don't worry, I'll take care of it."

"That's not the point, Roger! Why didn't you tell me—"

"Listen," he said, and he set his briefcase on the floor. On his white shirt was a large circle of reddish-brown blood, nearly dried, and at the center of the stain was a small, char-edged hole. "I'm not really in the mood to talk about this tonight. We'll save it for later."

"Oh my God. Roger—" She ran over to the phone.

What the hell was the extension for an outside line? She'd seen the ambulance number somewhere. One of the books, the "Welcome to Our Guests" brochure.

"No," said Roger.

She stared at him, the phone receiver limp in her hand.

"Bring me the phone," he said, so she did. "I've already removed the bullet, and the bleeding's stopped. It wasn't deep. If you call the hospital, they'll be required to call the police. We don't want police."

They didn't? If he'd been shot, why didn't they want the police? He said he was all right. Was he telling the truth? She'd never heard him lie, or at least she'd never caught him lying. How would she even know?

Kallur dialed the phone, eleven digits in a row. He waited, and said, "It's me . . . . Listen, the U.S. Descartesians weren't cooperative. . . . Yeah, and I'm afraid I've been shot. Settle down. People get shot every day. Listen, is . . ." Kallur looked up at Elizabeth. She didn't leave the room. "Is Henry there? Tell him I'm sorry. I'll be laid up for a while. A couple weeks, I'm really weak. Have Henry take the Descartesians personally, and get Kowolski to cancel Barry Neseroff . . . yes, the comedian. He's gone TV."

He set the phone down without saying good-bye.

"Do you want me to get you anything?" Elizabeth asked. What could she get? What did a man who took out his own bullets need from her?

"Actually, you could help me lie down. I've lost a great deal of blood and I'll be passing out soon."

She lifted him with her shoulder under the crook of his arm. He fainted even before they'd gotten to the bed.

The leather briefcase sat next to the chair.

Mark of the beast, and the number of God.

Under the fluorescent lights in the bathroom, the briefcase looked older, more faded than ever. There were two three-digit combination locks next to each of its metal latches.

Mark of the beast. She rotated the left-hand combination rollers to 6-6-6. Thank you, Clayton Pinkes, for being so clear about what the number of the beast was. The latch sprung open when she pressed the release.

The number of God. She lined the numbers up to 3-3-3. The release stayed solid, unyielding. She tried 7-7-7. Still nothing happened. Come on, she thought, this should be obvious. Then she felt disturbed; there was Roger on the bed, passed out, and she rummaging through his personal belongings. She should be calling the hospital anyway, no matter what he said. But there would be police. Roger Kallur didn't want police, and she felt protective of him right now. Protective? Then why was she trying to break into his briefcase?

I had a friend, said Clayton Pinkes fifteen years ago, *who didn't know if there was a God.* Your angel? *Yes.* Your angel didn't believe in God? *I think he wasn't sure.*

Not sure if there was a God.

A big zero, a metaphysical zero.

Elizabeth rotated the combination numbers to three zeros. The latch released.

These were the contents of Roger Kallur's brown leather briefcase:

- An airline ticket to Rochester, New York.
- A binder labeled "Descartesians," with detailed summaries of the group's origin, history, significant activities to date, and proposed lists of future activities geared toward what was labeled "Output: Global Prominence."
- A binder labeled "Christian Stewardship Ministry," with detailed summaries of the group's origin, history, significant activities to date, and proposed lists of future activities geared toward what was labeled "Output: Global Prominence."
- A change of socks and underwear.
- An X-ray of someone's left arm, one of the two bones in the forearm appearing considerably brighter than

the other. The bright one was labeled "ulna," the dim one "radius." Attached was a scrawled note saying, "Henry—no radiation. Can't compare genetic structures yet; need marrow for that. Interesting: Forearm temperature (subepidermal) consistently two degrees higher than body basal. R.K."

- A copy of *Baltimore Catechism No. 2, New Revised Edition*, 1962, from Benziger Brothers.
- A binder labeled, "Strategic Update, Project Earth-End." It had its own clasps and locks.
- A binder labeled "Comedy," with detailed analysis of high-visibility actions implemented by Solutions, levels of grass-root acceptance measured by national audience mean reactions to jokes focused on Solutions events. An appendix listed one hundred eighty comedians. The twenty-third name on the list was Elizabeth Goddard.

"I'm checking out."

The night clerk looked up, startled, and quickly crumpled over the pages of his *Penthouse* magazine to hide the cover. This left Elizabeth staring at a view of Miss August's breasts contorted in a bizarre manner that no blue movie, no matter how creative and athletic, could ever duplicate.

"It's three in the morning! Nobody checks out at three in the morning!"

Elizabeth tried to make herself look as calm and patient as possible. "Here I am, checking out."

He was a night clerk, so it took him fifteen minutes to figure out how to print up the bill.

"Thank you. The telephone charges. I'll need them itemized separately for business deductions."

That took another ten minutes. He handed her a list of three local calls (one to the restaurant, two to the club) and one long distance call made an hour ago. All phone numbers were recorded.

"You've listed an overnight visitor, Ms. Goddard."

"He's sleeping," she lied. *He's dead. He promised not to die, but he did anyway.*

"Oh. I see. Will your husband be checking out separately?"

"Yes. It's not my husband. It's just a guy I fuck." *Checking out? I guess he already has. If he hadn't lied about being all right, I could have called for help.*

The clerk was staring at her, a look of disbelief. *Why did he have that stupid expression? Had she said something shocking to him? She couldn't remember, didn't care.*

"Aren't you going to help me get my luggage out to the taxi stop?"

"Of course. Sorry. Yes, of course."

He came around the counter and lifted her two bags. He tried to reach for the leather briefcase.

"No," she said. "I'll carry this."

VAV:
Neil Perrin, Hard at Work

Neil Perrin worked very hard.

Not that he didn't always work hard. Every bit of energy Neil used was for Clayton, because Clayton was important, Neil could feel that deep in his gut whenever the work became too hard, too time-consuming. Neil had always believed in God, but it was through Clayton that he'd learned how to commit himself, to give his life over to the service of Stewardship every day, one day at a time. *One day at a time.* At times like this—sitting at his desk late, sorting through the hard copy of files he'd downloaded over the past four evenings, the data composites and sketchy bios of those who might be working for Henry Albert and Solutions—Neil would pause for a few moments and fantasize. He fantasized he was Clayton Pinkes, and did everything Clayton did to serve God.

It wasn't that crazy a fantasy, it really wasn't. Clayton was unmarried, Neil was unmarried; Clayton had nothing else in his life besides the Ministry, and neither did Neil; Clayton was thirty-nine, and Neil was only four years older and felt younger. He'd always felt younger, at least since he'd stopped drinking. He owed that to Clayton, too.

Clayton had found him in a gutter, literally, a real, live
gutter out of everyone's stereotype of a riches-to-rags
corporate executive who'd lost himself in his scotch.
Clayton fed him and let him live at the apartment while
Neil was drying out. Clayton drove him to Alcoholics
Anonymous meetings every night, *every night*, for ten
months.

No. It was just a fantasy. He'd never really be like
Clayton Pinkes. Clayton was too good a human being. Neil
could never match that, so he'd do the next best thing.
He could, he would, do anything for Clayton Pinkes.

Neil photoscanned the last set of faxed sheets he'd
received from Stephen Merritti, a systems operator for
Genotech Systems and a six-year follower of Christian
Stewardship Ministry. Neil OCR'd and transferred the
faxed information to the data base called, on his computer, SOLUTIONS.DAT. He sorted according to the
categories he'd established—that had been hard, the first
time, all the reading and tallying by hand to find the
patterns. The list, the original list on which all the
information was based, had been hacked from the
Princeton Educational Services database: all subjects in
the past seventeen years, since the inclusion of the
analytical section on the Graduate Record Exam, with
perfect analytical scores.

Neil called the newly sorted biocomposites to the
screen:

Lang, Caroline: Compton, CA
AGE: 38
EMPLOYED: Donald J. Reid Consulting
EMPLOYMENT DESCRIPTION: Account
    Executive—Police Interrogation Techniques
    Training Consultant. Federal Agent
    Interrogation Techniques Training
    Consultant. International Agent Interrogation
    Techniques Consultant.
ANNUAL INCOME: Unavailable.

RELIGION: Roman Catholic (practicing)
EDUCATION: MA Psychology, Bucknell U.
MAJOR MEDICAL: June, 1993 - Auto Accident,
      broken leg. April, 1990 - Suicide attempt,
      sleeping pills

Another one, then. This one would work for Solutions.
Number forty-nine.

Porter, Leonard: Boston, MA
AGE: 45
EMPLOYED: Fielding & Levine Associates.
EMPLOYMENT DESCRIPTION: Legal researcher;
      Criminal Law, some Corporate Law
      Applications.
ANNUAL INCOME: $69,400
RELIGION: Lutheran (practicing)
EDUCATION: Law Degree, Berkeley.
MAJOR MEDICAL: Angina symptoms,
      January, 1996.

Too old, solid salary information. Not one of Henry
Albert's people.

Bourne, Lawrence: Buffalo, NY
AGE: 30
EMPLOYED: Department of Health, U.S.
EMPLOYMENT DESCRIPTION: Genetic Research;
      also acting liaison to National Institute of
      Means and Standards.
ANNUAL INCOME: Unavailable
EDUCATION: MA Biogenetics, Clarkson.
RELIGION: Roman Catholic (practicing)
MAJOR MEDICAL: March 1992 - Suicide
      attempt, wrist/razor

That was it. Number fifty. Neil needed nothing else
from Stephen Merritti. He'd isolated the Solutions roster

and cleared all the extraneous biocomposites. He started
his final report.

Clayton,

Attached is a summary of fifty people whom I believe
to be members of Henry Albert's organization, Solutions.
Note that none of the bios lists "Solutions" as the
company of employment, and that there is no registration
of the company "Solutions" in any business database
available to us.

The data herein were derived from a listing of 117
people who have earned perfect scores on the Graduate
Record Exam's Analytical section. I isolated trends and
compiled this group based on unique patterns in the
data. Each bio speaks for itself, of course, but please
notice the following correlations in the fifty composites
included here:

Ages—Range from 22 - 39, average 29.3 years.

Salaries—Unavailable in information bases, even for
those who are public employees.

Religion: 100% Roman Catholic.

Medical: 100% with suicide attempts within last ten
years.

In summary, a typical Solutions employee is quite
young, analytically brilliant, Roman Catholic, and unques-
tionably self-destructive, at least during one recent period
of his/her life.

Am I begging the question, Clay, describing the
Solutions crew according to the same criteria I used to
determine that they are part of Solutions? Maybe, but
the correlations are astounding and, frankly, a little scary.
I'll have further information (i.e., correlational numerics,
validity tests, etc.) for our meeting next Tuesday.

Neil

There. That was thorough. That was one of the best
jobs he'd ever done for Clayton. Clayton would be
proud.

✧   ✧   ✧

"What the hell are these?" Clayton threw the bio-composites across his desk at Neil. Neil was standing because there was never any place to sit in Clayton's office, except for the coffee table, and that was too far from the desk.

Clayton seemed in a bad mood.

"They're a list of possible employees at Solutions. I thought you wanted to know about the company."

Clayton shoved the stack again, and the top six or seven pages scattered across the floor. "I wanted to know about *Henry Albert*. Dammit, Neil, why can't you just do what I ask?"

Neil felt his face getting warm, like tiny dots of perspiration becoming acid, starting to burn the surface of his skin. Well, Clayton *had* asked about Henry Albert, not about Solutions. But Henry Albert was president of Solutions. Clayton wanted to know about the company, didn't he? Why would he want to know just about the president?

"There was no available information on Henry Albert. Or on Roger Kallur or anybody nicknamed Papa Bear. I tried that first." Hadn't Clayton been supportive during the investigation? But Clayton didn't know what Neil was researching. Now Clayton was mad, and Neil felt useless, useless to Clayton Pinkes, who was important to him and to the Catholic community.

"Well, you should have tried harder! For God's sake, Neil, don't you ever use your head without someone else telling it how to work?"

Clayton never talked to him that way. What was eating at him? Why was he changing?

"Yes," said Neil. He tried to make his voice sound cold, professional, but he couldn't keep it from shaking. "I hit a dead end on Henry Albert, so I did the next best thing. I found his staff."

"Wonderful," said Clayton. "It was good practice for doing something useful." Clayton slumped in his chair and turned away.

Neil's hands shook. He worked hard for Clayton. He'd say that. "I work hard for you, Clayton."

"My garbage disposal works hard for me, Neil, but it doesn't give me anything useful."

A hollowness started and grew upwards toward Neil's mind. This wasn't Clayton. Something was wrong with Clayton or he wouldn't be talking this way. Neil and Clayton were friends, and Neil didn't deserve comments like that.

"Don't you think the people Henry Albert hires tells something about Henry Albert himself?"

Clayton was quiet; his face was in a sectioned slice of sunlight coming through the half-closed curtains. "I'm sorry, Neil. I'm being rude to you. I'm sorry."

Clayton, the apologetic. Now Neil was angry, for the first time in his life *angry*, with Clayton. "You're not being rude. You're being cruel. Apology rejected."

Clayton looked up; his eyes were helpless, but right now Neil was sick of helpless, Clayton eyes.

"Maybe you have a point, Clay. Maybe Henry Albert's staff says nothing about Henry Albert. Because my dedication and commitment to you sure doesn't say anything about Clayton Pinkes."

Clayton started to cry. That almost, almost, reached Neil, but not quite.

"You're crying, Clayton," he said.

"Yes," said Clayton. "There are so many things you don't understand, Neil. So many nuances that I wish I could share. But I think Henry Albert is the key to a murder I caused a long time ago."

A murder? That made a lot of difference. It did, it really did.

"A murder?" asked Neil.

"Of an angel," Clayton said.

"Oh," Neil Perrin said. The murder of an angel. Another Clayton Pinkes fantasy, another way to draw attention to, remorse for, the sad, trying situation of Clayton Pinkes.

Neil stiffened. "Stick my report in your garbage disposal, Clayton."

Neil slammed the door of his office behind him after he entered. He flopped down onto the office sofa and crossed his arms. He knew if he didn't cross them he would find something to throw and break, some potted plant or the small statue on his desk of the Virgin Mary or the answering machine.

The message light on the answering machine was flashing. He pushed the playback button—too hard, the machine slid across the desk a few inches—and Stephen Merritti's voice said, "Mr. Perrin? Mr. Perrin, please call me. Oh, God, please call me at home as soon as you can. I'll stay here and wait. Please."

Did Merritti have new information? Why didn't he just fax it? Neil dialed Merritti's home phone. On the sixth ring, a woman answered.

"I'm sorry," she said. The voice sounded weak. "I can't talk now."

"Mrs. Merritti?"

"Yes?" The word was hollow, lost.

"Please, your husband left me a very urgent message. Could I speak with him, please? I think it may be important."

She was quiet, and then he heard sobs. "They killed him! Right in our bedroom they killed him! Oh, my God, oh sweet Jesus!"

Her voice withdrew from the phone and was replaced by a male voice.

"Hello? This is Detective Allaire. With whom am I speaking, please?"

Neil slammed the phone down.

He studied the scotch, the way the ice melted and for a moment was separate from the alcohol, then how it became lost, dissipated throughout the rest of the drink. Losing itself to the strong fluid.

"You gonna drink that or meditate on it all day?" the bartender asked. Neil didn't answer. He stirred the drink and thought, Go ahead, water, just disappear in the scotch, as if you were never your own self anyway.

God, how he wanted to drink that scotch.

A man sat down on the bar stool next to him—there were bar stools empty all along the bar, but the man picked the one next to Neil Perrin and then didn't look at him. That was strange, but then again, Neil knew, no it wasn't, not at all.

"Are you going to poison my drink, or will you make it a spectacular moment, and blow my head off?"

The man looked over and laughed, unsure what Neil meant, at least sounding that way. The man smiled and nodded. He was a young man, twenty-seven, twenty-eight. Twenty-nine point three. He ordered a Budweiser.

"So I'm curious," said Neil. "How much does Henry Albert pay?"

"I don't know what you mean," the man said. "Are you drunk?"

Neil lifted the glass and held it to the light. Pretty, very relaxing. He would very much like to be drunk. "Your suicide attempt, was it satisfying? Did you feel disappointed that you failed? What was it? A botched hanging? Jump from a window that was too low?"

The man didn't look at him. He picked up his Budweiser and took a long draw. His other hand moved toward Neil, and Neil felt his heart speed up, pounding in his neck. But the man didn't touch him; he simply flipped his wrist upward, showing it to Neil. There was a thin, white scar in the small area between his hand and his wristwatch.

"I see," said Neil. "If you'd left it under warm water you might have succeeded."

"Yeah," the man said. "I know that now."

Neil nodded. He dipped a finger in the scotch and touched it to his lips.

"Your portfolio says you don't drink. I had a hell of a time finding you."

"Sorry," said Neil. "Could I at least have one last drink before you finish me off?"

"You could run away and head for the police," the man said, sounding very reasonable.

"Sure," said Neil. "Maybe I could experience some of their interrogation techniques first hand." The man said nothing, so Neil turned to him. "But that's not your field, is it? You're the biogeneticist. Have I guessed right? I figured they'd send you since you were stationed in Buffalo. You're the closest one to Rochester. Lawrence Bourne."

The man chuckled.

"How extensive is it? Are you guys everywhere in government?"

"Everywhere important. And not just government."

"No. I guess I knew that."

Lawrence Bourne gulped down the rest of his beer—it looked like a single swallow to Neil, just the way he used to drink his scotch—and then the man stood up. He tossed a dollar on the bar.

"You're not anything like your portfolio," the man said.

"Sorry. I've had a couple life-changing revelations. Call them religious experiences."

Lawrence Bourne started walking away. Neil grabbed his jacket. "Please," he said. "Don't leave me guessing. Just kill me straight out." He could feel himself losing control; there was no way to sustain the tough-guy, nonchalant pose. Neil just wasn't that way. He wasn't, at the core of his heart, anything tough, nonchalant, or glib.

"I'm not going to kill you," said Lawrence Bourne. "Precisely because you want to die. It's against our personal ethics."

Neil wasn't going to die. I'm not going to die, he told himself, and inside his stomach's relief fought against the faintest push of disappointment.

"I'll clear it up with Henry," said Lawrence Bourne, and then he was gone.

Back looking at the scotch: little slivers of persistent ice holding out against the final meltdown. Hopeless, stubborn ice. By now, Clayton would have read the letter of resignation Neil left on his desk. Clayton would be shocked, maybe even cry because he was so, so sorry about how he'd treated Neil.

Neil pushed the scotch away. If he was going to live, there was no good reason left to drink it.

ZAYIN:
Clayton, His Angel, and the Stripper Called Brandy Rae

Maybe God is completely opposite from me. Maybe He knows I exist but He doesn't believe in me. What about that? What if God doesn't believe in me?

Music started, something loud and rhythmic that Clayton wouldn't listen to if he weren't here. Then the voice of the DJ—familiar, a voice like every other DJ's in every other strip joint Clayton'd ever been to, as if the same guy worked at every one of them every night of the week. "Get ready, gentlemen," said the omnipresent DJ, "for the hot charms of Brandy Rae." He said it quietly; this was not the type of place that encouraged hooting and catcalls, and that suited Clayton.

Brandy Rae came on stage. She was beautiful and looked dangerous: a white blouse, strategically torn to reveal cleavage, a bare shoulder, a single black bra strap, the blouse tied in a knot below her breasts; denim shorts cut just below the bulge of her vulva, the cheeks of her rear end protesting the imposition of too small a size;

and legs, endless legs coaxed longer by stiletto spikes at least six inches long.

Clayton felt the buzzing—right away, on the very first dancer, first song!—and he saw himself with this Brandy Rae and she said, "I'm glad about it, Clayton. I'm really happy now."

He reached for the money clip in his right trouser pocket, and stopped. *I'm glad about it, Clayton*, she would say. *Clayton. I'm happy now. Clayton!* Using his name, his *real* name!

She was in front of him on the stage, gyrating her hips and reaching behind to unclasp the black lace bra she wore. When had she taken off the blouse, that white, dangerous, strategically torn blouse?

The black lace bra fell on the table in front of him. He looked up; he couldn't help it. Her breasts were mid-sized, with just the slightest hint of sagging; aging, and herculean efforts to ward off that aging. An older girl, closer to his age than to the ages of her dancer colleagues. There were glints of perspiration dotting each of her breasts, and Clayton began wondering what it would be like to bury his face in that warmth, between those breasts, and to feel her legs locked around his waist.

Clayton pulled out two one-hundred-dollar bills. He looked in her eyes to make sure she saw the money. She did; wide eyes with edges defending against the onset of first wrinkles, but damned if the world could see it twenty feet away when she was naked on the stage. The eyes went wider over Clayton's money, then slotted to slits, then joined the coy smile of her lips that said she'd accept the token.

It couldn't be a token, of course, or payment for anything, because the first look in those eyes reminded Clayton of someone, and that someone was Julie Ward from St. Catherine's Elementary School.

"Brandy Rae," said Clayton the Totally Other.

"That's right, sweetheart."

"Julie Ward, from St. Malachy's Elementary School," he said, a deeper, nobler part of himself breaking through and finding himself in a strip joint for the very first time in his life.

She stared for a while, trying to place him. He put the two hundred dollars in her hand. "That's so you can quit this place." He added another hundred. "To help you out until you find a respectable job."

She was still staring, and looked torn between throwing the money back at him and keeping it despite the bastard.

"I'm Clayton Pinkes," he said, and when she remembered him she placed an arm across her chest, hiding those mid-sized, still-beautiful breasts that Clayton the Totally Other had so badly wanted and would not be allowed to have.

Clayton did not believe in coincidences, but neither did he have the heart to believe in fate. Most of his philosophical effort went toward either (A) worrying that seeming coincidences were part of some great scheme to which he wasn't privy, or (B) worrying that life's seeming patterns and directions were happenstance, accidents of chance and habit. His philosophical position, he knew, was located at some point along a spectrum running from dubious fatalism at one extreme and nervous antideterminism at the other.

"Jesus Christ," said Julie Ward. "Clayton Pinkes. Jesus. Clayton."

Clayton blushed; she sounded as if she were trying to decide between the names. The two of them sat at a diner table now in a restaurant a few doors down from the HiLife Club. Too close, thought Clayton. Still too close to that place. But after her set, she had walked out with him, and Clayton wasn't sure if she was allowed to do that. Wasn't she supposed to serve drinks between dance sets? That was what other strippers usually did. She couldn't be finished for the night; it was only ten o'clock.

Julie Ward held her cup of coffee halfway between the table and her lips, and she did it without resting her elbows on the table. This made Clayton look down at her cup, and *that*, inevitably, led to his looking past the cup at her now-covered breasts.

Talk! Justify why you were inside the HiLife in disguise!

"When I heard you were dancing in this strip club," Clayton said sternly, "I came right away to convince myself it was just a vicious rumor."

"I've seen you on TV, Clayton. My mother watches you all the time. I do, too, sometimes."

"Yeah," said Clayton. "We've got a weekly show."

"I know. You're getting well known." She laughed once, short and harsh. "I mean, if even a sleazy stripper knows who you are . . ." She looked away from him.

"How long have you been a dancer?" Clayton said it to distract himself, to keep from staring at her breasts again.

Instead of answering him, she said, "Jesus, Clayton, you're a holy person and you're famous, and here I'm sitting, a sleazy stripper." She seemed stuck on that.

"God forgives everything. If you're really sorry, He forgives you." If He believes in you. If He knows you and believes in you.

"Take your wig off," she said. "I'd rather look at your own head."

He did. What did she think about the wig? "Jesus went into disguise to wander among the people," he said, but would that make sense to her? Bible story; would she remember things like that from so many years ago?

"So you rush into the lion's den to rescue me." She could have said that sarcastically, but she didn't. She believed that that was what he was doing. Yes, maybe he *had* rescued her, but she'd rescued him, too, just by being Julie Ward. He couldn't tell her that, of course; his rescuing her depended on her not knowing he'd needed to be rescued himself.

God, she was beautiful, and she was here with him. Just coincidence? Could be. He'd gone to so many strip joints by now that he was bound to run into her eventually. This was Rochester, where he'd grown up, where she'd grown up, so it wasn't so unlikely an encounter, considering her profession and his obsessions.

"God forgives everything," he said again. "Lewdness, lust, fornication, everything."

She looked at him again and smiled. "I'm clean with the fornication." She looked sadly proud, as if she had one piece of hope left in her.

"What?"

"Fornication. Sex." She leaned forward as if in confidence. "I'm saving myself for marriage," she whispered.

A virgin stripper? thought Clayton. Saving herself for marriage?

"I've only stripped for four years, you know." She sat up straight and was suddenly conversational and bright. "Before I started dancing, I worked for a collections bureau, getting ahold of people who were behind in payments. But that business folded. And before that I was an administrative assistant at Tarident Tool. That's a little manufacturing company. I worked for the guys who bought supplies and parts and stuff."

Clayton felt himself gripping his own leg tightly. She'd gone from distant and bittersweet to despairing to bright and chatty, and they'd only been sitting here ten minutes.

"I even went to college for a while, but it was only for three quarters of a year and it was just a community college. I guess that isn't impressive." She slumped down on the table, her arms crossed under her chin. This caused her breasts to flatten and spread under her, emphasizing her cleavage at the neckline of the tank top she was wearing now. Clayton tried to stare at her nose.

"You're a *virgin*?" he said.

Her face clicked back to despair. "Yeah. But that doesn't mean anything. I'm still a sleazy stripper. Am

I going to hell, Clayton? Is it too late for me?" As Clayton stared at her nose, a single tear ran down it.

"Julie," he said. "Julie, don't cry."

"Okay!" She sat up straight and wiped the tear away. She smiled wide, was beaming again. "So tell me, what do I do to keep from going to hell?"

She's an emotional wreck, Clayton thought. She's tossed about left and right by her own sins and she doesn't even know how to act.

"Just trust," he said. "Trust that God is willing to love you. That's all religion is, Julie. Accepting that God believes in you and would go to any extreme to draw you to Himself. That's what everything in religion is about—Jesus dying on the cross, people gathering at church to celebrate the mass together, all the prayers. It comes down to knowing God believes in you."

It stung to say that. But it was what she needed. What she needed, more than anything.

"I just want for everything to be calmer," she said.

That struck him, and struck him deep. "Yes," he said. "For everything to settle down. I know what you're feeling."

She stared past him now, chewing on her lower lip. A blank face; that must be what she looked like when she was thinking.

The waitress came and refilled the coffee cups without asking them if they'd like more coffee.

"It's true, isn't it?" Julie said it quietly. Her hands, folded on the table in front of her, were trembling. "What you're saying is true, Clayton."

"Yes," Clayton said. His voice sounded defensive to him.

"I need a job." Suddenly, she sounded logical, practical. "Now that I believe what I've heard you say on TV so often, I'll need to work for Christian Stewardship Ministry."

It was like watching a video on fast forward. "Julie, think hard about what you're saying. Real faith isn't a momentary decision. You need to consider it, to pray—"

"I was praying just now. You're right, Clayton. I knew that whatever you said would be right from the exact moment I realized it was you there in that wig. I believe." The tears started again, and soon she was weeping. Clayton glanced around the diner, but no one cared who the two of them were. "That's why I walked out with you. I went in back and said, 'I'm finished,' and then I got dressed and left. I knew you could make me believe." She put her hands over her face and wept into her palms.

"Don't cry, Julie. It's good to believe. It's a *good* thing."

She looked up at him, her shoulders still hunched. "Clayton, I'm happy. Can't you tell?"

Clayton drove around the dark city for several hours, taking turns where the signs allowed, jumping onto the Inner Loop of the 490 expressway, exiting randomly onto city streets, finding himself on the Inner Loop again. He was empty.

She'd been converted, sitting right there with him. And she'd quit her job and asked him to give her a new one. And he had, telling her to report to Mrs. Brunwig the coming Monday as an administrative assistant to Clayton's secretary. Then she'd gone home, a believer in God's forgiveness and love.

When it came right down to it—practically speaking, no morality and no lust involved—she should have been more grateful for the job. She should have at least thought to make a pass at him so that he could turn it down. He would have turned it down, of course.

Clayton's stomach went heavy when he realized he was letting himself think those things. What sort of person was he, anyway? How could he allow himself to lust after someone who had just found her faith in God? There was no hope, none at all, for Clayton Pinkes Whom God Did Not Believe In.

He missed Paolo. Paolo had to rescue him. That was all there was to it.

He stopped the car on East Avenue in front of Desireé Lounge. A bit distanced from himself, he acknowledged with chagrin that he had once again let guilt move him toward intolerable despair. Same old pattern. Same old Same Old, even on the night of Julie Ward's conversion.

But what does it matter, Clayton? She's happy now, and she thinks God believes in her. What does that mean to you? How does that help you?

Clayton nodded. Even if it seemed to matter, he would eventually convince himself to think it didn't. Clayton went inside Desireé Lounge.

"How ya' doin'?" she said. Clayton nodded. She had long, straight hair, strawberry blonde. She wasn't a stripper, or at least she wasn't working tonight. She was here watching and drinking.

"You're the big spender, aren't ya? Misty told me about you."

Who the hell was Misty? Maybe he knew her, but he couldn't remember. "Told me about you." Clayton-In-Disguise had developed a reputation somewhere along the line. Maybe some day he'd be as famous as Clayton The Just. Not that it mattered.

"You thinkin' about pickin' up one of the dancers tonight?"

Clayton looked at her. She wore too much makeup, but in the dark that wouldn't matter. She had a slim build, and maybe she was tall but he couldn't tell with her sitting down. "Yeah," he answered, and then purposely scanned her from head to lap. She smiled, not at all self-conscious. She even ran a finger up and down her thigh while he studied her.

"Tell you what," she said. "For a little extra than what you pay them, I can show you the wildest fucking time in your life."

Clayton laughed. She was probably a cop. That's what he deserved, to get arrested, to have everything made public and to live with the shame for the rest of his life. That would be atonement, atonement for Neil, for Father Dickie Lanpher, for Elizabeth—God, Elizabeth! He hadn't thought of her in years. And now Julie Ward, atonement for her having faith based on the say-so of a doubter and hypocrite.

"How much extra?" He'd given Julie three hundred dollars, which left him only fifty in his pocket.

"Four hundred, total. It's worth it for a lifetime experience." She reached under the table and gently squeezed his crotch. Clayton felt himself stiffening. Well, she probably wasn't a cop after all. Cops couldn't do that, could they?

"I'll have to stop at an automatic teller machine."

"That's fine with me." She'd unzipped his fly and had her hand inside his underwear.

Clayton Pinkes, what do you think you're doing? It was Sister Leo Agnes's voice talking inside his head from somewhere back in the mid-1970's. Clayton The Totally Other smiled. Praying, he thought.

He and the woman left Desireé Lounge. She had no car, so she drove to the bank with him.

God is not a game, young man. Father Dorman in the confessional.

She gave him directions to her apartment—out in Henrietta, one of the southern Rochester suburbs. As he drove she unzipped his pants again and lowered her face to his lap. He swerved a few times and tried to concentrate on the road.

Clayton Pinkes, you have the devil's own knack for getting into trouble. Sister Assumpta.

Clayton had an orgasm and almost swerved into the left lane. The woman—what was her name? He hadn't asked—sat up but kept touching him. The revival time was short, and she laughed aloud.

There is no devil. Demons are just a thought

experiment people use to shift blame. Paolo Diosana, the Archangel Raphael.

They came to the apartment complex and she took him by the hand. As they walked up the stairs she unbuttoned her blouse. Brazen. She wore no bra. Clayton's hand was on her rear end, and he brought up his other hand to play with one of her nipples. The climb up the stairs was awkward.

Clayton, maybe sex isn't the biggest evil in our lives . . . We both like it. Why would God make something so enjoyable for two people and then declare it one of the greatest sins in the world? Elizabeth. Elizabeth Goddard in 1980.

There was music coming from behind the woman's apartment door. Someone else there, her roommate? He didn't want there to be. He wanted her again, now. He didn't feel like driving out to find a hotel room.

The apartment door opened and a second woman, a spike-haired blonde in her late twenties, stuck her head out in the hall. "Cynthia!" the second woman said. "I thought you'd abandoned us!"

Cynthia—Clayton's date with the open blouse and exposed breasts—squeezed Clayton's hands. "Just bringing reinforcements," she said.

They went in. It was a sizable apartment, very large living room area, a kitchen almost as big as one you'd find in a residential home, and corridors leading to other parts of the flat. Clayton looked around the living room; good taste and well-equipped. There was a surrealist print on the wall of what appeared to be two bodies locked either in sex or combat; beneath that picture, on the floor, were two very real, very naked bodies, a young man and a dark-skinned woman engaged in more or less the same activity as shown in the picture. The sofa was expensive-looking, one of those three-piece sets that could be used either as separate furniture for a conversational cluster or together as a single stretch spanning part of one wall and turning the corner to span part of another. It was currently in the latter formation and occupied by two naked men with a woman between them, all three engaged in rhythmic movements, sweat, and various entries. The ceiling had a large, wooden fan turning slow circles, too slow to dissipate the sharp, smoky odor—sharper than cigarettes, probably marijuana, although Clayton could see no one smoking at the moment. Beneath the fan, a lone woman lay stretched on the carpet, masturbating with an anatomically correct vibrator. The carpet was colored a soft beige, probably extremely difficult to keep clean.

Clayton On Hold. He stood, observing. There was something down there, deep inside his mind, calling for attention. He didn't answer. He didn't know what to say.

"Well, hello," the hostess, the door answerer, said after he'd been standing there immobile too long. She was naked, had been when she answered the door. Her arms went over Clayton's shoulders and she kissed him, her tongue teasing his lips and her pelvis thrusting against his. "Welcome to the party," she said. Then she walked over to Cynthia and greeted her the same way, except that Cynthia responded and ran her hands over the hostess's back and buttocks.

"I've got to use your bathroom," Clayton said. The hostess nodded and pointed in the direction of a closed door inside the nearest corridor. Cynthia had continued her kissing down the hostess's neck, breasts, and belly, and was now making love bites on the hostess's hips.

"Keep the bathroom door open!" the hostess said. "That's part of the fun!" She sat down on the floor and embraced Cynthia. On his way to the bathroom, Clayton had to step over a couple in the corridor, she facedown on the carpet and he facedown on her. Clayton closed the door behind him and locked it. It took him a moment to find the light switch, and when he did, he stared in the mirror.

He tried to hate the person he was staring at. No hate came to him. So he tried to justify the person. No response to that either. He tried love, pity, anger, despair, compassion, guilt, but nothing worked any more.

Clayton In The Mirror. Clayton On Hold, visiting just another everyday orgy in a strange apartment. What did it matter, right? Except that even indifference had a threshold. He could feel that now. Indifference wasn't the absence of feeling; indifference was a very, very real thing inside his own head, its own emotion requiring its own level of energy. And now Clayton was pushed past the limit of sustaining it, and every other normal human emotion was too tired to make any sort of showing. That left nothing in him to feel, except for something extremely primal—that had been what he'd felt earlier, tugging at him for notice. It was something more primal than human emotion, an ancient thing. More primal than sex, it was even pre-sex. Pre-humanity, pre-world, pre-universe, something so primal that Clayton suspected it was *the* primal thing. Prime Mover. The Alpha part of Alpha and Omega. Something that could make a world as casually as it could destroy one. A curious feeling, he suspected, if he had been capable of feeling curiosity just then.

All of which was just metaphysical meandering through his soul. So Clayton decided it should have a practical application, this primal sense, to keep it from being mere psychological fluff. He lifted his right arm and willed it to work for him. The burning was immediate, from his elbow to his wrist.

"I'm going to Paolo," he said aloud to the arm. "Right now, god dammit."

And the bathroom, the apartment, the whole world blinked out, poof, just like that. There was darkness, and he hung in the middle of it. "Paolo?" he said.

It was a long time, floating in that nowhere. "Paolo!" he shouted.

"Pinhead?" The voice was weak, forever away from where Clayton hung.

"You *are* alive," said Clayton. "Jesus, you are alive."

"Sort of."

"Where are you?"

A long silence. "Not too sure. I don't know where I am."

Clayton's arm buzzed. "You're lying."

"Yes. I am lying. I'm in limbo. I'm where everything else *isn't*, except you, apparently. What do you want?"

"I want your help. I'm a slave of carnal desire."

"The result of being born with a body, Pinhead."

"My world is in little boxes, each part of me hiding from the other parts."

"Try therapy. But don't mention you talk to angels. They'll lock you up."

"Please, Paolo. Please. I need your help."

"Paolo helps those who help themselves."

"Raphael!"

A very, very long silence, about as long as the first two silences doubled. "What, Clayton? What do you want from me?"

"I need you as a friend. A mentor and confidant."

"A confidant? Oh, Clayton, my poor little Pinhead. You didn't learn anything from me, did you? I made it simple, one lesson, and you didn't learn a thing."

"I can make you come back." Clayton flexed his right hand to a fist. The buzzing in his forearm became more intense.

"Yes," said Paolo. "Yes, you can. You could make me come back."

"Then why shouldn't I?"

"Because I don't want to, Pinhead. I don't want to be anywhere near you. We're too much alike, us."

"How are we alike? You're an *angel*, for God's sake!"

"And you're a prophet, a Prophet for the End of Time. But we both lack faith, don't we?"

"I believe in God! You know I do!"

"That's not the issue, is it?" Clayton didn't answer. "It isn't, is it?"

"No. It's not. It's whether He believes in us, isn't it?"

Silence for a long time.

"I like it here, Clayton. It's peaceful. I can think. And every day I search, hoping to find Him here, out here in the nothing where He's hiding. You of all people should be able to understand that. I want to find Him and ask why He left, why He stopped believing in all of us."

Clayton now could feel only his right forearm, nothing else. "It's a lie. You're lying, Paolo."

"You know I'm not."

"Well, fuck you, then! Just fuck you! Float around in limbo forever, looking for your missing God! Who needs you? I don't fucking need you!"

A silence not quite as long as the other ones. "You keep looking, too, Clayton. Go back to your own limbo and search. And if one of us finds Him, we'll let the other know."

Raphael was alive.

Clayton was back in front of the mirror. He walked from the bathroom into the smell of sex and sweat in the living room. "Jesus, thought you'd drowned," Cynthia said. She took his hand and placed it between her legs. The hostess had wandered off to the sofa, where she was squatting over the two men and woman.

Clayton kept his hand there, considering. How did he feel now about touching her like this? Interested, yes. Guilty? No, he didn't feel any guilt about it. And how did he feel about swearing at Raphael? He felt quite good about it, not guilty at all. His anger toward God? Enervating, healthy, really *angry* anger. Guilt? Nope. None.

He could feel again, all the emotions he cared to summon. Except one. Clayton's guilt was gone.

Clayton gently pushed Cynthia away. "I don't want to," he said.

She nodded and kissed his cheek. "That's okay, sweetheart. If you prefer men, you can join Arnie and Alex in the back bedroom."

"No," said Clayton. "I *like* women, and I like *sex*. I just don't want . . . *this* . . . anymore. It's over."

She tilted her head and looked at him queerly. Did he expect her to understand? Of course she couldn't. "Keep the four hundred dollars," Clayton said. She shrugged and turned away from him. As he left the apartment, he heard her giggling like a little girl. She'd joined the group on the sofa.

CHETH:
Henry Albert, Hard at Work

Henry Albert scanned the daily variables reports of the one hundred twenty-three major projects currently active on the Solutions job log. Each variable report contained from three to fifteen key shifts in project structure and principal subject personality that could confound the experiment—the Grand Experiment, which was what Henry sometimes called it; the experiment that tested how many believing minds on the face of the Earth it would take to activate the hand of God for the purpose of knocking the universe out from under the feet of men. Minds, face, hand, feet; Henry liked that and decided to remember it. He would say it aloud some time.

Grand Experiment target: 2.76% of Earth's population.

Achieving that number was not itself the end. It was, said Michael, the Urim/Thummim threshold, where the physical met the metaphysical. Once achieved, and once an act of human faith broke the barrier, Michael's part of the project would kick in. Seven years! Famine, pestilence, war, all those untidy things before the destruction of Earth.

"It's messy, this Great Tribulation phase," Henry had said to Michael.

"It isn't negotiable. The Scriptures make it very clear what events presage the return of God. We need to follow it to the letter, so we need you to continue manipulating the Descartesians, the Asians, everyone else."

"We'd save a great deal of time just ending the world in a single, swift action."

"Nonnegotiable," Michael repeated. "Keep setting it up."

So Henry did.

Not that he fully *wanted* to. Not that he thought that Clayton Pinkes was the quintessential partner for his endeavors. But Clayton held the Thummim, and that was, according to Michael, everything.

And not that Henry thought that the Descartesians could amount to much. But Michael had promised that they would create a backlash, that they would be, unintentionally, responsible for a burst of faith, the faith of Clayton Pinkes. And that their faith would enable an act of God. An act of faith that precursed the end of the world.

Or that enabled whatever miracle wished for by the human race.

Or by Henry.

And that was what counted.

This morning, Henry read all one thousand one hundred eighty-two reported variables, thought for a while, and then went to his PrivNet console to type up the daily action items list. Of the one thousand one hundred eighty-two variables, only four hundred sixteen were Probable Influences that would confound the experiment process. Only twenty-two were Critical Causes. He issued seven hundred forty Negligible Item memos, four hundred sixteen Status Quo With Observation directives, and twenty-two Corrective Actions mandates. He sent them by PrivNet-Mail to his fifty field personnel.

Roger Kallur was dead, another administrative task. Henry cancelled Kallur's PrivNet account and erased backup reports Kallur had filed. He issued a universal systems purge that deleted all references to Kallur throughout the Solutions datanet. Then he issued his own variables report, a Vital Readjustment Response memo to all personnel to fill the gap left by Kallur.

Of the twenty-three Corrective Actions mandates, one read: LAWRENCE BOURNE, BUFFALO—BUFLBRN-666B LARRY, GOOD CHOICE ON SPARING SUBJECT NEIL PARRIN. APPROVED. CONSIDERING POSSIBILITY OF NEIL PARRIN SUB-TIER PARTICIPATION IN C. PINKES PROJECT. SEND INFO ON THEIR PERSONAL RELATIONSHIP, THE BREAKDOWN, ETC. MY BEST TO YOU, HENRY.

Henry left and flew to Milan.

There were many things to consider during the flight to Milan. Henry categorized each of them

Why did Michael demand global participation?

Simple: Because Michael, despite his posturing and flexing and maneuvering, was, above all else, a fair creature. That fairness extended to the breadth of the human race, something with which Henry could not be entirely concerned.

Why the Descartesians? Because, apparently, anything adverse would lead to just as strong a reaction. Newtonian, basically. The Descartesians were cerebral, and if there were anything the rest of the human race was *not*, it was cerebral. Despite himself, Henry had to admire the strategy—nothing bred loyal followers like a common enemy.

And why the rest of the world? Why Asia, and the remains of Africa? Because hedging bets was a good strategy. Michael needed 2.76% of the human race. A total of 2.76% would ensure that Michael's plan would be fulfilled.

That, too, Henry could accommodate. The power of

2.76% was not limited to an act of calling God back to the universe. That Henry had learned through Michael's unwitting trust. And Henry planned to use the 2.76% for his own ends. Not completely dissimilar ends. But unique, nonetheless.

Nonetheless.

So, Henry traveled. He traveled for the will of Michael. But, ultimately, for the will of Henry Albert.

"Good day, Signore Albert. It is a pleasure to see you."

They had searched Henry for weapons at the front gate of the villa. He'd carried a gun with him, just so they'd feel satisfied taking it away.

"Good day, Signore Marzoni. If you still weren't important to my plans, I'd kill you."

The two guards at the door, bulky Italian men twice Henry's size, stiffened and took a step toward him. Signore Marzoni waved them away, but they remained stiff and ready.

"Please, please, Signore Enrico . . . you are upset with me?"

"I'm upset with whichever one of your Descartesians put a bullet through my chief researcher, Roger Kallur. He was one of my most valuable assets."

The old man shook his head and made tsk-tsking noises. "Those were U.S. Descartesians, Enrico. We are growing quite large, and in the United States, we are still an underground movement. I cannot control every madman who associates with us halfway around the world."

Henry leaned forward in his chair. "You're wrong, Signore Marzoni. By my assessment, you can and will control them. If I didn't think you could, you would no longer manage this movement."

Marzoni's face reddened. "This is *my* movement, Enrico. You are merely a consultant."

Consultant. That stung, but only briefly. If it were

not for the parameters placed upon him by the Arch-angel Michael, such admonishments would not be actual. Would not be true.

"True," said Henry Albert. "But if not for Solutions, you'd still be sitting in the back of a café talking loud politics based on flimsy dreams. Still, you've paid for my services, so all of that is past business. Present business is that your United States associates have attacked my personnel, and that makes me very angry." Henry took out a ballpoint pen from his shirt's breast pocket. He twisted the top, and one of the guards—the one to the left of the door—screamed. The guard's head exploded, and pieces of skull whistled like shrapnel through the room.

Henry brushed at a spot of blood on his shirt sleeve. Marzoni was on his knees, shaking. The red face had become white.

"You see," said Henry, conversationally, "the bottom section of this pen sprays a liquid microstream of . . ." Henry nodded toward the headless corpse " . . . call it a rather volatile chemical mixture. And the other end of the pen contains a tight sonar projector tuned to twenty-two megahertz. That frequency drives the chemical reaction. I sprayed a little on your man."

Marzoni's eyes were nearly all white, too.

"In fact, I sprayed it on both guards, on you, on your gate, and on every inch of your villa as I passed through. So here's the message: one more scratch to any of my people that's traceable to the Descartesians, and I'll fry you so neatly that they shall edit Sodom and Gomorrah right out of Scripture and replace it with the meltdown of Milan. Capiche?"

Marzoni nodded, and Henry enjoyed the nod, even though it was only a compliance with what Michael expected of the European movement. Even though it was only a moot compliance with Henry's plans.

"Good. Now down to business. Item One: The schedule for the U.S. Descartesians' going public has been revised to eighteen months from today. Solutions will handle the American and European major presses; you're on your own for Asian states and South America. Item Two: You'll base your initial U.S. public activities in reaction against a growing American religious movement, the Christian Stewardship Ministry. They're a prime target, since you oppose nearly everything they stand for."

Marzoni kept nodding, stayed white.

After the meeting, Henry flew to Paris.

"Good afternoon, Monsieur Elobert."

"Good afternoon. The Société is in session?"

"You are expected." No one searched Henry here. The Société trusted him explicitly. They believed in him, for, after all, had they not created him, nurtured him, and did that not mean he was theirs? Had he not returned to them after his kidnapping by the CIA?

As he entered the chambers, Henry thought of his father and nearly hesitated. His father had worked for these people. He'd been killed by these people. But, no; Henry had no father, except, perhaps, for Papa Bear. That other world, that world on Kerguélen, had ended. Henry had ended it.

He made his *bon jours* to the twelve old men on the Société board. Rich men, richer than he, but they had no idea that money was a tool. They thought of it as power, in and of itself, as if its existence was enough, and that its intelligent use were a trifle, a detail.

"I have made my report for the month," Henry said. He passed out the twelve packets. "I am concerned that of my last seven action items, only four were carried out."

The oldest man, Monsieur Roque, cleared his throat. "Three were ignored, Henri, it is true. They did not seem to be relevant to the good of France or the good of Common Europe."

Henry touched his hand to his forehead, appearing

distraught; it was for show, but these men liked show and responded to it. "Gentlemen, you are all very intelligent people. You are not, however, as intelligent as I am." The heads around the table nodded. Here at the Société, that was a clear understanding.

"You are thinking according to the short-term profit of actions," Henry said. "Many of our items are based on the longer term. I'm certain that concept does not elude you." Twelve heads shook slowly, saying, No, it does not elude us. "I do not mean to scold. It is not my place. But partial implementation of our strategies could do more harm to the good of France and Common Europe than if we had done nothing at all to better the world." More nods, more meekly; they were humble before the scolding.

"Some of your plans do not make sense to us, Henri," said Monsieur Roque. "You have asked us to make financial assistance to several of the feudal states of Russia; what good does that do us, now that their own union has dissolved to chaos? And you ask us to sponsor the arts and to attempt to establish—" Roque groped for the English words "—comedy clubs? I do not see the importance."

Henry became grave for them. "Then the fault lies with me, gentlemen. I am remiss in my duty of explaining our more subtle strategies. Please give me your pardon. From here on, I shall be more detailed in my explanations."

Twelve more nods. They would like that, *merci.*

"I shall give an overview, and then I shall be pleased to answer all inquiries regarding the nature of this month's suggestions. Item One: An American subsidiary of the Catholic Church called the Christian Stewardship Ministry is making an impressive rise in influence and power. I would humbly advise that the Société do everything in its power to convince European politicians and principal to oppose this growing force of American Nationalism. The movement already has over thirty outlets on the continent and two in Britain. I submit that this is nothing more than Washington posing as Rome. Item Two: There is a growing movement throughout Europe known as the Descartesians. My information leads me to believe that they will become a strong political force within the next two years. The Société would do well to win the confidence of this group, and to cooperate with their political activities. They can be used as a strong arm of European unity. If the gentlemen would care to examine documents A and B in your packages, we shall review the histories and philosophies of both the Christian Stewardship Ministry and the Descartesians."

After the meeting, Henry flew to Rochester, New York.

"So you're Henry Albert. You're short, Henry. You look far too young to be running an intelligence operation."

He sat down across from her. He was at a Perkins restaurant in the suburb of Brighton, where he'd agreed to meet her. "How do you do?"

"I do shitty. Let's talk business."

Henry smiled, which struck him as significant—a real smile, not one just for show. She reminded him of Roger Kallur. No wonder Roger had liked her.

She pulled Kallur's beat-up leather briefcase from under the table and passed it to Henry. "There it is. Everything's where it was and nothing's been photo-scanned or copied. But I read it, so you may want to have me eliminated."

"Maybe. That hasn't been decided yet."

"Then let's decide now. The way I see it, you have two choices. You can either kill me or hire me to work for you directly. I now know too much for any other option."

Kallur and his obsession with hardcopy paperwork. If he hadn't carried it everywhere with him, this woman, this Elizabeth Goddard, would never have been involved. No, not true. She was involved in all this, somewhere. He'd read all the research on her. She'd been Clayton's companion when Clayton was involved with the Charismatics, a co-preacher. Except in the running of the children's religious group, they hadn't been close; that was clear from interviews with some of their old high school friends. She'd qualified and been enrolled in the comedy side of the Demographic-3 Opinion Formation projects that Henry himself had plotted. He hadn't taken much notice of her until she called the Solutions direct business line.

"Death or total involvement. You talk in extremes, Ms. Goddard. There are countless other ways to approach this. I could have minute alterations performed through brain surgery that would leave you mildly insane and too incredible to be believed. I could access your personal histories and destroy your credit and leave you completely destitute, a street person to whom no one would ever listen."

He felt a sharp, stabbing pressure at his groin—the pointed toe of her shoe. "And I could kick your balls up into the back of your throat and make your voice so squeaky that nobody will be able to listen to you without laughing."

He smiled again; that made two involuntary smiles in one conversation, and Henry was impressed. "You remind me of Roger."

The foot lowered. "I liked Roger. I didn't love him, and I've slept with other people over the years. But I really liked him." Her eyes didn't waver. "Roger asked for nothing outside of our business arrangements. We slept together, sometimes we went to museums, art galleries. Not often. You see, Roger could accept the fact that I was anatomically female and conversationally male." She waited, probably to see if he would react to that. He did, but he didn't show it. The reaction was bafflement; he didn't know what she meant.

"It's like this, Henry: Women talk around and around problems looking for connection, understanding, support. Men talk about problems, too, but the way they do it is to discuss solutions. They talk to battle the problems, while women talk to get some sort of rapport going with their own inner turmoil. I've never liked that about the women I've known. Or about the men who converse that way in an attempt to seem sensitive."

"Clayton Pinkes," said Henry Albert.

"Yeah. Clayton." Now she looked away. "Clayton is my antithesis. Physically he's male, but on the inside he dredges through the muck of his own slimy insufficiencies, going around and around and never attacking the problem. He's worse than any woman. Women will tap into a few close friends for sympathy and understanding. Clayton Pinkes expects the whole fucking world to be his support mechanism."

Henry nodded slowly, then stopped when he remembered the idiotic bobbing of the twelve heads at the Société. He waited.

"I miss Roger," she said. "I miss how straightforward he was and how he never felt guilt."

She was rather pretty, Henry decided. Comparatively, objectively analyzed against the prevalent standards of beauty in American society. "As a matter of fact, I do have a position for you," he said, a moment before he realized he really did.

"Good," she said. "This is what I want, then. For all these years, Roger has kept me from television. The way I see it, you're diluting your own potential. Through broadcast media, I could perform whatever the hell function it is you have me performing to a much larger audience. I've got the appeal, Henry, and you won't even need all the other comedians you have working for you. You give me the role, and I'll pull in the crowd. All you have to do is give me an opening, and I'll win the entertainment world over to you."

"Sorry," said Henry. "You've fulfilled your function on the comedy project. I need you to become a convert."

She leaned back in her chair, becoming guarded.

"You see, we've monitored public opinion quite well

through the comedy project, but we've also isolated those speakers who have the most talent for swaying public opinion. You're one of the best. In fact, I'll be honest: you're *the* best. You'll do television, all right, but you'll do it in the role of the strongest and most loyal believer in Clayton Pinkes's organization."

Her lips tightened. He read the nuances of her face to understand the reaction. He'd expected argument or anger, considering she'd made all her own plans before sitting down here. But Henry saw fear.

"See me Monday." He handed her a card with the Beach Avenue address. "Two o'clock. I have to go now."

Henry drove from Brighton to the house on Beach Avenue.

A concomitant conversation took place behind the locked door of Clayton's office at the Christian Stewardship Ministry headquarters. Clayton raised his right arm in the darkness and willed it to work for him. He was doing this immediately after listening to a voice mailbox message from Neil Perrin that said, "Clayton, maybe we should get together and talk. I was hasty, I guess. I really felt let down. Anyway, give me a call."

Clayton did not feel guilty when he heard Neil's voice. It was glorious, this feeling of not feeling guilt for the first time in his life.

The buzzing in his arm reached its peak, and Clayton said to it, "I want the Archangel Michael brought here. I want him right now." And then the room became dark, much like the darkness in Paolo's limbo, and there was a shape in the darkness that was darker still.

"Hey, what the heck! I was in the middle of a meeting!"

Clayton kept his arm in front of him. "Are you the Archangel Michael? That's who I called for."

The dark shape leaned toward him a bit. "Yeah, that's me. Who the heck—? Say! It's Pinkes, right? The one Raphael calls Pinhead? Pleased to meet you, pal."

"Paolo is . . . Raphael is refusing to help me. So I need you."

"You mean you've seen him? Raphael?"

"He's where I sent him. He could come back, but he won't."

The shape shrunk back a little. "Where you *sent* him? Holy cow. Ho-lee cow."

An angel who said "Holy cow"; Clayton was amused.

"I want to find God. I need your help. Do I get it?"

"Sure. Sure you do. In fact, pal, I'd be delighted."

The phone rang at Henry's Beach Avenue house. Papa Bear answered, but Henry suspected who would be calling.

"Henry it's—"

"Clayton Pinkes."

Papa Bear chuckled. "Right."

Henry took the phone.

"Henry," said Clayton.

"Clayton," said Henry.

"I've decided to take you on."

The simple, declarative assertion threw Henry for a moment. What was this? What was this simple, intuitive allowance of involvement by Pinkes? It felt vaguely cavalier, but somehow familiar.

"Why?" asked Henry.

"I'd like our ministry to be successful," Clayton claimed. *Claimed*. And then the real reason, the impetus, came after that. "I'd like to know if God really cares enough to come forward."

"I see," said Henry.

"No, you don't" said Clayton. "I have a calling from God, Mr. Albert. A calling I'm not sure I . . . approve of. But if it will help me . . ."

Clayton Pinkes' voice trailed off, subsided.

"Help you *how*?" asked Henry Albert.

Clayton was slow to answer. "Help me understand what life is all about. Is that too vague for you?"

It was Henry's turn to be slow, to be cautious. "Maybe it is too vague. How will this help your organization?"

"You know. Damn you, Henry Albert, you already know. Can I count on you?"

That was all Henry Albert needed to hear. "Of course. And I've been thinking as well, Clayton. Perhaps your situation calls for closer cooperation between the two of us. I realize I said that Solutions only provides plans and strategies, but I think Christian Stewardship Ministry could use a good deal of active direction from our firm. I'd like to handle the account. Personally."

"Naturally. I'd been thinking the same thing. And I wouldn't settle for anyone else."

Henry paused. All of this, all of the conversation, said that there was something different in Clayton Pinkes, in his tone, in the subtler levels of his psychology. Something was missing. From what little Henry knew, this didn't feel like a predictable Clayton Pinkes-type discussion.

"That's good, Clayton. Of course, we'll lower our rates to make them acceptable for day-to-day, full-time consulting. Otherwise the one hundred sixty percent return on investment would be impossible."

"Whatever you think, Henry. I could give you complete control over our fund-raising, if that would help the return."

"Yes," said Henry. Complete control? That meant Clayton would have to demote or fire whoever currently served that function. This was too easy. Which meant something was out of step somewhere. Which made Henry extremely interested. "My taking over fund-raising would be a significant move for both of us."

Some commotion arose on Clayton's side of the line. "I have to go now, Henry. My secretary, Mrs. Brunwig, is training a new administrative assistant. I guess there's some confusion out front. Why don't you have your girl call mine to set up a strategy meeting?"

"That would be fine," Henry said, but Clayton had hung up before he'd finished.

Henry folded his hands on his lap. He felt his mouth stretch to a wide grin, and he stared straight ahead.

"Something wrong?" Papa Bear asked him.

"Tell me. Do you think people's basic natures can change?"

Papa Bear seemed to be thinking hard to answer the question. "No," he said. "Not their *basic* nature. Do *you* think they can?"

Henry forced the grin away. "No," he lied. "Therefore, everything runs smoothly. As smoothly as I've planned it."

Henry woke up from a dream of her, the yellow-haired woman who had been Roger Kallur's lover. The one he had just hired on impulse. Impulse! Well, he'd reasoned it through afterwards, found how she could fit into the whole picture. But sitting there across the table from him, with her saying, "I miss Roger," tenderly, right after ripping Clayton Pinkes apart, saying . . . what was it? "On the inside, he dredges through the muck of his own slimy insufficiencies, going around and around and never attacking the problem." God, what a choice of words! It was exactly how he'd felt about Clayton Pinkes, exactly.

Until he started working with him.

Henry got out of bed and found he had an erection. That was nothing abnormal; sometimes he'd wake with erections two, three times a month. But something uneasy stirred inside him, telling him that this particular erection was connected to the dream about Elizabeth.

Of course it was. Because she was that First Woman, the one he had drawn to illustrate his theory of the existence of females, the sketch he'd shown to Rousas and Elobert and LeFavre and Bernardin, those people from his old world. That world was dead now, but she—she was alive.

He was disturbed that he was not quite sure *how* she had been his first picture of Woman.

He washed with cold water from the basin. The daily variables reports would be in e-mail soon. He would need to file major adjustments for the Christian Stewardship Ministry project.

He walked down the narrow steps to the kitchen and hesitated for a moment, a split second. Papa Bear wasn't in the kitchen. Henry half turned to go upstairs to check Papa Bear's room, and then remembered. Papa Bear had flown to St. Louis to claim Roger Kallur's body.

Why had he forgotten that? And although he had, why did it matter where Papa Bear was? Habit, probably. It wasn't that Papa Bear was a crucial cog in the entire project. Papa Bear was a habit, mostly.

While preparing his morning espresso, he smiled at a memory: For several weeks when he was thirteen, before he'd fully absorbed English, he had called Papa Bear "Père Bear." That used to infuriate Papa Bear, who thought it made him sound like a stuffed animal. But Henry had enjoyed the sound of the phrase, and didn't stop until Papa Bear yelled at him, loud. "Will 'a stuff dat fuckin' Pear Bear shit? Jesus, Henry, you fuckin' piss me off!" Henry had stopped after that, but the whole thing about fathers stuck with him. It was so important to be "Father" or "Dad" or "Papa" in this new world. Male progenitors used the terms, the founders of the country were spoken of that way, and even a number of the religious figures insisted on it.

He thought of his own father, Dr. Elobert, bent strangely on the floor with liters of blood pumping from his chest. Henry swallowed all the espresso and pushed back the faintest touch of panic. He couldn't identify the panic's root, but it had something to do with Papa Bear and being afraid.

He descended from the kitchen to the house's second level, the operations room. He sat at the system console to call up the E-mail, then noticed a flashing priority audit code on the upper right corner of the screen. He accessed the system's audit utility and scrolled the message:

EXTERNAL ACCESS ATTEMPTS, 7/10/99
1:07 A.M. telephone attempt, access denied
SOURCE: (716) 867-9191
1:45 A.M. telephone attempt, access denied
SOURCE: (212) 442-3571
2:13 A.M. PrivNet link attempt, access denied
SOURCE: IBM PRIV*9765
6:14 A.M. PrivNet link attempt, access denied
SOURCE: ATT PRIV*4412
WORKSTATION ACCESS ATTEMPTS, 7/10/99
6:22 A.M. System terminal A, access denied
Failed Password #1
7:12 A.M. System terminal A, access denied
Failed Password #3

Terminal A? Henry scrolled the message again and confirmed. But *this* was workstation A, so how could the system be registering access attempts this very morning? Someone would have to have been sitting right here, in this chair, less than twenty minutes ago—

Henry spun. He faced three guns, and not very small ones, either.

"Good morning, Elobert. For a man who doesn't exist on paper, you sure are one hell of a busy cowboy."

Elobert—they knew his old name. Henry scanned their faces, read them. The first one, the one who spoke, wore a scrawny mustache that made the rest of his head look too large. His facial muscles were relaxed, but his eyes were alert, a bit on edge; he tilted his head to the right side, a long-established habit, maybe a slight hearing problem. He was East Coast American, CIA.

"How can I help you?" Henry said, politely.

The second man, to the first's right, Henry's left, was definitely Caribbean: dark, short, his hair slicked back and greased in the Latin *nuevo imagen* style. He was the only one with a defined stance for holding a gun on a dangerous enemy: legs at twenty-five degrees, feet at ninety, elbow of the firing arm crooked at a right angle, finger poised above the trigger but not touching it. A definite soldier, special forces of some kind. SouthAmer Guard.

"You can help us by cooperating in a nice, long discussion about your activities, current and past. I'm sure you'll be quite reasonable about it."

The third man was different. He had Germanic features, maybe Swedish, and his face was stern. He was young and exceptionally thin; his hair was nearly white. He was tilted half toward Henry, half toward his companions. The part of his body facing Henry was relaxed—his holding arm drooped, his left leg casually bent. But his other side held all the tension: taut neck muscles, a locked knee, a quiver in his right eye that almost became a twitch. This third man was ready for action, but not against Henry. Interpol, thought Henry. Someone infiltrating from the Société to protect him.

Henry leaned back in the chair. He did it swiftly, swinging his arms up behind his head. The Caribbean man crouched as if to leap, and the third man, the German, pulled back his firing arm the slightest bit, ready to swing in the Caribbean's direction. Henry was right. This third man did not fit with the other intruders.

"Don't get cute," the CIA man said. His eyes moved quickly around the room, probably seeking weapons they might have missed earlier.

"Oh, I'm not cute," said Henry. "I just look cute when I'm bemused. What do you need from me?"

"We represent a growing concern, Elobert. There are people anxious to know—"

"Cut the shit," said Henry. "You're with international intelligence agencies. Now discuss your output

requirements and I'll see what I can do. If you can't get
to the point, leave."

The CIA man's face stopped relaxing. "All right. We
want access to all your information files. You've been
tracked on trips to Japan, Africa, Italy, Germany, Venezuela, and Christ knows where else. Political trips, business
trips, fucking religious trips even. We want trip content,
mission, goals, priorities, and established action plans."
He came close to Henry and put the muzzle of his
submachine gun against Henry's crotch. "We want to find
out what the fuck you're trying to pull off behind the
scenes."

"Oh, is that all? I'm taking over the world."

The CIA man stared at him a moment, and then
burst into a hacking laugh, half snorts, half coughs. "Jesus
Christ. Jesus H. All-American Christ. You're a fucking
mad scientist."

"A political scientist," said Henry. "Social studies."

"A mad scientist," the CIA man said. "Just like Roland
said. Before you killed him."

Yes, Roland. Roland had been CIA. Had they been
tracking Henry from that long ago? This was not good.
He'd have to access their Langley headquarters files to
erase references to himself. A tedious job, and it didn't
ensure hard copy could be eliminated.

"Roland was like a father to me," Henry said.

Why had he said that? Impulse again, and he didn't
like the feeling. Ever since that Goddard woman had
turned up, he'd felt himself slipping backwards, slipping
back to that place, to Kerguélen.

"If he was like a father, why'd you kill him?"

Henry grinned. "He was a loose end. I admired him
very much, but he was a risk." He stared directly at the
CIA man. "A risk I apparently underestimated." Henry
stretched out his legs and chewed his lower lip for a
while. He felt himself drifting a little, and then he said,
"Ever notice how everyone is busy killing his father in
one way or another? Not just Oedipus, that's too obvious.

But others, like the early anti-monarchists abandoning and executing their kings. Or people like Hitler, who espoused a perfect race that physically and genetically had nothing to do with him. And Nietzsche. Now *there's* a father killer, the most important in the world. It's a big world, gentlemen. It's very hard to control."

The Caribbean was getting edgy. The CIA man's head was tilted even more than it had been at first. "We want your game plan," the CIA man said. "Download all your files to us. I'll give you the number for hookup." He pressed the gun harder against Henry's groin. "And no viruses or worms, asshole. We sweep clean, and it would only piss us off."

"My own father," said Henry, "was a good man. Not a great one, but good. More than anything, he loved the natural world. Science! Any natural law, any plausible theory. It was his entire life. So is it any wonder I'd one day find myself burning to destroy that natural world and claim the supernatural for myself? I think we all practice patricide, gentlemen. Every man kills his father at least once in his lifetime, especially if he loves him."

The CIA man looked at Henry with disgust. "Jesus, I thought you were the one who said cut the shit." He relaxed, just a little. "Why don't *you* quit stalling and get to the output, Elobert?"

"Oh," said Henry, putting surprise into his voice. "You must have missed it. This *is* the output."

Henry's right foot caught the barrel of the gun and swung it under the man's chin; with his left foot he kicked hard against the man's hand, the fingers still poised at the trigger. A short burst; chips of bloodied plaster fell from the ceiling. There was an immediate spray of gunfire from the Caribbean, and Henry rolled forward toward him. A stinging, then, in his left forearm, but he ignored it and came up from his roll, knocking the weapon from the SouthAmer Guard's hand.

The third man stood there, watching.

Henry swung an open hand at the Guard's throat, well

aimed, deadly. He missed. The Guard was under him, now, and his legs scissor-clamped Henry's lower back and abdomen. A numb fire shot through Henry's groin, and he spun to break the pressure, landed on his back. He kicked and caught the Guard in the shoulder. He'd been aiming for the chin.

"You could do something, you know!" Henry shouted at the white-haired man. He rolled to an upright stance, the fallen guns to his back. But he couldn't reach. The Guard was up and lunging.

Through the pain of a foot slamming into his stomach, Henry heard the third man say, "Not really. I can't do anything at all. I'm ethereal."

An angel? Henry thought. This guy's an angel? The hesitation gave the Guard an advantage; Henry tasted blood, was staring at the ceiling now.

"I should kill you," the Guard said, a Latin accent. Henry lifted his head to focus on him. The Guard wasn't even breathing hard. "If I didn't have orders, I'd break your neck right now."

"Do something!" Henry shouted.

"He can't even see me," said the white-haired man.

"I am doing something," the Guard said. "I'm letting you live." The Guard spat.

"Then *make* him see you!"

"If you think it will help."

The Guard's eyes narrowed to slits. The third man didn't change at all, no twinkle, no smoke, but the Guard suddenly spun, startled, and crouched to a stance.

"Hi!" said the white-haired man, the angel. "Ever hear the one about the string who walked into a bar?"

Henry lunged, found neck, and collapsed to the floor. The Guard's body fell beside him, eyes still open.

The ceiling was still out of focus; Henry lay on his back, his chest heaving. Now he felt the pain in his arm and lifted it to look: three bullets, two in the lower arm, one in the upper. "Give me a hand," Henry said, and then swore at himself. Ethereal. The angel couldn't do anything but stand there and converse with him. Unless it was the angel he'd been waiting for. "Are you Raphael? If you are, heal me."

"Sorry. Raph's still AWOL. Besides, you're not my client. What happens to you isn't my responsibility."

"You'd have let them kill me," Henry said. He tried to stand, felt dizzy, and rested on his knees, his good arm flat against the floor to steady himself.

"They weren't going to kill you at all. I've been watching them for about an hour now. If you had died, they'd have died. Orders, you know. God, human beings are so violent."

"Who are you?"

The angel started glowing, and sweeping robes replaced his shirt and trousers, waving in a wind Henry couldn't feel. "Hail, Henry, full of bullets. The Urim is with thee." The fluttering stopped, the light dimmed, and the angel stood once more in trousers and shirt.

"Charming," said Henry.

"It's great for parties," said Gabriel.

"What do you want? I didn't ask for you, I asked for the one called Raphael."

"We can't give what we don't have, Henry. Besides, I'm here on my own business. You've just acquired the services of Elizabeth Goddard. I'm her managing angel."

Henry stood. Elizabeth? She was involved at this level? Had her own angel?

"I want to know if you plan to keep her in comedy."

Henry saw blood on the leg of his pants. No pain, but he checked anyway. He couldn't find a wound, so the blood must have been from the CIA agent. "No," he said. "She's going into religion. I want her to play an up-front role."

The white-haired angel frowned and stepped forward. "You can't do that. With just a little more time, she could become the greatest comedienne of the age. The *final* age, Henry. It's the last chance for the world to laugh."

"To laugh? I'm bleeding to death, and you're worried about global chuckles?"

"You're not bleeding so badly."

Henry looked down at his arm. There were two fading scars on his lower forearm—not wounds, not bullet holes, scars on the Urim arm healing themselves. The third hole on his upper arm still bled, and he pressed his right hand against it to stop the flow.

"Now back to laughter. Your entire comedy program exists merely for the sake of monitoring public reaction to political activities, and I say, sincerely, that you've made impressive headway using that approach. I'm not suggesting you discontinue the whole thing; I'd just like to see the limitations removed from Elizabeth. Let her play top clubs, let her do networks and cable appearance. Consider it an act of mercy for the ending world, if you like. People need to laugh. For example . . ." The angel waved his hand, and the two assailants were standing next to him, the SouthAmer Guard and the CIA agent. Henry tensed, but then saw their bodies were on the floor still. But they stood beside Gabriel nonetheless.

"Okay," said the angel, "now you two are dead, right?"

The men—no, the spirits of the men—stood silent, terrified.

"So give us an end-of-life perspective. Would you have wanted more laughter in your life?"

"Madre de Dios," said the SouthAmer Guard, making the sign of the cross. "You are an angel." The CIA man was staring down at his own semi-headless body.

"Yes," said Gabriel, "but we don't have a lot of time before you cross over. What do you say? More laughter in your life?"

"What happens now?" said the CIA man. "What happens to us?"

Henry sat down. He was tired, hurting, and now confused.

"How would I know what happens now? You cross

over. I've never been there. Maybe you go to paradise or maybe you wallow in eternal torment. Just answer the question!"

Another wind started, one Henry could feel, and the two men began to glow, just as Gabriel had earlier. They were startled, throwing their hands out to try to grab something that would anchor them to the room.

"Yes," the SouthAmer Guard said, nodding vigorously, obediently. "I would very much have appreciated more laughter in my life."

"Me, too," said the agent.

Henry's forearm tingled, and he felt the Urim beating steadily, thumping, a heartbeat. The spirits of the men glowed brighter, and he couldn't look at them any longer. Then they were gone, the wind with them.

"So there," said Gabriel. "Even the dead vote for laughter. Think about it." Then the angel, too, was gone.

Henry didn't stir, and his mind returned to him, the sharp, rapid mind that had been slipping away since he'd met Elizabeth. There were different levels of the metanatural. More than one. A level of angels. A level of human souls that angels couldn't understand or access. And beyond that, who knew? More levels, endless levels, each more subtle and sublime than the last, until that final level where God hid. One world after another for Henry to enter, claim, and conquer, until he was face-to-face with the Father of the Universe. Then, what next? Patricide, perhaps.

Despite the bullets and the beating, he felt very good.

"Major changes," he said, and they all wrote that in their notebooks. Well, not all, not Papa Bear, who never took notes. But the fifty others, the core of Solutions, they meticulously recorded anything Henry had to say. Especially this time. This was the first occasion the entire organization had ever been gathered.

"Number one: Methodology. We're at the point

where we've permeated vital organizations throughout the world, and that has been sufficient until now. But leaks become more of a risk the thinner we spread ourselves. The most recent leak to the CIA is one for which I take full responsibility. Now I've been warned and you've been warned. I'll handle that breach personally."

They stared, unblinking, unnodding. Henry approved of that.

"We are well established now. The first stage of the project, Permeation, has closed. The next stage begins. The concept is that of the Vital Few."

They had a hungry look; Henry would have preferred dispassion. Hunger led to impulse. When he'd started the company, he'd had sixty-three employees. Now there were these fifty, himself, and Papa Bear. Only Roger Kallur had been killed. Thirteen others had taken their own lives. No patience, no vision of the Grand Suicide. How many more would go before the end?

"The world is not something we need to destroy molecule by molecule. Our Vital Few approach identifies those key areas of balance upon which the stability of the global society depends. Areas that may seem as disconnected as this table leg"—he patted the table before him—"that row of books"—he pointed toward the top shelf of the bookcase at the left of the table—"and that chair" (he nodded toward a shabby ladderback beside the bookcase.

He waited a moment to let them consider. "Do you see it?"

Lawrence Bourne raised his hand. "I do."

"Show me."

Bourne left his seat and came to the table. He studied the table leg a moment, then swung an open palm halfway down its length. The leg snapped; the side of the table dropped, hitting the second lowest shelf on the bookcase; the bookcase shook, freeing the bookend on the top, sending seven or eight large encyclopedias toppling onto the seat of the old ladderback chair; the chair collapsed from the impact.

"Good. Your new assignments narrow Solutions' scope, but increase its depth. Now number two: Need to Know. Until now, we've all known basically how all the pieces fit together. As we come closer to our goal, the threat of leakage becomes more dangerous. I'm establishing three levels of information to limit the risk of any one of us becoming a problem. See sheet three."

There was a brief shuffling of pages from the packets he'd given them. Sheet three was read quickly. Their eyes came back to him.

"You'll notice a new level for our organization, the one listed as L-3. This level involves those people who believe our end goal is to bring the world under our control in a single government, such people as Neil Perrin of Christian Stewardship Ministry, Andre Roque of the Common Europe Société, Salvatore Marzoni of the Descartesians." He paused a moment. "Elizabeth Goddard, the comedienne." Several eyes shifted, one or two heads tilted; the name was new to them. "It is important these people believe they are fully in the know. They play important roles, and would not be as willing if they knew our end. Level L-2 constitutes each of you. The L-2 group knows the true goal of Solutions and knows the Permeation phase of the operation. From here on you will not be privy to the interconnection of the Vital Few operations. That information is classified L-1."

The L-1 list showed himself, Clayton Pinkes, and Papa Bear.

Several hands raised, and Henry waved them down. "I'll tell you why Clayton Pinkes is on there. Because I have no choice. Clayton will know things whether we tell him or not."

"Why?" asked Caroline Lang. "How could he possibly know?"

"I'm sorry," said Henry. "The explanation of that is L-1 information."

After they'd all gone, Papa Bear grabbed him by the elbow.

"You're never going to tell them, are you?"

"Tell them what?"

"About the angels, and God, and that whole side of things."

Henry pulled his elbow away. "It would complicate everything. These people are suicidal maniacs. If I throw a metaphysical variable into their worlds, they'll be swayed from their single-mindedness."

"Um," said Papa Bear. Henry felt anxious, although he had no reason to. He didn't.

"Look, you know the importance of all this. We're bringing God back to the universe."

Papa Bear smacked his lips thoughtfully. "That's what Clayton's doing. It's even what Michael's doing. But you, Henry? You're just controlling and destroying. And you're doing it without the least bit of hate. The destruction is motive enough for you, all by itself, boy."

"Don't call me boy!" Henry shouted. "You're not my . . ."

Papa Bear smiled at him. "Um," he said.

The room felt too small and too dark. The Beach Avenue bedroom had had windows facing west, toward the street lights, always a dull fluorescent glow and a humming on summer nights when the windows were opened. That house was sold now—gone from the life of Henry Albert, on paper never even having been owned by him. This new bedroom in this new house (on paper not his either; owned, rather, by a fictitious Bernie Brightwater originally from a non-town called Oak Flats, Illinois) faced away from the street. His room was on the second floor, and had slanted ceilings that vaguely bothered him.

"You're not my father," he had been about to say to Papa Bear. Idiocy. Papa Bear hadn't said "son," he'd said "boy." Even if he had said son, what would it matter?

"He's not my father," Henry said. He could see his father—kind, old Dr. Elobert—dying, twisted, bloodying a faraway floor in another world. In his mind he stood Dr. Elobert up, cleaned off the blood, straightened his hair and shirttail.

Thank you, Henri.

"There's no reason to thank me. You're still dead."

No one is ever really dead, son.

"Yes they are. Don't be absurd."

Your viewpoint is limited. Think of the theories of relativity. You are observing from a fixed location. To you, the dead are dead. To the dead, you're not even alive yet. To the unborn, you never were.

"You use relativity as a metaphor, not factually."

By your perception. Yes.

"Then why should Papa Bear care? If the dead aren't dead, my ending the world shouldn't matter."

He questions your motives.

"*My* motives? Look at everyone else's! Michael wants God back and could care less about humanity; Pinkes wants God so he'll feel justified in holding opinions not based on facts; Neil Perrin wants to be somebody, anybody, because he's nothing in himself."

You've left someone out.

"I know. I . . . know."

What are Papa Bear's motives?

"Who can tell?"

Come on, Henri. You know.

"Who can tell?"

He likes you, Henri. He cares about you.

"Why, Father? That's no motive. What's his reason?"

There doesn't need to be a reason. People have reasons for disliking others, but liking them, caring about them, those are motives all by themselves.

"I don't understand. I can't comprehend that."

Of course you can't. You're a sociopathic monomaniac.

"I'm very good at what I do."

*Indeed. That you are. But I think you care about
Papa Bear.*

"Maybe. Maybe I do."

God help him.

"Father, I . . . Father, there is this woman. Elizabeth
Goddard."

I know.

"She's the one I sketched, Father. The day I invented
women."

I know.

"She interests me. I've found myself acting impulsively
since I met her."

Indeed.

"I'm trying to ask you what I should do! I need your
advice!"

My advice, Henri? Be reasonable. I'm dead.

Henry pulled out Dr. Elobert's shirttail and mussed
his hair. The blood seeped back over the shirt and
trousers. Henry carefully set the doctor back down on
the floor, bending his leg to an unlikely angle, opening
his mouth and tilting back the head.

Henry climbed from bed and turned on the light. He
sat with his back against the headboard for a long time.
After that, he slammed his fist a single time against the
bedroom wall. The plasterboard cracked, broke, became
a hole. In less than half a minute, Papa Bear ran into
the room.

"What's going on? Are you all right?" Papa Bear
looked from the hole, to Henry, to the hole.

"I'm fine." Henry lay flat and pulled the covers to
his chin.

"Good," said Papa Bear. "I was just . . . you know,
after that incident last week on Beach Avenue, I was
worried."

Henry said nothing. After Papa Bear turned out the
light and left, he rolled over on his stomach, facedown
in his pillow. "What do you care?" he said.

❖   ❖   ❖

A week later, early morning at the offices of Christian Stewardship Ministry, he walked with Elizabeth Goddard toward Clayton's office. She was dressed wrong and he told her so.

"You should have worn a business suit."

"This is a Betsy Johnson. I spent a hell of a lot on this dress. Besides, you're one to talk. Do you ever wear anything besides black pants and black turtlenecks? You could spend a little on clothes yourself."

He didn't doubt her dress was expensive; he just didn't like how it looked for the situation. She would be seeing Clayton Pinkes face-to-face for the first time in nineteen years. It was a business meeting, and she looked like she was ready for an expensive evening on the town.

The dress was floor length, nearly, a white background with tasteful blue flowers in irregular patterns. The sleeves puffed a bit, not a lot, and they were off the shoulder, almost even with the horizontal neckline. The neckline went a little too low, showing just the beginning shading of what would become cleavage in another two or three millimeters. She wore her hair down—it had been tied up when Henry first met her, or tied back, rather, a single blonde ponytail hanging limply between her shoulders, down her back. Now she had done something with it, made it more attractive. "Had it done," whatever women meant when they said that phrase. He didn't know the words to describe the style because he'd never bothered to research female hair. Maybe he should. It couldn't hurt; all knowledge was beneficial.

He halted that entire line of thinking.

In the reception area, Julie Ward looked up at them, smiling. Then she studied Elizabeth for a moment. She was more cautious. Henry noted the change.

"Tell Clayton we're here," Henry said.

Julie Ward shuffled some papers on her desk and asked, far too casually to really be casual, "*Both* of you have an appointment?"

"I do. This is Elizabeth Goddard. Clayton's not expecting her, but Ms. Goddard will be sitting in."

Julie's shoulders and head did something funny then: She straightened her back while at the same time lowering her chin; her right shoulder came forward a bit so that she was slanted ever so subtly toward the two of them, him and Elizabeth. Her eyes remained lowered as she hit the intercom button and the phone. Henry could tell she was, for some reason, on her guard. He glanced quickly, peripherally, but saw no threat. He dismissed it; the woman was manic.

"Clayton, Mr. Albert is here for his appointment. He has a Ms. Elizabeth Goddard with him."

The way she said it—MIZZ e-LIZZ-abeth GAH-dard, slightly punching the stressed syllables—caused Henry to glance at Elizabeth. Was she the threat?

"Are you serious?" Clayton's voice said over the intercom. "Send them in." Clayton sounded flustered, but not nearly as flustered as Henry had anticipated.

As they walked to Clayton's office, Elizabeth said, "Well, Clayton still has an eye for women. Did you see that secretary?"

"Of course I saw her. I've spoken with her dozens of times." But the question hadn't been information-seeking, it had been exclamatory. Elizabeth had a guarded look similar to Julie Ward's.

"Hello," said Mrs. Brunwig, who was walking past Clayton's door carrying a stack of printouts. "Oh," she said to Elizabeth, and Henry watched the old woman's eyes go through evaluation, comparison, resignation, and slight melancholy. "Good day." She walked on.

Competition, thought Henry, a bit astonished. Competition, not guardedness. But none of them knew each other, really. How could they go right into competition without any one knowing a single fact about the other? And even Mrs. Brunwig.

Fact: Elizabeth knew Clayton, and had attended school with him during their high school years. They'd worked together for a short time running a small youth group in Brighton. All reports indicated they were never particularly good friends, simply colleagues.

Fact: Julie Ward had attended elementary school with Clayton. They were friends during a short summer recess but lost touch after Julie went off to Catholic high school.

Fact: Mrs. Brunwig never lived in Rochester, New York, until the late 1980's.

Tentative Conclusion: Elizabeth never knew Julie, Julie never knew Elizabeth. Mrs. Brunwig never knew Elizabeth. They felt competitive because . . . because . . .

They were at the office door; he would think about it later.

Clayton was standing when they entered. He looked as if he were about to say something, something to Elizabeth, and Henry cut in. "Clayton, this is Elizabeth Goddard. You may remember her from back in high school."

Clayton nodded. Henry wasn't sure what he was reading on Clayton's face—not nostalgia, not surprise, not attraction, not guilt, nothing with a name, but something significant. That made two times, two times in three minutes, that he couldn't immediately assess a situation.

Elizabeth stepped forward and offered her hand. "Pleased to see you again, Clayton. I've admired your efforts for years. I've often watched you on television."

Banal enough. Two acquaintances meeting again.

"Thank you, Elizabeth. I've heard you were an entertainer. I apologize I've never had the opportunity to see you perform."

She blushed gracefully. "I'm afraid you would have found my material inappropriate. I did comedy, and it called for a rather ribald style."

"Ah. You sound as if that's a past occupation."

"I've given up comedy. I've recently returned to my faith, and I'm looking for work more in line with serving the Lord."

Henry felt more stable; now he could follow the nuances. Complete banality. "I brought Elizabeth here because she has a natural gift for communicating with audiences. Her talent, her faith, and your past friendship make her an ideal choice for our itinerate spokesmen program. She's accustomed to extensive travel and has no family ties."

"No husband?" Clayton asked. "No children?"

"No," Elizabeth said.

"I see. Well, why don't the two of us take a moment to get reacquainted. Would you like some coffee?"

"That would be lovely."

They both looked at Henry. For a moment he thought they expected him to run out for the coffee. But there was coffee right there, in Clayton's pot. Then he realized: He was being dismissed.

He stood there.

Clayton walked to him and put his left arm around Henry's shoulder, steering him toward the door. "You know something that's always bothered me, Henry? The word 'nonchalant.' If we have that word, shouldn't we also have the word 'chalant'? Doesn't that seem fair? Why don't you take about fifteen minutes to develop a strategy for introducing the term 'chalant' into the English language?"

The office door shut, and Henry stood in the hall. He could understand Clayton dismissing him, but Elizabeth? Why would she want him out? Just a few weeks ago, when they first met, she'd been frightened of the name Clayton Pinkes. It made him feel . . . made him feel . . .

Henry walked to Julie's desk.

"Do it," he said.

"Oh, God, not again! I'm in such a good mood, Henry."

"Do it and keep in a good mood."

She scrunched up her face in a childish way. "But I can't stay in a good mood. I mean, if I listen in, I'll feel guilty, and that will upset my stomach, you know. And if I hear something I don't like I'll get upset, or maybe I'll even get angry, and that always give me a headache. I have too much work today to feel sick."

Henry leaned on her desk with both hands balled into fists. "You know you want to listen in as much as I do. Come on, Julie, it will be fun."

She considered it, then whispered, "Yeah, it *would* be fun!" Her face strained to suppress glee. She pushed the sequence of numbers on the phone that Henry had set up to make the intercom one-way, a monocom.

" . . . travelling, which gets tiresome without a real life goal." Elizabeth's voice.

"I know what you mean. Henry has nearly tripled my travel schedule since we contracted Solutions." Clayton.

"He's told me the work will be strenuous. But if the Lord is calling me to toil, who am I to run away?"

"Tell me, have you kept up on reading the Scriptures?"

"On and off. I've started a rigorous program of study and prayer to bring me back to better understanding of the messages."

"Study and prayer! If only I had time. Henry keeps me booked solid. I can't begrudge him, though. I guess . . . this will sound strange, but, I guess I think of him as a father figure. He's so well organized, knows exactly what to do in any situation. Yeah, he's like a father."

Henry stepped back from the intercom. Business, they were discussing simple business. He was interviewing her. Henry'd expected something else, didn't know what, now cursed himself for expecting anything he imagined. Anything that wasn't established by facts. "Turn it off," he said.

Julie Ward looked up, surprised. "We just started!"

"This is a waste of time. Turn it off."

She pouted and pushed the switch. She sat there a moment, hunched over, chin in her palms, sulking. Then she spun in the chair, beaming with hope. "Say," she emoted, "do you think you could talk Clayton into going on a date with me?"

Henry turned his back on her and walked to the chairs in the reception lounge. *He's like a father figure.* Henry picked up a morning newspaper and read an article on a systems crash at Langley, CIA headquarters, over the IBM PrivNet link. "Less than one thousandth of one percent of critical data has been lost," a spokesman said. The article speculated on possible threats to national security. The CIA spokesman was quoted as pointedly denying such a situation existed. The loss mostly involved archival accounts, two decades old. The media were making an issue out of a non-event, and the source of their information would be severely censured.

Henry put the paper down. It said nothing he hadn't learned in the Daily Variables Report from Lawrence Bourne.

He clicked his tongue and crossed his arms. Father figure? How could Clayton even pretend to believe that?

This is what Henry Albert missed by turning the monocom off when he did:

Clayton stood across from Elizabeth. They talked stiffly for a while, then Clayton pulled his chair out from behind the desk. She sat in it, very proper and poised. He sat on the edge of the coffee table.

His arm was buzzing, and when he blinked he could see the vision of Henry Albert standing, listening, by the intercom.

So they talked pleasantries. She seemed to not want any reference to their past, and he would play along. It was a game of some sort. A big game, though, because Henry was outside controlling it.

Then the buzzing in Clayton's arm stopped; Henry had given up listening.

"I certainly hope I can learn from Henry's and your

guidance," Elizabeth said. "There are so many people in the world to be reached with the message of God's love."

"And then we can destroy it," Clayton said. Her face dropped a little. "Once we get the ball rolling, we'll summon God back to the universe and cause the end of the world. Or maybe the other way around. We start destroying it and He comes running to settle everything down." He held his right arm out to her. "I'm not entirely sure how it works yet, but when the time is right I'll know. Henry will tell me."

"Your arm," she said.

"Yes. The almighty Thummim of God. You remember the day I took the rock—?"

"I remember," she said, too quickly.

"Henry's got something like it, but we're the only two. Limited edition."

Elizabeth adjusted herself in the chair. "As long as you use your gifts for the greater glory of God."

"Quit fucking around," said Clayton. He saw her shoulders tense. "Face the facts. Whatever your motives for being here, you're only playing Henry's game. Maybe you came to kill me; Henry wants me alive, so you'll be blocked. Maybe you want to dishonor me; Henry needs me to be a respectable, hell, a worshipped public figure. So you'll be blocked. Maybe"—he summoned his arm and tried to look deep into her soul—"maybe you have a fantasy that goes like this: You become well-known as my partner in preaching; you seduce me and become my lover; you anonymously tip the press off that we're having sexual relations; they investigate and you break down and confess, tell the whole story; I'm ruined, my tiny empire shattered; you get talk show appearances, where you again get to demonstrate your gift for comedy, now riding on a crest of notoriety; Elizabeth Goddard lives happily ever after."

She was pale now, because he'd taken such care to describe in detail exactly what her fantasy was. He could feel spite and anger rising, and he withdrew from her soul.

"I hate you, Clayton Pinkes," said Elizabeth Goddard.

"I know. But I won't say I'm sorry."

"You're a worm, you're pure slime. Every time I think of you my stomach lurches."

"Better find a doctor. You'll get ulcers one day."

"It doesn't matter that you won't hire me. You can live with the knowledge that I hate you every single day for the rest of your life."

"I guess that's not too long. I'll bet Henry's got Armageddon scheduled already."

"And I hope when you die that your God keeps you in hell forever."

"Fuck God, Elizabeth. Fuck Henry and me and you."

Her mouth was open, ready to go on, but nothing came out. She looked silly like that, so he reached over and pushed her jaw shut. Then he stroked her cheek, lightly, once.

"You've changed," she said.

"Yeah, about two months ago. I decided suddenly that life was far too complex for me, and that Henry Albert, despite himself, might have some of the answers. It was a Thursday, I think."

"You're different. Not just your behavior. Your basic personality."

"I guess you'll just have to spend the rest of your life with the knowledge that you hate someone who doesn't exist." He walked to the office door, started to open it. "Your first broadcast will be the day after tomorrow. prepare a six-minute message and I'll go over it with you."

She didn't rise from the chair.

"You're hired," said Clayton.

Book III:
The Age of Reason

"A believer assents to things proposed
to him by another, but not seen
by himself; so that the knowledge
of faith resembles hearing rather
than seeing . . .

"There is therefore some knowledge
of God that is higher than the
knowledge of faith."

St. Thomas Aquinas
Summa Contra Gentiles, XL

Tritologue

Stockholm 2005—The Grand Finale!

At last, at last! The Angelic Convention to end all conventions—literally!! You'll need to get your reservations in early, folks! This is the last convention before the scheduled return of God, so the convention committee is bringing you the highest quality programming ever imagined in the history of angelkind. Act now!! Don't lose your spot at Stockholm 2005!!!

For reservations contact Mandi, Convention Team Liaison.

Scheduled Program Highlights

Entertainment

"I'm Still Not Very Funny"—The Archangel Gabriel performs his comedic smash hits "The Metaphysical Bummer" and "Why I Read Anselm's Ontological Argument Backwards."

"My Clients Crack Me Up"—A knee-slapping look at

the whacky world of Management Information Systems, presented by Bob of the Heavenly I.S. Division.

Personal Growth

"Employment Under the Almighty"—A seminar conducted by the Archangel Suriel discussing career development opportunities in the coming Kingdom of God.

"Behave Yourself!"—Wonder about the social graces needed for an audience with the Ancient of Days? Distressed over a possible divine *faux pas*? This panel lecture by the Ethics Committee discusses the poise and charm that will make you the pride of the Sanctum Sanctorum! Proper attire required.

Informational

"Urim/Thummim: Latest Theories"—Get the latest theories firsthand from Heaven's greatest thinkers about the last of the holy relics, the Urim and the Thummim of old. How do these two items link the physical with the metaphysical? What makes them a key to contact with the Almighty? Why do they only respond to human acts of faith? Scholars of the Metascience League debate one of the hottest endtime issues ever!

"Human Politics: Key Players of the Last Days"—With such busy work schedules lately, an angel can easily lose touch with the human political scene so vital to our own efforts. The archangel Azariel gives an easy-to-follow overview of the United States, Common Europe, the SouthAmer Economic Coalition, and even the scattered Russian/Asian states. Insightful biographical information will be presented on such key players as Salvatore Marzoni of the Descartesians, Andre Roque of the Common Europe Société, French-American strategist

Henri Elobert (aka Henry Albert), and, of course, the enigmatical Clayton Pinkes.

Business Meetings

"Solidarity Now!"—Union meeting for the Amalgamated Angelic Workers Union, Local #1. Keynote speaker: Abaddon the Destroyer.

!!! Special Event !!!

"The Trial of Raphael"—For the first time in the history of angeldom, the full judicial Council Most Holy will be gathered to pass judgement on a Senior Executive! Senior Staff member Raphael the Archangel faces charges of mutiny and treason in this once-in-a-universe event. Don't just hear about it from your friends! Be there firsthand to see Raphael face possible eradication from all levels of the space-time continuum, physical or metaphysical!

Presiding judge: Michael, Prince of Angels.

ALPHA:
Clayton After the Turn of
the Millennium

On the second verse of the "Star Spangled Banner,"
Clayton Pinkes edged the chair in front of him a few
inches backwards, then piously faced the flag at the front
of the ballroom until the end of the anthem. It was a
plush chair with rich-looking dark wood and rich-looking
red upholstery, and it probably had the sort of name
that rich-looking people casually dropped into the middle
of furniture conversations—a Chippendale or a Duncan
Phyfe or a Queen Anne period piece or something.
There were a whole class of people who would never
deign to say the word "chair" all by itself, and here he
was with them at the . . . what was this they were at?
A "fête." Not a "party" or a "shindig" or a "get-together."
A downright "fête," which meant this wasn't a ballroom
after all. It was a fêteroom, which sounded to Clayton
the tiniest bit obscene.

He pulled the chair of uncertain nomenclature back
a few more inches.

The gentleman in the row before him intended to

sit on this very chair as soon as the room finished the third verse of the national anthem—that was how America was now, a three-verse anthem minimum before any function, fête or not. That gentleman was none other than Walter J. Underwood, Secretary of Commerce of the United States of America. Secretary Underwood was a staunch supporter of the American Patriot Party, which by implication made him a staunch supporter of Clayton Pinkes's Christian Stewardship Ministry; but the Secretary had never donated a dime to the Stewardship cause, and his build proclaimed him to be primarily a staunch supporter of the Underwood belly and three hundred other pounds of Underwood. Not that Clayton cared, really. But holdouts like Secretary Underwood disturbed Henry Albert, so Clayton made a point of addressing offenders directly.

At the close of the third verse—the phrase that asked where the enemies of America were now, and then answered itself that their "blood has washed out/their foul footstep's pollution"—Secretary Underwood and the rest of the gathering settled back to their chairs, and Secretary Underwood continued settling past where his chair was supposed to be, down to the floor, a muffled *flumph* that caused heads to swivel and then politely glance away.

"My God, Walter!" said the wiry, bespectacled man to the right of where Walter had assumed he'd be sitting. "You've missed your Duxbury!"

Ah, thought Clayton. A Duxbury.

"Give me your hand," the wiry man urged in a panicked whisper. "People are glancing!"

"Allow me," said Clayton, who kneeled as a humble servant of God and gently lifted the Secretary's shoulders, mass, and volume, much in the manner that one would gently lift a sack of dry cement. Papa Bear and Neil Perrin, stationed respectively and as always at Clayton's left and right, moved to help. Clayton waved them away.

"Thank you," Underwood mumbled, breathing so hard

that Clayton made it a point not to. The Secretary looked up, and when he realized that Clayton was Clayton his eyes widened. "Mr. Pinkes! Why . . . thank you, thank you ever so much. I'm honored."

Clayton gave him a serene nod that could have meant "Shucks, it was nothing," or "Indeed, you *should* be honored." Clayton sat, and Underwood sat, so everybody in each of their parties sat, too. They faced the podium (which probably had a different name at this function, but Clayton thought of it as just a podium) and the speaker—who was, in fact, *the* Speaker, the Speaker of the House—began his pre-fête speech: Blah this, blah that, and welcome to his Honor so-and-so and also to our dear friend and blah-blah public servant, all of whom were this-and-that about the growing pride of Americans and so-and-how committed to what was, after all, still a delicate experiment in democracy, and etc., etc. about balanced responsibility and freedom, which wasn't, after all, license, to whit and, ibid., et al., c.f. what I said last year, so please welcome for our invocation the respected and beloved Clayton Pinkes, who has brought the hearts of America back to the spirit of God, faith, and country.

Clayton got up and invoked briefly, and then on impulse he suggested that it might be a good practice to include the fourth verse of the "Star Spangled Banner" whenever it was sung, considering it was the only verse that mentioned God. Hundreds of rich heads nodded, and by the end of next month it would be an unpardonable social blunder to omit the fourth verse.

A half hour into the party, Clayton was speaking again with Secretary of Commerce Underwood. "You must be more careful," Clayton said. "Secretaries of Commerce have an unfortunate track record with accidents."

"Indeed?" said Underwood, uncomfortable.

"Yes," said Clayton. "There was that one Secretary . . . Neil, what was his name, the one with the horse?"

"Baldrige," said Neil.

"Yes, Baldrige. Twenty years ago, I think. One day a happy, healthy government worker, and the next—bam, thrown from a horse and dead of a broken neck. Makes you wonder what it's all about. Makes you wonder if at any moment you'll find yourself in the presence of God, giving an accounting for your life."

Right on cue—Henry Albert's cue, no doubt—the Secretary of Education, Allen Delathe, approached Clayton and made a short speech about the importance of Christian Stewardship Ministry's social and spiritual programs throughout the world and especially in America. With pointed nonchalance, a sort of broadcasted subtlety, he slipped Clayton a check and said, "I hope this token helps some way in God's work." Then he left.

Clayton looked at the check and nodded. "Well, my goodness," he said aloud. He handed the check to Papa Bear, who promptly stashed it in the inside pocket of his suit coat.

Underwood obviously saw what was happening, but social rules were still social rules and he had to play along. "That reminds me," he said. "Has my administrator gotten around to sending you my own . . . little token?"

"Why, no," said Clayton, now appearing embarrassed over such open talk of money.

"Indeed, my apologies. The schedule has been so hectic of late."

Clayton kept looking amiably at Underwood.

"Why don't we take care of that right now?" Underwood said. "David?" The wiry man rushed to Underwood's side and handed him a leather hand purse from which Underwood drew a checkbook. Clayton thanked the Secretary profusely. The check was for twenty thousand dollars.

"You could have accomplished that without making him miss his chair," Neil Perrin said after the Secretary wandered away. "Don't such adolescent pranks make you feel childish?"

"You mean, do I feel guilty, Neil?" Clayton considered. "Nope. I feel jocular, puckish, déclassé, and pleasantly petty. But I'll keep trying for guilt. I promise."

"It's time to go," Neil said. "You're going to miss the ten p.m. with Archbishop Taccone."

"Sure," said Clayton, gazing distractedly after the Secretary. The fat man moved over to a gathering seated around something that elsewhere would be called a coffee table. Clayton nudged Papa Bear and asked, "What would you say are my chances of sneaking over there and tying Underwood's shoelaces to the legs of the Duxbury?"

Papa Bear scanned the crowd. "Not too good. Too many people around. Of course, I could cause a commotion across the room, maybe ask some old white lady to dance."

"Clayton!" said Neil. "We'll be late." And then to Papa Bear: "Don't you encourage him."

This is what it's like when you walk through the world suspecting there is a God, knowing there are angels, and understanding that the faith you had in yourself, once, back in your innocence, is shattered—not by God, not by angels, not by demons once invented to shift blame, but by yourself:

You wake up each morning and put on the required suit, not an extremely expensive one like everyone around you now wears, but an old store-rack one that has finally started feeling comfortable after three years. You meet a guy named Henry Albert at the building you own—a whole building now, and the richer you get the plainer you want your eating and living and dressing; in the final accounting, you're a rebel to yourself. This guy, Henry, goes over a list of strategies and speeches and engagements that fit into a plan to end the world. You don't really concern yourself with that part, the bit about ending the world. If that's what it takes to see God face-to-face, so be it. You really do believe that. You do.

Sometimes you wish you could feel guilty, but that's not a feeling you can access any more.

Another guy named Neil Perrin, a guy who once respected you, is always close at hand to make sure you meet all of Henry's appointments. Neil used to worship you, but now he does everything in his power to become like Henry. This doesn't make you jealous, only intrigued. Neil Perrin seems like a guy who needs to aspire to something greater than himself, and on that one day when you weren't any better than he was, he rejected you and latched on to Henry. Which, by implication, makes Henry better than you. That doesn't bother you either, because Henry amuses you.

The whole world is Neil Perrin. The whole world aspires to something greater than itself, and you, Clayton Pinkes, are becoming the icon of their hope. You proclaim God as no one on Earth has proclaimed Him since Peter, Paul, and Silas. You point to Heaven, the world looks. The world follows your extended arm, gazes at the hand, out along the tip of your index finger and beyond to where you insist God is standing. And they, this world of Neil Perrins, they all start nodding, saying, "Yea and verily, there God is."

Occasionally you look out that way, too, past your own fingertip, but you don't see anything.

There's a third guy in this life of yours, the one who acts as your bodyguard, a black man named Papa Bear. He's human, maybe the only one who's human out of all these Henry Albert clones you see appearing in hallways of your own organization. Papa Bear cannot be explained. He's here by the grace of Henry, but he is nothing like the others. He laughs. He tells stories about the past days in the Bronx. He plays extravagant poker with you in the back of the car (you owe him thirty-eight billion dollars). But you can't quite decide what he's doing in the middle of all this. What he means to Henry.

There are two women, two you look at and wonder why you feel no guilt. The first is Julie Ward, your very first love, and the second is Elizabeth Goddard, your very best. Julie admires you, likes you, has even tried (but failed) to get romantic with you. Her moods are as stable as weather in Seattle, but you like that. Julie is someone different every three minutes. She drives Mrs. Brunwig crazy, and you find yourself smiling because you'd always believed that that was exactly what Mrs. Brunwig needed most. The only difference between Julie and the rest of the world is a measure of honesty that expresses the unpredictability of the human soul. Yes, that's how you would explain it; you laugh and feel philosophic for having thought that.

And there is the other woman, Elizabeth Goddard. She is kind to you, gentle, attentive, compassionate, and she hates you down to the marrow in every one of your 297 bones, maybe even the one in your right arm that isn't your own.

Or maybe she doesn't hate you at all.

She has become one of your best preachers during the last six years. Her "talks"—Henry says not to call them sermons—draw as big a crowd as yours, and you have watched her reduce a congregation to tears and instantaneous repentance. She is better than you in some areas of preaching. She reaches the more cynical souls. The two of you are a perfect balance, both reaching to the core of different types of people—she the cynical, you the guilty. It couldn't have been a better pairing if it had been planned. Which, of course, it had. You are convinced she is one of Henry's people, too. You distrust anything so perfect and precise. You distrust Henry, you distrust angels.

So in this world of the year 2003, Henry tolerates you. Elizabeth despises you. Neil Perrin rejects you. Julie Ward lusts for you. You try to react to all of that, try to feel angry or frustrated or lonely. Or guilty. Thinking about it makes you feel like telling jokes and pulling pranks.

At night you go to bed alone. You've gone to bed alone since the conversion of Julie Ward. Father Dickie Lanpher is probably getting bored with your confessions. You pray, flat on your back with the lights out and naked beneath the covers. "God, bless Henry," you say. "God bless Julie and Dickie and Neil and Papa Bear and Mrs. Brunwig and Elizabeth and Paolo and Michael the Archangel and, most of all, God bless God. Take care of Yourself. Have a safe vacation. Stop by for a talk sometime. Amen."

Day in, day out, you feel pretty much the same way at any given moment. You feel glib, downright glib.

Clayton whistled as he walked down the twenty-third-floor corridor of Christian Stewardship Ministry inside a building that was, until last year when Henry bought the entire thing, the Chase-Citibank tower in downtown Rochester. He paused and straightened la Tour's *Mary Magdalen with Oil Lamp*. He'd moved the painting here from his apartment last August. There was a bit of dust on the bottom lip of the graven wood frame, and he wiped it away with his handkerchief. "How d'you do?" he said to the woman in the portrait, bowing slightly.

"You're ten minutes late!" Julie Ward said when he came to the reception area. "Henry's in the office already, and you know how he has a conniption whenever anybody's late!"

Clayton patted her head. "And how are you today, Ms. Ward?" She squinted her eyes and put a finger to her lips; Clayton knew it would take a long time for her to decide. "All right, then, how are you at this exact moment?"

She beamed. "Fine, thank you. Say, do you wanna have dinner together tonight?"

"I'm honored. But no thank you."

"Rejection number four hundred and five," she said. She slumped over her desk, swinging from just fine to just turned down.

Clayton walked past Mrs. Brunwig's desk to his office. Henry sat there in a chair he must have dragged in—no getting Henry to sit on the edge of the coffee table. Henry's hands were folded in his lap; he was unmoving, like stone.

"Mrs. Brunwig!" Clayton called back into the reception area. "Mrs. Brunwig, would you mind waddling over here a moment?" She came. "It would appear, Mrs. Brunwig, that someone has donated another statue for one of our churches. Marvelous craftsmanship! When did it arrive?"

"Mr. Pinkes, really!" But she smiled. He could get her to smile all the time now.

Henry said nothing, and Clayton neared the chair. "Which saint would you say this is, Mrs. Brunwig? Francis of Assisi? No, wrong attire, too many black clothes. Perhaps a Dominican, then?" Clayton began circling Henry. "Good Lord, what a piece of art. The eyes . . . they seem to follow you around the room." From behind Henry, he said, "Indeed! He's even got them in the back of his head!"

"Oh, Mr. Pinkes, you *are* incorrigible."

"You're late," said Henry, and Clayton jumped away, grabbing his chest above the heart.

"It speaks! It speaks, Mrs. Brunwig! Just as the Scriptures foretold: 'And there was given unto the beast a mouth to speak great things and blasphemies.'"

Mrs. Brunwig chuckled and left. Henry glared until Clayton sat. Then he drew out a folder with graphs and tables. "We have to plan a major assault. Not enough people believe yet."

"We have millions of followers." Clayton played with the plastic, three-inch statue of St. Francis of Assisi he kept on his desk.

"We have thirty-six million four hundred and nineteen

thousand seven hundred and twenty-two members of Stewardship. That's not enough, not even a quarter of the way there. Even the Descartesians have that much of a following. We've got to come up with something really big."

Clayton put his feet up on the desk. "Just how many do you want, Henry? How many until you figure God comes back? You can't convince everybody."

"I don't need to convince everybody. I only need a certain number." Henry was staring away now, a clear signal that he didn't want to pursue the topic.

"How many? How much belief will draw God to Earth? What's the scientific equation for that one, Henry?"

Henry drummed his fingers on his knees. Clayton felt good about that; drumming fingers were Henry's equivalent of screaming tirades.

"Tell you what, Henry. I'll get the numbers right from the source." Clayton looked toward the ceiling. He summoned the tingling sensation to his right forearm. "Michael! Get on down here, old boy!"

The room dimmed after a moment. "I really wish," the darkness said, "you guys would learn to schedule appointments."

Henry was slumped in his chair now, his arms folded across his chest. Clayton smiled. Now Henry would be *really* pissed off.

"Couldn't you even try to stop him from summoning me?" the dark shape asked. Henry shrugged. "Yes, you *have* tried, and you can't do it, can you? You match his strength but not his faith."

Henry adjusted himself in his chair. Nasty, thought Clayton. Now he's feeling downright nasty. "I've noticed," Henry said, "that you can't seem to stop him either."

"Just a quick question," Clayton cut in. He'd wanted to pick on Henry, but he didn't want to make Henry feel inferior to anyone. That would crush Henry. "My advisor here was explaining the mathematics behind this whole God project. What percentage of the human race needs to believe God is coming before the Urim and Thummim actually force Him to appear?"

"Two point seven six percent," said Michael.

"That much!" said Clayton. "I hadn't imagined. With the population moving past six billion, that would be about . . . gee, just a whole *lot* of people!"

"One hundred sixty-five million two hundred thousand," said Henry. Then he glanced at his watch, as if keeping track of the exact birth rate and population growth.

"Then Henry's right. I guess we need something really big."

"May I go now?" the dark shape asked dryly.

"Just a second. How'd you arrive at that number? That two point whatever?"

"Correlational," said Michael. "The population of the villages called Sodom and Gomorrah at the time of their destruction was 362. God told Abram that he would spare the villages if only ten righteous men were found. That was because the Urim and the Thummim were among them. The same with the Israelites escaping Egypt: 17,179 true believers out of 622,416 leaving. And the defeat of Saul: David's chief warriors, the Thirty, out of an army of 108,650. It's all paradigm, pal. Two point seven six percent to use Urim and Thummim to sway God to your purposes."

"To end His absenteeism."

"Yes. I guess He wants to see if the universe will keep ticking away without Him now that He's wound it up. I think He's going through this Newtonian deity phase of life."

"So you get millions of people to invoke the end of the world through the Urim and the Thummim, and He's got to come running to do it."

"By His own established terms."

Clayton leaned back in his chair, hesitating. In his

younger years he'd argued with a Calvinist about whether or not human beings had free will. He found himself on the edge of arguing with an angel whether God Himself had any. He decided against the whole debate.

"Tell me," said Michael, and Clayton felt his arm tingle. The angel was going to ask it again, the same old question. "Have you heard from Raphael?"

"Not a word," said Clayton, the same old answer. "He may as well be in limbo for all I know."

"I'd truly enjoy speaking with him."

"Maybe he'll send you a postcard."

Henry's fidgeting had stopped. The black shape drew closer to him. "How can you tolerate working with this person?"

Henry made a casual wave with his hand. "You learn to deal with him. He's actually enjoyable after awhile."

The shape faded, and Clayton held back his laughter until all light had returned to the room. "It's pathetic, isn't it? With the Urim and Thummim between us, he'll do practically anything we say." Clayton stood to walk around to Henry's side of the desk. He found himself falling face forward to the floor, and he barely threw his arms out in time to absorb the impact. He looked toward his feet: somehow, some way, during the conversation with Michael, Henry had tied Clayton's shoe-lace to the leg of the desk chair.

"You amaze me," Clayton said. "You constantly amaze me."

Henry made no acknowledgement. "Where were we?" he asked, opening the folder on his lap.

That afternoon, Clayton sat in the back of the '00 Cadillac Extremidor in which Henry insisted he be chauffeured: Neil Perrin to the right of him, Papa Bear to the left of him, a guy named Frank with a blue cap before him at the wheel. He was on his way for a one o'clock confession at St. John the Evangelist, Father

Dickie Lanpher's new parish. As they rode, Clayton talked over the PrivNet Communications Console with Julie Ward.

"Have Mrs. Brunwig send out condolences on the Orient Famine, 'Dear Sovereign State of blank in Old China, we continue our prayers and fund-raising efforts on your behalf, we are speaking with representatives of the United States government to aid you in every way possible, just as we aid your brothers and sisters throughout Asia and Africa, our hearts are saddened by what we know is the greatest trial in the noble millennia of your history, etc., etc., Clayton Pinkes, Christian Stewardship Ministry.'"

Japan reduced, China reduced, Africa and the Soviet Union reduced. In his heart and in his arm, Clayton believed the specter of Henry Albert hung over those nations and continents. Henry'd done everything possible to use Stewardship money to support a standoff strategy; each time an independent Asian state rose to take power—usually by means of European Descartesian funding—Henry would flood that state's neighbors with Christian Stewardship Famine Relief donations. The balance kept the Asian states unwarring, parochial.

For all Clayton knew, Henry could have even caused some of the original falls. Not Russia, surely, since that collapsed of its own weight, and not Africa, which disintegrated under disease and famine before it had ever gotten a chance to consolidate. But Japan made Clayton wonder. He closed his eyes, summoned his arm, and called forth the vision again: Henry seated across from an aged Japanese man, saying to him in French, "I would respectfully suggest that you purchase as many of the defaulting U.S. properties as possible. The insurance alone will minimize risk, and you will find America significantly in your respected debt, both morally and financially." In each reiteration of the vision, there was a different Japanese businessman listening to Henry. The words were always the same.

It had taken Clayton a few weeks to translate the French using a worn Larousse's dictionary. But once the final word was in place, it only took a moment to *really* understand, to grasp the message of the vision: Japan had been crippled when the last administration issued the Durghing Amendment, unilaterally suspending repayment of Japanese debt for a fifteen-year recovery hiatus. Conveniently. Right on cue. The U.S. media recoiled at the breach of trust, then quieted when it found itself adrift in a contented America free of yen debts.

"Clayton? Did I lose you?" Julie Ward's voice over the PrivNet console.

"Yes. No . . . sorry. Just thinking."

"Is that everything you need?"

Now there was a question. Of course it wasn't everything he needed. Clayton needed God. Needed Him here no matter what it took—Henry playing with the world to get it just right, Clayton playing with souls to get them lined up and ready to declare and demand Parousia, the appearance of the Almighty. Was that wrong? He tried to feel guilt, failed. It came over him like an aroma new each time: Henry Albert was a very powerful person. At Henry's whim, Clayton was becoming just as powerful. And Clayton couldn't feel the least bit guilty about it.

"One more thing," he said to Julie on impulse. "I'd like you to issue a memo in my name directing everyone employed by Christian Stewardship Ministry to attend confession no less than once a week from here forward."

Clayton could feel Neil and Papa Bear turn to stare at him.

"Oh, God," said Julie. "I think I'm starting to feel depressed."

"That's for all field offices, too. Effective next Monday."

Clayton signed off the PrivNet console. The two still looked at him. Papa Bear was smiling.

"You can't just tell everyone when they have to go

to confession," Neil said. Behind the words, his face said, "Can you? Can you *do* that?"

"Why not?" said Clayton. "The church used to do it all the time before Vatican II. Remember? Back in the Baltimore Catechism days?"

Neil's face struggled to formulate an answer. It surrendered. Stop trying to be Henry, Clayton thought. Stop trying to be anyone who isn't Neil Perrin. I wasn't very good to you, Neil. But you were good, a good person, all by yourself. Be Neil.

That train of thought became too intense for Clayton. He spun around toward Papa Bear. "Say, do you ever read the classifieds?"

"Sometimes. Not often. No real reason to."

"In the personals, they've always got six or seven letters that say 'Thanks to St. Jude for favor received' or 'Thank you, St. Jude for answering my prayer.'"

"I've seen those."

"Well, take a memo for publication. Hit forty or fifty of the major city dailies. I want it to say, 'My Beloved Faithful: You are all quite welcome. Regards, St. Jude.' Send that out tomorrow."

Dark box. Cold screen. Hard kneeler. "Dickie forgive me for I have sinned."

"Hello, Clayton."

"Hello, Dickie. I'm forty-one years old. It's been six days since my last confession. These are my sins."

"Clayton, why don't we do this face-to-face? The church has been doing it that way for twenty years now."

"I'd like to preserve my anonymity."

A sigh from the darkness beyond the cold screen.

"I have sinned against Henry Albert by taking pleasure in picking on him."

"How exactly have you been picking on him?"

"Could you say, 'my son'? That sounds a lot more priestly."

"Clayton . . ."

"Please. For me."

"How exactly have you been picking on him . . . my son?"

"Well, Dickie, it's like this: I can't really tell you, because the details are confidential, but I really enjoyed it and I'd probably do it again."

"Do you feel sorrow for this sin?"

"Um . . . not really. But the score's been settled. He tied my shoelaces to a chair leg."

"I see."

"My son?"

"I see, my son."

"And I've sinned by taking pleasure in turning down Julie Ward's dinner invitations. It really isn't fair of me to keep enjoying her pursuits."

"Clayton, does it ever strike you that every time you come in here you tell me the same things?"

"Yeah. I'm trying hard to feel bad about that."

"Do you feel bad about anything any more?"

"No. Never." Clayton's right forearm tingled. "Okay, that was a lie. I feel myself close to feeling bad, but I can't quite push over the edge."

"You're saying you have a barrier to guilt?"

"Yeah. Isn't that ironic? Me, of all people."

A tapping sound from beyond the screen; Dickie's foot on concrete floor.

"Why don't you try to get closer to Julie? You obviously find her attractive. Would the world be so shocked if the incomparable Clayton Pinkes fell in love and got married?"

"She's crazy, Dickie. Her emotions don't come in waves, they come in tsunamis." That made him think about the Japanese again. He wanted to feel bad about them, but that was Henry's sin, not his.

"I'm going to be really candid, Clayton. Don't take this wrong, but I really miss your guilt. I miss your feeling what a sin feels like."

"I don't. I really don't. My morality took a turn for

the better the day I stopped feeling guilty. The only thing I miss is innocence."

"What do you mean?"

"Innocence," said Clayton. "Back when God believed in me."

BETA:
Swaying the Masses

They stood before a thousand. Tens of thousands of others—or hundreds of thousands, millions, who knew any more?—watched live through the techno eyes of the network and PrivNet link cameras. She stood only three feet away, but he could feel the wall, the years between them. Elizabeth wore a blue gown, floor-length and neck-high but subtly more erotic than if she were in a microskirt with a translusilk blouse. Subliminal sexuality without a hint of malice or intent, a dress meant to cause male registration without male conscious acknowledgement.

Across the stage, the two U.S. Descartesian representatives wore gray and beige European fatigues. The male was named Mr. Franklin and the female Ms. Adams. Clayton cringed. Franklin and Adams, no subtlety at all.

"What our opponents despise," said Elizabeth Goddard, interrupting, "is that Americans, exercising their free will, have exercised it to reject the political and spiritual philosophies of the Descartesians."

"That is false!" said one of the Descartesians, screaming a little too loudly for the microphone and causing a brief squeal of feedback. "We despise the mental coercion practiced by the followers of the Christian Stewardship Ministry and by their bed partners, the American Patriot Party! Christian Stewardship Ministry has been a deluge to the minds of the public, a deluge so forceful and all-encompassing that there are few who can think in terms other than those set down by Clayton Pinkes!"

"Listen up, America," said Elizabeth Goddard. "This gentleman is using all his oratory skill to declare you stupid."

Laughter from the crowd, and the moderator, a member of the waning Republican party and therefore neutral to the debate, banged a gavel. "Point of order," he announced. "The Descartesian party still has the floor for six minutes."

Elizabeth nodded angelically—God, she could be beautiful at will! And Clayton thought, A gavel. I should get myself one of those. They're impressive. He pictured himself gaveling Henry quiet at a full staff meeting. It wouldn't work, but it would be good for some laughs.

"Thank you, Mr. Moderator," said the gray-and-beige Descartesian who'd become too passionate. "We are honored that the Christian Stewardship Ministry would grant us their presence at this public debate, but we are less than impressed by their practice of the virtue they call patience." A few laughs, but not nearly as many as Elizabeth had gotten. "There are many issues we could debate endlessly to no resolution, but our differences lie at the heart of our philosophies. Descartesians feel that the decisions and beliefs of a political party must rest on fact, not religious fancy, and on contemporary ethics, not ancient codes of morality. Our philosophical forebear, René Descartes, once proclaimed the following: 'In our search for the direct road to truth, we should busy ourselves with no object about which we cannot attain a certitude equal to that of the demonstrations of arithmetic and geometry.' In plain English, this means that we do not base our laws or policies on religious speculation. We do not base our laws and policies on ethereal concepts like patriotism and nationalism. We start from facts, we end in facts, and no imagined pantheon or proposed deity ought to serve as the basis of society. We strive for *one* nation, one *world* nation, under the control of reason."

Applause, some of it enthusiastic, most of it polite.

"Mr. Pinkes, you have a ten-minute rebuttal."

"Thank you, Mr. Moderator." Clayton spread his arms and clasped both sides of the podium. He came close to the microphone so he could speak gently. "I don't recall," rebutted Clayton Pinkes, "ever setting up anything that could be called a system of morality."

He backed away and stood facing the Descartesian representatives. The silence lasted for about fifteen seconds, and then conversations broke out throughout the hall. The moderator finally intervened. "Silence on the floor, please. Mr. Pinkes—is that all?"

"For now. I guess it's their turn."

The second Descartesian moved to the podium across the stage; she looked unsure, thrown by having expected ten minutes to prepare herself to speak. Elizabeth looked at Clayton and nodded once, very slightly. She'd seen what he'd done, signaling approval. There was even a touch of genuine admiration in her eyes.

"Mr. Pinkes claims that he has never proposed any system of morality. Perhaps that is true; we would need to check past tapes of his performances more closely to verify his statement. So let me put it a little more bluntly: I believe I have a right to an abortion whenever I demand it. What do you say to that, Mr. Pinkes? I yield for open discussion, Mr. Moderator."

Clayton smiled. "I'm forced to disagree. From a purely factual viewpoint, you'd only be able to demand an abortion if you were pregnant. I believe that would be the most proper approach for a fact-based Descartesian."

Some applause from the audience.

"You're sidestepping the real question, Mr. Pinkes."

"He's sidestepping nothing." Elizabeth took the podium. "His point is an excellent one, Ms. Adams. You claim to be a political movement whose policies are derived from fact. You reject ethereal concepts like patriotism and nationalism. And yet you speak of your right to have an abortion. A *right*, Ms. Adams? Can you demonstrate that right to me using arithmetic and geometry? Can you demonstrate that a child is not a living human being in the womb? I think not. You merely shrug and say, 'No one has proven that the fetus is a living human,' and so you decide to go ahead and endorse abortion *based on your ignorance*. Your philosophies and policies are no better or worse than our own, except perhaps in the realm of hypocrisy. In that ethereal concept, you've beaten us hands down."

Applause, thunderous cheering. God, she was good. Clayton would never have thought to say those things. She was good, good, good.

"Tell me more of hypocrisy, Ms. Goddard. Tell me about your own abortion."

Now there was not the tiniest noise anywhere in the auditorium. The network and PrivNet link cameras swung to focus on Elizabeth. Clayton felt his guts churning, and moisture beaded on his left palm. *Say something! How the hell did they find that out? Talk! The longer you stand there, the worse it will be*. But Elizabeth was frozen.

"Please, give us an answer, Ms. Goddard. Do you oppose abortion on religious grounds, or is it just because you've already had your own turn at being a slut and a murderess?"

Clayton pulled Elizabeth away from the microphone. "Please," he said, very quietly. He summoned a gentle tingling to his arm, a surge of persuasion. "If you want to insult my organization, feel free. Insult me, even insult

God if you like. But don't insult this friend of mine in my presence."

"I'm simply testing her newfound respect for facts—"

"Here's your fact. Yes, she had an abortion as a young woman. And fact two: The baby was mine. And fact three: We've both suffered over it in our own hearts for years."

"I'm glad about that, Mr. Pinkes. It pleases me that you suffer."

Clayton decided it was time to lose control. He slammed a fist on the podium and shouted into the microphone. "How much do you people want? You've got a united Europe, you're influencing select Asian states through your donations, and now you want North America! Well, I'll tell you something, great lovers of fact, you can have every single bit of it! Because God is returning and this world as we know it is coming to an end in just a few years!" Noise from the crowd. Clayton waved his arm and they settled to murmurs. "Have your land and your government and your money and power, because in only a short time the kingdoms of this world will fall to the power and presence and glory of God! *This* is the *word* of the *Lord*!"

Several hundred voices spontaneously responded: "Thanks be to God."

"Mr. Pinkes, if you'd settle down, we could return—"

"No, Mr. Moderator, I will *not* settle down! *They* called for open discussion!" Clayton spun toward the nearest camera; the adrenaline pumped hard and his arm was on fire. "All of you who are watching, all believers and followers of God and the Christian Stewardship Ministry, and all Jews and Muslims and Theists of any brand name: What these Descartesians want is the power of the State and the influence of Mammon! But we know better! We know that power is only in God, whatever rules or rituals we observe to worship Him.

So give these people what they want! If they want money, then let them be cursed with it!"

"Mr. Pinkes, you are out of order!"

"Every single one of you who clings to faith and the power of God: Get out your checkbooks and right now, today, send as much money as you can afford to the U.S. Descartesians' political offices! They want power and wealth, let them swim in it! I want no less than ten million . . . no, *twenty* million dollars sent to our friends of the U.S. Descartesian party so that they can speed their way to the corruption and disgrace of clinging to this world and its marvelous facts!"

"We don't want your money!" the Descartesian Franklin was yelling. "We don't need religious dollars . . ." But his voice trailed off, either because Clayton was shouting over him or because he wasn't certain he wanted to argue away twenty million dollars.

"Send the money today, and don't indicate that it comes from a believer. Don't let them have the pleasure of sorting out the donations of Christians and Jews and Muslims and believers of any sort. Swamp them with what they lust after most!"

"Mr. Pinkes!" The moderator was banging steadily, insistently. "I'll be forced to call this whole debate to a halt!"

"No you won't! *I'm* declaring it over! Enjoy your world, Descartesians. It's ending soon and God is on His way!" Clayton took Elizabeth's arm. "That's a fact," he said.

Forty-six miles away in the living room of the house that served as Solutions headquarters—the fifth house to serve that function since Solutions merged with Christian Stewardship Ministry—Henry Albert sat grinning at the television screen. "This is bad," he said. "This is very, very bad."

The PrivNet console signaled. He grabbed the receiver.

"Did you hear that? I'm out at the car. People are going nuts over here!" Neil Perrin was not composed.

"I heard it," said Henry.

"What are we supposed to do? The press is flocking here like crazy! Cars are starting to pour in, and news crews—"

"All right, just give me one second to think."

Henry took three seconds, actually.

"Number one: Get those two out of there at whatever cost. They talk to nobody, clear? Number two: Get Burnes, Martin, and Catalini over to my place right now. We're doing an all-nighter to write the autobiography of Clayton Pinkes, full disclosure of any of the seamier episodes, and essays on what a Christian Steward can learn from them. Number three: Call Backstern Publishing and make it very clear that this thing goes to press Thursday latest. Have them file a press release that the book has been a year in the making, and that the Descartesian information came from an in-house leak of things Clayton was going to tell the world anyway. Who did the background research on Elizabeth Goddard?"

"Morelli."

"Number four: Ask him nicely why he missed the abortion information and then . . . well, I'll handle it from there."

Neil hesitated, and Henry expected him to ask what "handle him" meant. He didn't, which was for the best. Neil wasn't the sort of employee who dealt well with death.

"Look, Henry, what about the money? What about the twenty million?"

Henry took three more seconds. "I don't know."

Perrin said nothing, and Henry let him say nothing for quite a while. That phrase was one Neil Perrin had never heard Henry say.

"Get moving," Henry said, and cut Neil off.

He was still grinning, he could feel it. He could think of something about the money. But he couldn't concentrate on it. All he kept thinking was, "They had sex.

Clayton and Elizabeth were lovers once. Clayton was almost a father. They had sex."

The church was full, every pew packed and Catholic bodies lined across the back wall. It was a strange church, St. John the Evangelist in the Rochester suburb called Greece. Its late-sixties design—expansive, imprudent—showed total ignorance of impending energy crises. Clayton gazed upward toward the top of the two-hundred-foot tower above the altar area; it was a strange tower, a sort of fat, concrete silo surrounded by a roof whose design waved and tilted irregularly outward, forming a circle with low edges near the eight sets of double doors. "It looks like a robot in a skirt," Clayton said when they drove onto the grounds. Papa Bear had laughed; Neil Perrin remained silent.

"Ten minutes," said a man wearing a baseball cap tucked under enormous audio earphones. Clayton had no idea who the man was. It didn't distract him, though; new faces were old news.

At the back of the church, the small balcony that usually functioned as a choir loft held network and PrivNet link cameras. Ten minutes to Mass, thought Clayton. Tell God He has only ten minutes to get ready for the ritual. No sooner, no later, O Lord of the Broadcast Frequencies.

Clayton walked back to the vestry. Father Dickie Lanpher was adjusting his chasuble, the sleeves of his alb caught under the outer garment. Dickie smoothed them out slowly, piously, as if it were the most important thing he could ever do in his life. Maybe it was. Clayton thought of Paolo on that day, God, it must be twenty-some years ago now, the day Paolo rolled up his sleeves and healed Dickie Lanpher's shoulder. And now Dickie, Father Dickie, doing the same sort of thing to deliver the body of Christ to the hungry audiences. What did Dickie think about? Who was Dickie? Clayton wanted to know, suddenly. He wanted to know why Father

Dickie Lanpher could be so solemn, so staid . . . so *reasonable* . . . about his faith.

Behind Dickie, near the shelf that held the chalices, patens, palls, and purificators, stood Henry Albert. He held a red and green book entitled *Stewardship: Hard Lessons on the Path to God, An Autobiography of Clayton Pinkes*. Clayton's photo was on the back.

"Henry!" said Clayton. "What a surprise to find you joining us for the celebration of the Mass! I'd never considered you the religious type."

"Maybe I've taken a spiritual turn," said Henry. "I've been going to confession every week, per your mandate." Henry sounded bitter, which meant he was in a neutral mood.

"Good. That's good for you, you know." Clayton tapped Dickie's shoulder. "Say, you don't suppose I could learn what vile and nasty things Henry Albert would consider sins, do you? Maybe you should break the secrecy rules just this once."

Dickie turned to the back shelf and began filling a chalice with communion wafers, and when he did that, Clayton's forearm began to tingle. Clayton concentrated and caused it to settle down.

"This has just been published," Henry said, holding the book out to Clayton. "You should read it."

Clayton laughed. "I've already read the reviews. Seems the critics think my style is refreshingly honest, succinct, and passionate without being overly melodramatic." Clayton took the book and weighed it with one hand. "It would probably take me twice as long to read it as it took you to write it."

Henry grinned; Clayton felt himself tensing, going on guard. "That book wouldn't have been necessary if you hadn't lost your cool with the Descartesians. We could have easily replaced Elizabeth, but you decided to implicate yourself as the father of her aborted child."

Dickie's shuffling of religious implements got louder.

"Guess you took care of that little slipup, huh?"

Henry nodded. "The *Washington Post* called the Descartesian revelation 'petty, in light of Pinkes's upcoming autobiographical confiteor.' Being the exposer rather than the exposed has elevated you to the status of America's Most Honest Man." Henry's grin was larger, as large as Clayton had ever seen it. "Even your bit with the donations to the Descartesians has won you some acclaim. Their donations jumped one hundred twelve percent the week after your contributions mandate, and they've kept all the money. It makes them look bad. There's a statistically significant shift in sentiments among the secondary and tertiary stanines."

The secondary and tertiary stanines. That was how Henry saw the world, people on a bell curve that either favored his manipulations, opposed them, or were still undecided.

"So the outcome was positive, overall," Henry said. "And if you ever pull anything like that again, I'll put you in more pain than you've ever felt in your life."

Dickie turned around. "You two can disagree as much as you wish," he said. "Personally, I don't like either of you very much. But if I hear one more threat of violence in my vestry, I'll throw you, your cameras, and all your manipulations out of here for good."

Clayton felt as if he'd been kicked. Had he just heard that right? Did Dickie Lanpher say he didn't like Clayton very much?

"I'm sorry, Father," Henry said, his face losing the grin and becoming solemn. "Being around Clayton has caused me to lose track of my manners."

"Well, that's understandable. But find them again."

Clayton tilted his head. What had he ever done to Dickie? They were friends. Had been for decades. Again he wanted to crawl inside Dickie's head, to see the world as Dickie saw it. To see himself through Dickie's eyes.

"I'll be personally attending all your public engagements from here on," said Henry. "Until I'm convinced you're not dangerous to your own cause, I think I should be on hand to resolve difficulties."

"I don't need you here."

"Also, Father, there will be some changes to the Mass schedule. From now on Clayton will be speaking after communion. The introit will include a short talk by Elizabeth Goddard."

One corner of Dickie's mouth drooped. "I would need some sort of confirmation from the bishop that including a sermon in the introit is—" Even as he was saying it, Henry handed him a letter with the seal of the Diocese of Rochester in the upper left-hand corner.

"But I *always* do the introit talk," Clayton said. "It gets them in the mood for my keynote message."

"Elizabeth will do it better. It adds variety. She's perfect as a warm-up for you."

"I don't need a warm-up act!" Clayton was shouting.

"After communion," said Henry. Clayton's arm was buzzing again. "You'll speak after communion, and *only* after communion."

Clayton closed his eyes and let his forearm, his Thummim, take over: a vision of Henry, standing in a business office with a portly, balding man. The man said, "I don't understand the formula." Henry said, "It's a yohimbine base. It crosses the blood-brain barrier, gently blocks and alters peripheral serotonin receptors." The man said, "Yes, yes, but why? Why would anyone want this in communion wafers?" "To increase the suggestibility of communicants," said Henry. "To build faith; and at the same time, you get to build your business. You'll be distributing ninety percent of the communion wafers in America by the end of the year." "I can't do this," the man said. Henry leaned closer to him. "Oh, yes," Henry said. "Of course you can."

The vision ended, and Clayton was staring at the communion wafers beside Dickie's paten.

Henry's face showed confusion, and then clicked back

to a neutral gaze, indicating to Clayton the exact second that Henry knew that Clayton knew.

"It's just support," said Henry. "Of course you need them. You've prematurely announced the end of the world. These will help speed up what would have happened naturally."

Dickie's head swiveled back and forth between the two of them. Clayton thought for a moment that he would tell him, tell Dickie, that the communion wafers were drugged. But Dickie didn't really like him. So screw Dickie.

"You don't need tricks to accelerate people's faith in God. You just have to ask me, and I'll do it."

Henry raised an eyebrow, condescendingly.

"You doubt me?" said Clayton. "You think you need tricks? Fine, five bucks."

"What?"

"I'll bet you five bucks that I can walk out there without your"—he glanced at Dickie, then at the communion wafers—"manipulations, and that I can get this crowd to proclaim that 'up' is 'down' before the first hymn."

Henry leaned against the back shelf and crossed his arms. "Be reasonable, Clayton. This isn't some face-off over your machismo and pride."

"For me, no, it isn't. For me it's about what people want to believe, need to believe. But that's not how it is for you, is it? For you it really *is* about pride. The grand pride of Henry Albert, Sole Controller of the Minds of Men."

Henry was still as a statue. "That's not how it is at all, Clayton."

Clayton's arm tingled. Henry Albert was lying.

Clayton extended his right arm. "Then shake on it," he said. "Bet five dollars."

They had never touched in the years they'd been together. Henry held out his own right hand, but Clayton drew back. "No," he said. "Shake with your left hand, Henry Albert." Henry hesitated, but then held out his left hand. Urim met Thummim.

✧ ✧ ✧

The Hebrew word "thummim" is derived from a primitive root, "tamam," which means "complete" in both a positive and negative sense. It therefore connotes such disparate concepts as coming to an end, falling into complete failure, arriving at fullness, and perfection. As "thummim," the word takes on the connotation of Complete Truth.

Urim connotes flame, fire, judgement, light, and brilliance.

It could be demonstrated, then, that the light of knowledge, the very fire of rational judgement, is something different from, even inferior to, the Complete Truth.

Henry's eyes were wide and his face pale when Clayton released his hand. Clayton himself felt nothing, but Henry's expression demanded some sort of response. Clayton grinned, wide.

"For a moment," Henry said, and then halted. "For a moment, I could comprehend . . ." He shook his head, gave up trying to explain what he'd felt.

A man stuck his head through the vestry door and announced the two-minute warning.

"Five bucks," said Clayton. He walked out of the room, around the enormous stone divider that ornately shielded the vestry from the congregation, and to the podium.

"For God, all things are possible."

Nods from the congregation.

"For God," louder still, "all things are possible."

Some shuffling, and a few vocal amens.

"You don't believe it, do you? You don't believe that statement, not one bit."

The shuffling stopped.

"For God, all things are possible! Possible! All things! For God! All things! For God, all things are possible! For God, all things are possible!"

Some of the crowd were joining in the chant, and

Clayton threw his hand up. "Don't . . . you . . . dare!" Silence again. "Don't you dare say that with me! Don't you dare confess what you do not believe! I don't want a single person out there saying this thing unless he really, really believes it. Is that clear?"

Nods, some confused, some timid.

"For God . . . all things are possible!"

He said it alone this time.

"Only if you believe it: For God . . . all things are possible!"

Several people joined in.

"Only if you *completely* believe it: For God . . . all things are possible!"

Even more. And more still. And everyone, even some of the members of the network crews. The repetition grew stronger, louder, frenzied. Clayton had a peripheral view of the stone divider. Henry Albert was standing beside it, watching.

"Do you really believe it?"

"Yes!" "Amen!"

"Do you really, truly believe it?"

"Amen! Amen!"

"All things?"

"All things!"

"*All* things?"

"All things!"

"For God, day is like night and night like day!"

They repeated it.

"For God, up is down and down is up!"

They repeated it.

"For God, black is white and white is black!"

They repeated it.

"For God, good is evil and evil, good!"

They repeated it. He yelled it again. They shouted it back and burst spontaneously into cheers, amens, hallelujahs. Clayton pushed himself from the podium and ran to Henry. He threw his arms around him and held the embrace as the congregation rose to its feet.

Henry's arms stayed at his sides.

"Congratulations, my evil friend Henry." Clayton squeezed him harder. "Evil has just been declared a good thing. I've justified you in the sight of God."

"Indeed," said Henry, but his voice was far away.

Clayton released him. "Cheer up, Henry. It's only five bucks."

Henry's eyes became focused again, his lips tight and straight.

"So tell me you'll cancel the drugged communion wafers. We don't need them. Tell me you'll let me handle the faith."

"All right. No drugged wafers. You're going to Rome."

Clayton stared. Where had that idea come from?

"You're the single most powerful force in Catholicism today. Catholicism, hell, in all western and Middle East religion. You need to appear in Rome."

"To see the Pope?" Clayton felt vaguely cheated of a victory he should be enjoying over Henry right now. "C'mon, Henry, I can't even get Dickie the Priest to like me, and he's my oldest friend. How can you expect the Pope to like me?"

Behind them, the congregation had started the entrance hymn, hundreds of voices proclaiming: "With the God as the Way/I will walk through the torment/ rest by the river/fly with the wind;/With the Lord as my Way/I'll control every summit/drink from the flowings/ of peace deep within."

"He doesn't have to like you, Clayton. He just has to see you, and he will. I don't think we should do it just yet, maybe not even next year. But when the time comes, he'll agree to see you. The Pope's no idiot. He must realize that one word from you and all these people would demand *you* be made Pope."

"With God as the Way," sang the crowd, "I will comfort my sister/uphold my brother/learn through my pain;/With the Lord as our Way/we will conquer together/steward the weakest/heaven regain."

"Maybe we'll do that, Clayton. If we don't like him, maybe we'll make you Pope."

"I'm not even a priest, Henry."

"It doesn't matter. Throughout history—"

"It's not really in your plan, Henry. You're just making this up on the spot."

"All right. Making you Pope isn't part of the plan. But if we wanted to, why not? Standing here right now, you're as much to the world as the Pope, the Archbishop of Canterbury, every single Patriarch, and Buddha himself all put together. How would you like it? Pope Clayton the First. Holy Father."

"No," said Clayton. Henry grinned.

"With God as the Way," sang the masses, "I will use all my talents/grow through the balance/of who I am;/ With the Lord as my Way/say yes to the calling/fear not the falling/cling to His plan."

GAMMA:
2005; Clayton Pinkes, Prophet for the End of Time

Clayton shuffled into the office building, past the guards. "I'll just be a few minutes," Clayton told Neil Perrin and Papa Bear. They stayed downstairs.

He was tired: three tapings today, a live presentation, and a Mass with Father Dickie. The message was always the same now: Prepare for the Lord; prepare for the End of Time.

"No dates," Henry always told Clayton and Elizabeth. "Establish the expectation; establish the glory and rewards of the believers; announce the imminent end of suffering, longing, loneliness. But promise no dates."

Elizabeth worked with him at each taping. God, she was good. She was magnificent. She could make an audience laugh, cry, shout . . . he admired her and felt no envy.

She was always quiet now, when she wasn't on stage. Ever since the debate with the Descartesians two years ago and all the hoopla surrounding it, she had grown more introspective. All pretense of the proper, pious church woman was gone. She asked Clayton if he was tired, he asked her if she was, they'd both say yes, and one time—it was only once, but it was recent, only three weeks ago—he had said he was extremely tired, and she reached over and massaged his neck. He'd closed his eyes and wanted it to feel erotic, but it hadn't. It felt like friendship and support.

Apparently, more was gone from him than the ability to feel guilt.

He went down the hallway to his office. A light was still burning down there, even though it was past eight in the evening. Clayton stopped at the portrait of Mary Magdalen, gave a short bow, and said, "Good evening, ma'am."

He walked up behind Julie Ward. "Darn thing!" she was saying, trying to force a paper clip onto too large a stack of contribution reports.

"A little late," said Clayton.

"I am *so* angry about this paper clip! I've been trying to get it on for ten minutes and it keeps popping off!"

Clayton took the clip, bent it open, rebent it with a larger gap between the small and large loops, and clipped the papers. Julie's face brightened. "There. Now I'm a happy person again. Especially since you're here."

Clayton patted her shoulder and walked toward his office. Elizabeth must be tired, too, he thought. Henry'd pushed them both too hard for the past few months. She had to be sick of this work.

"Hey," said Julie Ward behind him. "What do you think about dinner?"

Clayton turned. "That's a good idea. A relaxing dinner. Do me a favor, Julie. Call Elizabeth and see if she'd like to meet me somewhere. Transfer it to my office line when you get hold of her."

Julie sat still for a moment, then yanked the phone receiver from the cradle. "Fine," she said, "just fine."

❖   ❖   ❖

"The reason I hate you," Elizabeth said, reaching across the top of the table to touch his hand lightly, "is sheer habit. Deep scars from long ago. Maybe it shows I never really grew up."

Clayton examined her—he could have kept himself from doing that, but he didn't want to. Why would she think she'd never grown up? She was classy, beautiful, poised, charming, ironic, self-sufficient . . . he stopped. It was starting to sound like a Boy Scout oath.

"You want more coffee?" asked the waitress, chunky, short, aloof in a way that said she didn't care if Elizabeth had more coffee or not. The two of them were at a small diner, randomly chosen as they drove through the Rochester suburb of Gates. "Don't dress up," he'd told her over the phone. "Wear jeans and a casual top. Something messy, even. We're gonna sneak off and go eat somewhere the waiters don't call me sir and you ma'am." He'd left the office through the State Street entrance, leaving Papa Bear and Neil waiting at the doors of East Main. He'd swung to his apartment and thrown on an old pair of trousers and a green T-shirt, then picked her up at her townhouse outside the city. They'd laughed, turning street corners quickly and doubling back with the car to be sure no one was following. After a while it was obvious nobody was, but they kept it up just because it felt fun, felt free, felt like they were playing tricks on the world: two celebrities, incognito.

"You still hate me, then," he said. The waitress filled his cup and stared between the two of them. She was instantly interested.

Clayton smiled at the waitress, pointedly. "Thanks for the coffee, sugar," he said, using an accent that sounded, to him, like a guy on a street getting coffee. Elizabeth laughed. "Maybe we could get some of that pie you got in the spinny thing over there. A couple of pieces, hon."

"Oh, God, Clayton, I couldn't eat another thing!"

"Baloney. Make that three pieces of pie, sugar."

The waitress peered at him over the tops of her bifocals, glanced at Elizabeth, then left.

"I think," said Elizabeth, "that half of me hates you and half of me—"

"Loves me?"

"No. Hates myself."

"Great," said Clayton. "That sums you up at one hundred percent hate. I don't believe it."

She smiled, but it was a sad and tired smile. "What am I doing this for, Clayton?"

"Because you're good."

"I only started because I wanted to hurt you somehow. I felt like you were controlling my career from somewhere far away. All my material was pulled from our past together, and then all my performances were getting set up by Roger Kallur who worked for Henry who works for you. You kept showing up and making claims on my life."

From deep inside Clayton, an old feeling stirred. *You could sleep with her,* it said. *She's obsessed with you.* Clayton acknowledged the long-silent voice. *Yes,* he told it. *I could sleep with her. Or I couldn't. Or I could think about it and masturbate later. Any combination of those, too. I guess it really doesn't matter.* The old stirring agreed it didn't matter, not a lot, but maybe just a little. *Ah,* Clayton told it. *That means you lose. You've become indifferent.*

"It's not me making the claims. It's Henry. He claims both of us. I told you that when you started."

She dropped a fork she'd been playing with; thin steel clunking on the table. "He doesn't control us, Clayton. He's just another person. Me, I came to him first, so I don't feel any obligation. And you! Every time I turn around you're annoying him for the sheer fun of it." She studied him, her head bent, her eyes up and saying she liked that, she liked how Clayton always annoyed Henry. "Christ, Clayton, why were you such a shit when we were young? Why can't I look at you now without seeing

Clayton Pinkes, child preacher? It could be different. But it isn't. Those times are over, but they were there, they were real. They made both of us what we are. And it was just a stupid childhood affair."

This time when their hands touched, he was the one who reached over.

"It can't be erased, Elizabeth." He squeezed her hand, and neither of them broke the contact. "We're two people who built our lives on the intensity of a brief moment. That's not so strange. Look at all the people who follow us now. Most of them had a single, intense religious experience, and they'll spend the rest of their lives basing things on that. None of them will go backwards and say, 'Gee, maybe I overreacted.' It's too scary to go back to the start, to admit everything has been based on the intensity and belief of a single moment."

She looked disturbed by that. "Clayton, we've got millions of reasonable people hanging on our every word! These aren't idiots following us, bringing the Stewardship message into their churches."

"Madmen are reasonable. Geniuses are reasonable. Hell, you and I are reasonable. But if you trace anything reasonable backwards you'll find the moment of insanity that started it all. The moment of faith. That's how life is, Elizabeth. That's just how it is."

He suddenly felt very sad. He released her hand and sat back in the booth, sharply. "Shit," he said.

"What? What's wrong?"

"I said it. I said, 'That's how life is, Elizabeth.'"

Her face was knit with concern; she leaned forward. "What's wrong with saying that?"

"I always knew I would say it. But I was going to avoid it. As long as I never said it, there would always be a world and there would always be you, sitting, talking with me."

He could tell she didn't understand; she was trying, but she couldn't. There were only a few visions, flashes from his childhood, that remained to be fulfilled; the one with that phrase had been the most important to Clayton.

Henry—as always, perfectly on cue—came through the front door of the diner and walked to their table. He sat down on Elizabeth's side. Closer to her. The booths were too small here, Clayton decided, although they'd seemed fine when it was only himself and Elizabeth.

"This was a good idea," Henry said. "Getting away, not telling anyone where we are. It feels relaxing already."

"How'd you find us?" Clayton asked. Henry. Omnipotent Henry. Omnipresent Henry. Thanks for stopping by, Henry, visit again some time.

"Come on, Clayton, even you should be able to figure out I'd keep the cars bugged and electronically traceable."

The waitress came with three pieces of pie. Clayton cursed himself; now it looked as if Henry were welcome, as if they'd been expecting him to show up eventually. Maybe Clayton had been.

No black jeans or black turtleneck tonight; Henry wore a pair of blue denim shorts and a white tank-top. He was wearing sandals. His hair was a little mussed, purposely mussed to not look like a proper, well-groomed Henry Albert. He's not a celebrity, Clayton thought. He's just mocking me.

"You're heading to Rome tomorrow, both of you. I've got business in Los Angeles. Pope Pius will see you at 6:30 P.M., Rome time." Clayton sat up; Elizabeth stared out the window, completely disassociated from the discussion. Henry started eating one of the pies.

"Tomorrow?"

"Sure," Henry said. "I mentioned you'd be going."

"You mentioned it two years ago!"

"How much advance time do you expect?" Henry asked, looking sincere. "It's billed as a private, spontaneous meeting, which will give us twice as much media coverage once we leak the news. Planned meetings aren't nearly as interesting to the press." He put down his fork, looking as if he were suddenly finding himself out of line. "I shouldn't be talking about business. Tonight, we're just three normal people enjoying ourselves. Let tomorrow worry about itself." He put a chummy arm around Elizabeth's shoulders. She shifted a little closer to him, and Clayton thought he felt his heart flutter. He'd hoped she would pull away a little or look cold.

"Yeah," said Clayton. "Three normal people getting ready to end the world." Because now he knew it would really happen. He was the Prophet for the End of Time. That's what Clayton's life was. That's just what it was.

At the very moment the three sat in Gates at the diner, the Count of the Faithful, as recorded by the Population Numerics Data Base in Heaven, Management Information Systems Division, read as follows:

WORLD POPULATION: 6,423,700,915
ROMAN CATHOLIC WORLD POPULATION: 1,246,837,412

FAITHFUL [DEFINED IN THIS CONTEXT AS THOSE WHO HAVE BASED THEIR LIVES, HOPES, OR BELIEFS ON THE WORDS OF CHRISTIAN STEWARDSHIP MINISTRY'S CLAYTON PINKES AND ELIZABETH GODDARD]:

ROMAN CATHOLICS:	46,973,421
PROTESTANTS:	23,258,970
ORTHODOX, ETC.:	3,212,943
OTHER CHRISTIANS:	2,828,103
TOTAL	76,273,437

TOTAL PERCENTAGE OF WORLD POPULATION: 1.187%
TARGET PERCENTAGE FOR URIM/THUMMIM: 2.760%
TARGET NUMBER FOR END OF TIME: 177,294,356
NET NUMBER NOW NEEDED: 100,020,919

❖   ❖   ❖

After landing, they were driven across several airfields to a small, gray hangar with a mottled black tar and gray tile roof. The Italians—who were these people? Solutions personnel? Vatican representatives? both?—took Elizabeth's hand to help her from the limousine. They let Clayton stand up on his own.

A short delay: passionate debates in Italian with arms flailing and voices rising and a conclusion of comradely slaps on the back; Clayton had expected a fist fight. None of the entourage spoke English. Had Henry forgotten? Simple culture shock made Clayton wish for an interpreter, like he'd had before on trips outside the U.S. Then he realized he usually had nothing important to say to the interpreters anyway, so he stopped caring.

Elizabeth looked beautiful, wearing a simple, modest off-white gown and a plain brown scarf with tassels. Maybe the Pope wouldn't even look at Clayton. Maybe he'd spend all his time staring at Elizabeth and cursing celibacy.

Next they were in a helicopter, and Elizabeth rested her head on his shoulder. They hadn't slept the entire flight over; they hadn't talked.

"Now you lookit down here," the helicopter pilot shouted to Clayton. "This is the Vatican City."

"You speak English?" A stupid question, Clayton knew right when he'd asked it.

"There you see of course the very beautiful dome of San Pietro, okay? It looks a lot better on postcards, 'cause they always take the postcard picture on the sunny day, yes? We don't get that many sunny day here, not as much as we are wanting, but what can you do?"

Clayton said he didn't know what they could do.

"In front of the big basilica, you got the Piazza, see, the plaza like the big circle? Is to the left of the river, see? It's a muddy river, I think, but other people they say that lots of river is muddy everywhere so is nothing to be ashamed of. How you take the mud out of a river anyway?" The pilot laughed. Clayton nodded and tried to smile. It all looked dreary to him, gray sky, dull ancient rock, thousands of bodies packed into and mulling around the Piazza. At the center of the Piazza was a tall, red obelisk, looking as if it were just stuck there because someone felt the need to mark the middle of the circle. A granite phallus, Clayton thought, the last erection in Vatican City. He laughed quietly, and Elizabeth looked up at him.

"You're not thinking of a practical joke, are you?"

"Not really, but good idea."

"This is the Pope, Clayton. Be nice."

She didn't put her head back on his shoulder. He wished he hadn't chuckled.

"There's a lot of people in the Piazza today because you be coming here. A lot of . . ." The pilot glowered. "Ah, you know."

"No, I don't," said Clayton. "A lot of what?"

"Politicals. Descartesian people. They are making a protest."

Clayton looked down again. A lot of the bodies seemed to be carrying signs. He'd assumed it was a normal San Pietro Piazza crowd out to catch a glimpse of the Pope. They were here for him; they were the enemy.

"And here we got the beautiful Vatican Palace, all the important things nice and tight together, yes? We land to the west, and the Swiss guard take you to the Raphael Rooms. There you wait for His Holiness. We got some Italian police, too, just in case of trouble, but if I was you I would trust the Swiss guards a little more. The Italians don't like you too much, see? The Descartesians, they started here in Italy. You know Milano? Up there."

"Where are we waiting? Whose rooms?"

"Raphael Rooms, for His Holiness wish to stroll with you." Clayton felt himself straining against the seat straps. "Oh, the rooms?" the pilot said. "Named for the great

Italian painter Raphael who in the early 1500s was asked
by Pope Julius II to—"

"Okay," said Clayton. The moment of panic left. He
felt relieved; disappointed.

The rooms were smaller than Clayton expected. Actually they were sufficiently sizable by American office
space standards—his usual environment—but here they
seemed small, four chambers amid hyperbolic architecture and artistry. "Stanza d'Eliodoro," one of the three
Swiss guards said in a scratched, tenor voice when they'd
entered the first chamber. They wandered, and the guard
continued his raking utterances for each room: "Sala
Constantina. Stanza del Incendio. Stanza della Segnatura."
Clayton stopped wandering and didn't go near any of the
walls, mostly because the walls were all covered with
paintings and Clayton didn't want to listen to the Swiss
guard's scratchy voice announcing the name of each and
every scene. Elizabeth did approach the walls, and the
guard followed her stiffly. "Parnassus," he announced,
following her. "Disputà." Elizabeth was nodding, as if this
were all familiar but still fascinating. Clayton watched her,
her head bent back to gaze at the four figures of Justice,
Poetry, Theology, and Philosophy painted on the ceiling.
Her hair hung to the middle of her back, long, straight,
golden. One ankle crossed delicately behind the other,
just the toe of the first foot touching the floor. She should
have put her hair up, Clayton thought. This is too solemn an occasion for loose hair.

From outside the north door of the Stanza della
Segnatura, someone called in, "Heezahoe Leenus, Popey
Usda Turteenta." A code phrase, thought Clayton, artistic
language, but then to the portal came His Holiness,
Pope Pius the Thirteenth, accompanied by still more
Swiss guards. Clayton felt his knees lock, and he
reviewed protocol: Down on one knee. Then Pius XIII
will offer his hand. Kiss the papal ring. Bow the head
slightly. But his knees were still locked. This was the

Pope. The spiritual descendant of St. Peter. Yes, he'd kneel now.

The Pope walked past Clayton, directly to Elizabeth, who was still turned toward one of the painted walls.

"Yes, that is one of my favorites, also," the Pope said to her in English. "It is called 'School of Athens,' and there is Aristotle, there Plato."

"Why do the walls all show groups locked in debate?" She had not turned. Clayton fought the urge to call over, "Hey! There's a Pope standing behind you! Give a curtsy for God's sake!"

"Ah," said the Pope, "it is because this is the room that tries to give form to abstract ideas. Justice, Philosophy, Theology, Poetry. These ideas cannot be like things you hold in your hand and show. The painter chooses to display images of the men through history who have most struggled with ideas. Men who would, I fear, be lost in this age of machines."

Elizabeth looked over her shoulder, then, and recognized Pius XIII. She bent to one knee and kissed the papal ring. Clayton felt his heart calm. "Your Holiness," she said. But then the Pope bent at his waist and kissed her hand. That wasn't in the protocol, Clayton thought.

"I am delighted you would join me," the Pope said to Elizabeth. "I did not wish to meet you in formal audience, so I thought we would take a walk and chat as friends. I hope I do not presume to act as a friend. We have but met just now."

"Thank you, Your Holiness," Elizabeth said. "I'm flattered."

Clayton chewed his lower lip. *Flattered?* One was not "flattered" by a Pope. "Honored," maybe. "Grateful."

Pius XIII walked over to Clayton and held out his hand. Clayton kissed the ring. "Your Holiness," he said.

"Miss Goddard," said the Pope, returning his attention to Elizabeth. "I trust your flight was not too unpleasant?"

"No, Your Holiness. But please, call me Elizabeth."

"Thank you. Call me Dario. It is my Christian name, and it would please me to hear you use it."

"Dario," said Elizabeth, and she blushed girlishly.

Clayton felt annoyed, embarrassed for her, protective, irritated, and lonely. All at once. Rising annoyance directed at the Pope, and coming up with that annoyance—*Guilt! Spontaneous guilt!* Clayton nervously scratched his left leg. He thought about it awhile and decided what he really felt was jealousy—not jealousy over Elizabeth receiving all the attention from the Pope, but jealousy toward the Pope himself, of the Pope being so charming with Elizabeth. "So," said the Pope, "your friend here is the Prophet for the End of Time."

That was Clayton's chance, so he stepped up to the two of them. "Yes, Your Holiness," he said. "I have been called by God to proclaim His return."

"Imagine," said the Pope, still addressing Elizabeth. "I have prayed my entire life for a word from God, but have gotten only reverent silence. Your friend must be quite proud to have heard from Him directly."

"He received his calling from an angel of the Lord."

"Ah, then this is different. Angels are angels, but only God is God." The Pope folded his hands above the pouch of his stomach, as if expecting acknowledgement of his last statement's profundity. "You have seen these angels, Elizabeth?"

"No, Your Holiness. Dario. I have never been graced with such a vision."

"Or perhaps you have." The Pope took her arm, and they began walking into the Sala Constantina. Clayton followed them, and the guards followed him. "You know the Scripture, 'Many have entertained angels unaware.' Perhaps your angel is a secret to you, someone you know well who has not revealed himself."

"Do you think so?" Elizabeth laughed. "Perhaps Clayton is my guardian angel."

The Pope laughed, too. "I would doubt this. He is not even a very good prophet."

Clayton bristled, then calmed. He couldn't argue with the Pope. Even thinking about arguing made him feel guilty, like distant days ago being scolded in the confessional by Father Dorman.

Guilty? thought Clayton. Did I just feel guilty? I must be mistaken.

So why would the Pope insult Clayton? Clayton had worked hard building up Catholicism in the world. Clayton had done more to unite Catholics and Protestants than anyone in the twentieth century, perhaps more than anyone ever if you looked at the simple numbers.

Clayton couldn't hold it back any longer. He stepped in front of the two and stopped them. "Your Holiness. Are you displeased with me? Have I somehow offended you?"

The Pope frowned, large fleshy lips, almost what one would consider a parody of lips. "I am hoping, Elizabeth, that your friend and I can end this day as enemies. If we do not, then he is a fraud."

Enemies? Why would the Pope want that? Clayton fought against a guilt with no object (but another part kept saying, *Guilt? I'm feeling guilt?*), and he once again knelt. "I feel nothing but respect and loyalty to His Holiness and to God's Holy, Catholic, and Apostolic Church."

"As I feared," said the Pope. He released Elizabeth's arm and for the first time addressed Clayton directly. "You are no better than a priest."

Well, that was a strange sentiment. Extremely strange considering it came from a Pope, himself a priest, leader of priests. Clayton considered three or four things he could say in response, but none of them seemed, on second consideration, to have any relevance.

The Pope turned to the Swiss guards—there were six of them by now—and waved them away. A few anxious words were exchanged in Italian, and the guard who seemed to be the captain reluctantly led his men out of the Sala Constantina.

"I am sorry," the Pope said gently to Elizabeth. "The guards do not mean to be intrusive in the talk of others. They are quite nervous today with so many visitors in the Piazza." He looked sidewise at Clayton. "A good many hostile visitors. Seeing so many people who are your enemies, Clayton, it gave me hope for you. But then I thought, no, anyone can have many enemies. Only a true prophet can have the correct enemies."

This man is obsessed with enmity, thought Clayton, who then corrected himself and thought, this *Pope*. Maybe that was the problem. Maybe he was focusing too much on this man's title and not enough on his human nature.

"Dario," said Clayton. The Pope tilted his head slightly and crooked a smile. "You're speaking obscurely. If you would come right out and tell me what your problem is, I'd do a much better job of deciding why I should be your enemy."

"Thanks be to God," said the Pope, "you are finally being reasonable." He took Elizabeth by the arm again, and they walked. They walked a long way, through narrow hallways, into grand salas, past artwork so priceless that even Henry's financial empire would pale in comparison. Suddenly Clayton realized he was lost. He could never find his way out of here, and he felt panic, and felt guilt about feeling the panic since he was in the safe bosom of Mother Church. When they stopped they were several flights up. The room was plush, overstated, chandeliered and carpeted and portraited and sculptured and all that in a space of no more than four hundred square feet. Too many colors, thought Clayton; gaudy, expensive in an ancient, multichronistic way.

And there was an archway, gridiron gates closed but revealing a balcony looking out over thousands of Descartesian protesters in the Piazza San Pietro.

It was sensory and emotional overload. Clayton couldn't stand for much longer, and he walked to a—

what was it? He'd learned the names for most American aristocratic furniture, but this was an old world, a new world, seats and sofas from too many different eras. "Dario, may I sit in this . . . this what? What do you call this?"

"A chair," said the Pope. "Please do."

Clayton sat, the Pope sat, Elizabeth sat. She sat closer to the Pope than Clayton did.

"There they are, out *there*, all your enemies. By my accepting you here, they are my enemies also. You see, Clayton, the Church has two branches of authority, and you and I represent both of them."

"I claim no authority in Church matters, Dario."

"Bullpoop." Clayton blinked, then decided he had, in fact, just heard the Pope say "bullpoop." "The first branch of authority is priesthood. From the newest deacon up the ranks to me, that is all priesthood, the ones appointed to maintain the status quo. You know that term, *status quo*? It's Latin."

"I know the term."

"The second branch is prophethood. That branch is a little harder to point out to you because it is not regimented. It can't be, because of its very nature. Prophethood is the force of change, which of course always puts it in conflict with priesthood. One side serves the function of maintaining, and we would be scattered and lost without it. The other side forces a function of continuous progress, and without it, we would become stagnant and die. So you see, the whole philosophy behind Christianity is inner conflict, drag against velocity, preservation against entropy. You see?"

"I see," said Clayton.

"No you don't. Because if you really saw, you and I would be the bitterest enemies on the face of the Earth. But we are not, Clayton. You have deep respect for me, and I find you charming and harmless. The whole thing makes me sick to my belly."

Okay, thought Clayton, here I sit with the Pope, who's

saying the drive of religion should have us ripping each other's throats out.

"I'm trying very hard to dislike you, Clayton, but I'm afraid you're just not doing your job. You claim to be a prophet, but all your actions make you nothing more than a priest."

Controversy? The Pope wanted Clayton to be more controversial and contrary? All right, maybe he could try that when he got back.

"Tell me, Clayton, which is the true Church of God?"

"Ours, Your Holiness."

"You think so? What is your proof?"

Long-ago lessons filtered across the years, pages in the Appendix of the *Baltimore Catechism No. 2*, Benziger Brothers, Inc. "First," said Clayton, "only the Catholic Church possesses the marks of the Church established by Christ, that is, unity, holiness, catholicity, and apostolicity. Second, the history of the Catholic Church gives evidence of miraculous strength, permanence, and unchangeableness, thus showing the world that it is under the special protection of God."

The Pope slumped strangely—elbow on his left knee, his left hand rubbing his forehead; other arm raised and the hand scratching the back folds of his aged neck; one eye hidden by the first hand, the other staring up at Clayton. "Unity? Every time someone disagrees within the ranks, we've thrown them out. So of course we have unity, since they're not Us any more. Holiness? If one discounts the torture, killing, and maiming of our adversaries throughout the centuries. Catholicity? We shall certainly accept any human being who completely agrees with our ideas. Mind you, it took some time for us to decide that blacks and Indians and aborigines and pygmies fell into the category of 'any human being.' Apostolicity? We claim to come directly from the ordaining hands of Peter. So do the Orthodox and Episcopalians. Even Luther was a priest. Once we sever them from the descendency, I suppose they don't qualify for apostolicity any more. There goes your first argument, Clayton."

Clayton felt anger. "How can you say those things about the very Church you lead?"

"My question is *why* do I need to say them? Why am I not sitting here defending against those charges from *you*? As a prophet, Clayton Pinkes, you are a failure. No priest would even *want* to make a martyr out of you."

Through the gridiron gates and the balcony opening, Clayton heard the sound of chanting. It grew louder, broke away into disorganized shouts and screams. Anger flooding from the mob, so much anger that Clayton couldn't sustain his own. There was a distant tinkling of breaking glass, and finally there were the thin wails of Italian police sirens.

"They're becoming more violent," Clayton said.

The Pope waved a chubby hand of dismissal. "What about you?" he asked Elizabeth. "Which do you say is the true Church of God?"

"I think it's arrogant to assume any church is truer than any other. Or even any faith."

"Yes!" said the Pope, and he rose from his chair and strode over to her, patted her on the shoulder. "Now I have at last heard a statement I can disagree with! Perhaps, Elizabeth, it is *you* who are the prophet."

She blushed again. "No, Dario. I am simply a servant of God."

"You are something more, though. You are something important in this whole escapade. Otherwise you would not associate with this fool of a false prophet and his improper apocalypse."

"Your Holiness," Clayton said, brushing past the insult and moving toward the gates of the balcony, "the mob is becoming barbaric. There's a riot." Even as he said so, the red granite obelisk at the center of the Piazza San Pietro was shaking, teetering. It fell, and Clayton tensed when it hit. For the briefest of moments, less than a second, he was confused—no sound with the impact. But then it came, like thunder after lightning, an echoing thud that resonated and was finally drowned out by the even louder cheers of the rioters.

There were gunshots, too.

"The obelisk?" said the Pope, dragging a chair to the balcony gates and sitting to watch. "Good. I've always hated the thing. Ugly."

"Please, Your Holiness, move from the balcony! There are guns—"

"I know," said the Pope. "Look how foolish they are. They can't kill us without killing each other first."

Even Elizabeth began to look nervous. "Dario, it's not safe."

"I'm an old man, Elizabeth. If the world is ending, I wish to miss none of it, even the most insane." The Pope stood from his chair and opened the gridiron gates. He walked onto the balcony itself. Clayton was petrified. The old man was waving, smiling at the crowd! Without thinking—feeling only, moving on emotion (moving on guilt)—Clayton ran to the balcony and grabbed the Pope, spinning around so that his own back was a shield to bullets. He was ready to push, to force the man back inside, but his hands were suddenly empty. The Pope had run back in, of his own accord. The Pope was safe. The Pope was closing the gridiron gates. The Pope was locking them, locking Clayton away from safety.

Wow, thought Clayton, and then a few seconds later, not sure what to think, again thought, Wow.

"Clayton!" Elizabeth screamed, and she began pulling on the gates, grabbing the bars and throwing her full weight backwards. She fumbled with the latch, but it had a key lock, and no key. The Pope stood beside her, serene.

"Talk to them," the Pope said. He chuckled. "You are the Prophet for the End of Time. How would they dare not listen to you?"

"Your Holiness," Clayton said, slowly, calmly, much

more calmly than he wanted, "please do me the honor of letting me in. Right fucking now if you don't mind."

The Pope's chuckle grew to a heartier laugh. "That's it! Swearing in front of the Pope! Now you really *are* loosening up!"

Don't lose your temper, Clayton thought. He's gone mad, and losing your temper will only make him crazier. Try to reason with him. From behind the sound of gunfire increased, automatic weapons now, and people screaming, either the police shooting Descartesians or Descartesians shooting themselves in confusion. Any moment a bullet would be sent toward him, *him*, standing here exposed on one of the Pope's balconies.

The Pope again sat in the chair facing the gridiron gate, looking complacent.

"I realize Your Holiness finds this amusing," Clayton said, remembering the phrase even as he spoke it and unable to keep it from coming, "but this is my *life* we're discussing."

Another vision from his childhood. Another step closer to the End of Time. Another milestone in the path to God.

"Have faith," Pope Pius XIII said soothingly through the bars of the gate, using a tone he had until now reserved for Elizabeth. "Do something."

Far back in Clayton's mind, in an area beneath his immediate awareness, two memorized verses of Scripture met one another and fell into conflict. They fought for a while, one wielding a weapon of common sense, the other wielding common decency.

The first came from the Book of Revelations, chapter 11: "I will commission my two witnesses to prophesy. . . . If anyone tries to harm them, fire will come out of the mouths of these witnesses to devour their enemies. Anyone attempting to harm them will surely be slain in this way."

The second was much simpler, coming from Exodus,

chapter 20, reappearing for an encore in Deuteronomy 5, and leap-frogging itself all the way up to Matthew 5:21 for a moment of elucidation. That verse said, "You shall not kill."

Not an impressive verse, really, in terms of word count. But it won.

Clayton stopped being afraid. He felt the arm, its vibrations that reached out and, quite irrationally, calmed him. An even deeper tingling—more like a note of music just under the human range of hearing—rose up from somewhere Clayton arbitrarily called his "soul."

They were killing each other down there, and it was his fault. He felt intense guilt about it. He had to act.

He raised his arm—that arm, the Thummim arm that was a conduit to God—and shouted to the masses, proclaiming them to fall into silence and heed his words.

It was a stupid attempt, of course. Nobody could hear him.

So Clayton raised his arm higher, stretched parallel to the line of his body now, and willed for some way to get their attention. That didn't work either. They kept killing each other, and by now some of the shots were coming up his way, ricocheting off the masonry and architecture no less than thirty feet away. They had all lost their reason, he decided, like battling, mindless dogs on which you would turn a hose.

With that thought it started raining. Not a light sprinkle, not a gradual increase from steady fall to a violent torrent, but straight, heavy, pounding, windless rain like a million buckets dropped from Heaven in a single instant, then dropping again, then again, and again.

Boy, did it rain.

It rained that hard for a full forty seconds. Not a drop fell on Clayton, not even on the balcony, but it rained so hard he couldn't see anything going on in the Piazza. All he could hear was a sound like you hear if you turn the knob on the shower head to its tightest stream and let it run directly on one ear. Clayton heard it with both ears.

It stopped (poof, like that), and a two-foot puddle of water spanning the length and breadth of the Piazza ran off through various drains, gutters, streets and alleys, leaving a crowd of ten thousand drenched, flat on the ground to a person, and too disoriented to move yet.

"Settle down!" yelled Clayton into the silent Piazza, his voice now booming, resonant, impressive as God speaking from Sinai. He said it in English, of course, so most of them wouldn't understand. It felt satisfying anyway.

A third of the Earth away, Henry Albert ran to the television and changed channels rapidly. He'd watched the live PrivNet broadcast up to the very second the rain began to fall. At Clayton's command? It certainly looked like that, like he had summoned the rain. But then the picture cut out, and none of the other satellite channels had sustained transmission either. He kept turning, furiously, until finally, after five minutes, the IBC-Net resumed. Clayton was gone from the balcony. Thousands of Descartesians were wandering away from the plaza. Drenched, confused, demoralized.

His own console screamed for attention, the PrivNet satellite link to Europe. Henry activated the scramble grid before receiving the transmission.

"Do you know?" an Italian voice screamed. "Did you see this?"

"Yes," said Henry.

"What do we do? How can he perform miracles like that?"

"This changes nothing," said Henry. "In fact, it makes your assignment all the more critical."

"Yes, of course," said the Italian voice in a way that meant, no, maybe not.

"You can do it," Henry said. "I wouldn't have selected you if I didn't know that for certain."

"Yes. Of course." Calmer now and more resolute.

Henry disconnected the link and disengaged the scramble grid. He sat down and flexed his left hand. It almost felt real. It wasn't, of course. It wasn't flesh anymore, it wasn't bone, it wasn't Urim.

How can he perform miracles like that?

He couldn't, of course. The Thummim could, and had.

When Clayton came in from the balcony—how long since it had been unlocked?—a small force of Swiss guards was again around the Pope, now leading him away from the room on the perimeter and ignoring his protests. "Dario!" he yelled, and the entourage halted, the Pope's head sticking out between the shoulder blades of two very tall, colorful uniforms. "Sufficient," the pope said. "Perhaps you have what it takes. Maybe your Apocalypse isn't as inappropriate as I'd wished."

"You're insane," Clayton said. Elizabeth came beside Clayton now, and she held his arm. "And if you're not insane, you're the cruelest son of a bitch in the world."

"Wonderful," said the Pope, looking genuinely pleased. "A pity, though. What is the Church coming to when a priest must teach a prophet how to be disrespectful and rebellious?"

"Screw yourself, Your Holiness."

That chuckle again as they led the Pope through the doorway. "Delightful! Simply delightful! There's hope."

She kept holding his arm, and as a second group of Swiss guards led them down, left, right, north, west through the Vatican, he became more and more aware of the danger. Not the danger at the balcony, because that didn't frighten him any more, just made him angry. But the danger of his right arm—*his* right arm, because certainly if Henry's left arm, Henry's Urim, could do the sort of thing Clayton had just done, then Henry would already be doing it.

No human should have that power. The human Clayton Pinkes did.

"I'm frightened," he said to Elizabeth.

She rubbed a hand between his shoulder blades, slow and soothing. "It's all right," she said softly. "It's over now. They'll get us to the helicopter. You're safe now."

She didn't understand? She hadn't felt it, the raw force of Thummim. He'd only grazed it, brushed it gently, and a full piazza of Descartesians met a deluge. He was safe now, sure he was. But the rest of the world? This damn thing could destroy the world, and a part of him recoiled, realizing that was, after all, the whole point.

He felt guilty, and believed he had every goddamned right to feel so.

There was no helicopter, only a car. "Gone ahead," said the Italian pilot. "Not safe, see? We thought they shoot at it, and already is happening, you know? The politicals think they are shooting at you, but we sneak you out." The pilot tapped two fingers against his temple and winked.

The Italian opened the back door for Elizabeth, gently helping her in. He opened Clayton's door to the front seat and helped him in with just as much chivalry. Clayton thought of the Pope and his attention to Elizabeth, but the thought didn't work. It didn't distract from the fear of that deadly relic, that Thummim, that was his right arm. He felt lonely, wished he had sat in back with Elizabeth. Why had he let the Italian seat him up front?

They were soon clear of the Vatican, clear of Rome and the outskirts themselves, headed at more than 120 kilometers per hour back toward the airfield. The Italian drove faster, and when the car passed 130 kilometers per hour the door on Clayton's side began to rattle.

The Italian shook his head, exasperated. "It a bucket of bolts, you know? That's the saying, I think, for car that stinks. You got to hold on to the arm thing to stop the shaking." Clayton did, and as soon as he'd stopped the rattling, a band of metal sprang up from under the door's armrest and latched his wrist to the door.

"What the hell!" Clayton yelled.

The Italian spat. "Hell, exactly. I see you there." When the speedometer needle touched 150 km/hr., an explosion blew the door off. Not just the door, but that was what Clayton was looking at at the moment of the explosion: the door flying away, landing a few dozen yards from the rest of the car. It was almost a comic sight, since he could still feel his arm strapped tightly to that door, the pressure on his wrist. He turned to see the Italian driver in flames, and beyond the driver, out the window, an odd, spinning world, blue sky, horizon, solid ground, another horizon, blue sky again with plumes of smoke, a cycle of rotating landscape caused by the rolling of the car. Clayton felt vaguely detached from it all.

He thought of Elizabeth, and that made him feel attached again, downright involved. He screamed because the sensation of still having a right arm was beginning to fade, and when he screamed it was not her name. He screamed for someone to help her, to keep her from being hurt, from—dying.

He screamed for Paolo.

DELTA:
Away from the Mess
and Confusion

They sat down for coffee inside a four-star café/restaurant in Madrid, just after the war—well, the war that counted here, in Spain, the one right before the war that counted for everyone else in the world, the Second World War, the one that led to nuclear weapons for those who could afford to invent them. Clayton ordered the paella. His friend asked for something vegetarian.

They got a table near the window with the best view of the aftermath.

"It's my favorite place and time," his friend said. "Do you find it peaceful?"

Clayton did find it peaceful, but didn't know why. His mind must have wandered for a moment. He wasn't sure why they'd come in here. But it was nice. Well-lighted. Pretty clean. How about that? he thought, realizing he didn't even remember coming in. He must have been a little tight last night, a little tight.

"Just relax," his friend said. "Take some time. Want some jerez?"

That sounded good to Clayton, so his friend poured a cup for each of them. Clayton drank it in one flip of the glass. Always enjoyed jerez, he thought, which was also strange, considering he wasn't sure what jerez was. Sherry. It tasted like sherry, so that's what it was. But he'd never tasted sherry either. What did it matter, though? This was a good time, very relaxing.

"Why are you wearing sunglasses?" he asked.

"They know me here. Thought I'd shade myself incognito. Spend time with you for a bit. No interruptions."

That was nice, and very considerate of such an important man.

Man?

"You're an angel, aren't you?"

"Yeah. I'm an angel."

"I knew that."

They sat quietly, drank. I could stay here forever, Clayton thought.

"No, you can't," said the angel. "Nobody can stay anywhere forever. Not even me, I guess."

He's kidding. Clayton thought. Angels can do anything.

"Cannot. Angels are just angels. Only God is God."

That sounded familiar. Someone had just been saying that to him a little while ago before the explosion. Yes, the explosion. He didn't feel like thinking about it now, not just yet. Everything was so calm.

"Let's walk," said the angel. The paella and the vegetable plate hadn't come yet, but they walked out to the street anyway. It was a dusty street, not crowded, narrow and lined with buildings that didn't rise any higher than four stories. Clayton looked for a sidewalk, but there wasn't any. There were some soldiers laughing and slapping each other on the back down the way, near the corner of the main road. They went there, up to the main road, and the angel called in Spanish to the soldiers. They waved to him and shouted back something that made him laugh.

The whole city was at peace.

"The whole world," said the angel. "Not an act of human violence anywhere on the face of the planet right now. There are wars declared, but no one is firing. There are brutal men, millions of them, but right now not a single one is beating his wife or camel or dog or neighbor. A rare moment. That's why I like it here, this place, this time."

Clayton knew he didn't belong here. He wasn't even born yet, not for another twenty-three years. It didn't seem to matter.

Besides the soldiers, there were few people on the street. A couple of street vendors. Two men walking arm-in-arm away from where Clayton stood. A man and women naked, slowly making love in the middle of the street. No cars or horses or trucks or wagons or sirens or horns or loud explosions that could kill anyone.

"This is the only time of worldwide peace in the twentieth century. It lasts seven minutes."

That seemed incredibly short for such a good thing. They passed a fruit cart, and an elderly señora gave Clayton an apple, patted him on the back, and cheerfully explained why she was giving it to him. Clayton didn't understand a word, of course, but he suspected she'd simply wanted him to have it because she felt good. Seven minutes? So short.

"It is short. In the nineteenth century it was seven hours. The century before that, seven days. In the seventeenth century it was seven weeks, and seven weeks every century before that for 77 consecutive centuries, back to when human civilization first started getting organized. You know; the wheel, stone blades, simple tools, the first of the human machines. But then we lost track of God, somewhere back in the seventeenth century. We angels, I mean. He just up and fled, and no forwarding address. After that, the periods of human global peace got shorter and shorter. I suppose the 21st century will have only seven seconds. Seven lousy seconds of peace."

"I last saw you," Clayton said, remembering now, "in limbo."

"Yes," said Raphael.

"I didn't really see you though. We were in nothingness. Outside everything. The last time I *really* saw you was in 1976. You were young then, you were Paolo. Now you're an adult."

"It's just a material adjustment. No real aging."

"You were at peace in limbo."

"Yes." Raphael looked around the *madrileña* avenue. "It was like this all the time. No pain, no willful hurting. No need to heal anyone."

That's right—Raphael was the angel who could heal. He could really touch humans if he wanted.

"Why did you come back?"

"You called me. I had to come."

"No," said Clayton, not sure why he disagreed.

"You're right, Pinhead. Always catching me in lies. I didn't have to. I heard you call, and I was being forced to come, but I could have fought for a few seconds more, clung to limbo until I was safe. You were losing your power to summon me."

Yes, Clayton was aware of that. He had power, but he'd lost it. Why? Why had his power to call this angel gone away?

On the street they passed two drunkards, two men, solemnly waltzing down the center of the avenue. The shorter one was leading.

"Paolo," Clayton said. "I don't have an arm. Look, Raphael. My arm is gone." Clayton gazed at the blackened, withered stump that hung from his shoulder. It didn't hurt, but Clayton gasped nonetheless. This was the first moment he'd noticed there was no arm there.

Raphael nodded.

"This means I can't send you back!"

"I know."

"But it isn't safe for you outside of limbo! They're looking for you!"

"I know."

"You shouldn't have come! You should have fought me! I didn't know what I was saying!"

"I came. Elizabeth is fine, just a few bruises. You might have died, I don't know. I didn't want to take that chance. Where else in the universe am I going to find someone like you?"

Elizabeth? Yes, there was a woman by that name. In fact, Clayton loved her. He was pretty sure he did.

"Now just relax for a few more seconds. Peace is so rare, Pinhead."

So Clayton relaxed and felt the peace. It *was* rare, fleeting, but for that moment he felt peace across the Earth, goodwill toward just about everybody.

Then a shot was fired, a girl screamed up the way, and Clayton saw the soldiers from the corner laughing and beating a young Spanish woman. They ripped her skirt and finally let her go, yelling after her. A thin stream of blood ran down the side of her face. The two drunkards lost their waltz in midstride and resumed a hand-to-hand struggle.

"That's it, then," said the Archangel Raphael. "Seven minutes of worldwide peace. All done."

Around them the air shimmered, and there stood a human shape of deep blackness, another human shape that was a pillar of fire, and another not-so-human shape that resembled a weather-beaten gargoyle broken loose from an ancient cathedral.

"You've finally come back from vacation, then," said the icy voice of the dark shape.

"Greetings, Michael," Raphael said. He bowed slightly to the other shapes. "Archangel Suriel. Seraph Abaddon."

The pillar of fire rose a touch higher, like a man straightening his pose for a formal greeting. The gargoyle did the opposite, slouching as if ashamed. "Hey, Raph," the gargoyle said.

"You are now placed in the custody of the Executive Council, pending your upcoming trial." The dark shape drew nearer, and Clayton stepped backward involuntarily. "We were gonna try you in absentia, pal, but it looks like we're gonna have a much nicer party."

"I'm sorry, Raph," the gargoyle said, moving around Raphael and pulling Raphael's arms behind his back. The two sets of arms, Raphael's and the gargoyle's, merged. The gargoyle lifted Raphael with ease. "You was always good to the workers, Raph, to the union angels. I hate this more than you do."

"I doubt that," said Raphael.

"The Thummim!" The roar from the dark shape was unexpected, deafening. The soldiers from the corner looked over toward the group, and a moment later they were running away down the alley, shouting in terrified Spanish. "Where in perdition is Pinkes's arm?"

"I think," said Raphael, smiling through the strain of being lifted by Abaddon, "you should check with Henry Albert."

"Damnation! This has gone too far! That psychopath has finally gone over the line!"

"How do you plan to stop him?" Raphael asked. The world around Clayton began to fade, and there was pain sprouting in small spots over his body. The small spots grew and joined each other. Body pain. A whole body in turmoil.

"C'mon, Michael," Raphael's waning voice prodded. Just his voice: Raphael and all of the others were gone now, and so was pre-World War II Madrid. "C'mon," said the voice. "How do you think you'll ever stop him now?"

Blackness.

And light again.

His left hand was being held, but he immediately checked for the right. It was no illusion. When he looked, the arm he thought he could still feel wasn't there.

"Amazing recuperative powers," a deep, male voice said. Clayton squinted. A doctor, an American. And there, holding his hand, was Elizabeth Goddard. She had a small bandage above her left eye. Otherwise she looked healthy. She looked wonderful. He loved her. He decided right then, once and for all time.

"Elizabeth."

"You'll be fine, Clayton. Hush. You'll be fine now." She bent and kissed him gently on the lips.

He was flat on his back, he could tell. In a bed, probably a hospital bed. There were metal railings on each side.

"It's like I can still feel it."

Elizabeth ran a gentle hand through his hair. "You lost the arm, Clay. It's gone."

EPSILON:
The Faith of Henry Albert

Papa Bear was furious. Henry didn't have to read his body language deeply to know that; the clenched fists were message enough. "You did it, didn't you?" Papa Bear demanded. "You're the one who set up Clayton."

The two of them were in Clayton's office at Christian Stewardship Ministry. Henry put his feet up on Clayton's desk. To make room, he kicked off a copy of Clayton's autobiography, now a bestseller, and the small statue of St. Francis of Assisi. "What makes you say so?"

"I wondered why you didn't send me and Neil with him to Rome. I wondered why he suddenly didn't need bodyguards while traveling to the area of the world most hostile to him. Jesus, Henry!"

"I'm glad you noticed all that," said Henry. "You're the only one who did. Sometimes, I fear I'm surrounded by bigger idiots than I've suspected."

Papa Bear shoved Henry's feet off the desk. That startled Henry. The man had never done anything physically aggressive for as long as Henry'd known him. "I don't see what the concern is," said Henry, really not seeing, really trying to. "Clayton is perfectly safe. So is

Elizabeth. The explosion was never intended to kill." He reconsidered. "Well, except for the driver." That could be it. Maybe the death of the driver was what bothered Papa Bear.

"Don't you even care? You've crippled him for life! You're done with him, and you rip off his arm and dispose of him. It might have been better if you just killed him outright." Papa Bear's eyes closed tight. "Listen to me. Can you believe it? Listen to what I just said."

Henry felt he should be consoling Papa Bear, but he wasn't certain how that was done. "I'm not disposing of Clayton. I just took the Thummim away from him and put it in more competent hands. Mine. Clayton himself I still need. He's the one who activates the faith of the masses. My trigger mechanism." Papa Bear's face didn't soften. Henry tried another approach. "Clayton's arm isn't an issue. We can replace it. Do you realize the advances we've made in cybernetic limbs? I've got one myself." He held up his left arm to show Papa Bear. "See? Completely normal, at least on the outside. It's artificial, but I can do everything I've ever done before."

"You cut off your arm?"

"Yes, we surgically removed it. Last week. The point is, Clayton will get one just as functional. Sure, it doesn't have as much feeling, but does that matter?"

"Henry. You *cut off* your *arm*?"

This was not so hard a concept, but Papa Bear didn't seem to be grasping it. He should know Henry had a plan. He should know Henry well enough by now. "The arm has to be studied. I can't very well spend all my time in the laboratory. So I removed it. Why are you so irritated?"

"Irritated? I'm fucking aghast, Henry! Do you just . . . just *do* things, whatever you feel like, without thinking about the consequences?"

"Of course I think of the consequences. Everything is calculated. I've thought things through so carefully that very little could stop the flow of events now."

"Christ, Henry, the *human* consequences! How people feel!"

Papa Bear thundered from the office before Henry had a chance to answer that. Henry followed, of course, but not fast enough to catch up to the man. Henry stopped beside Julie Ward's desk. She was disconnecting the monocom. She'd heard the entire exchange.

"You were listening?" He didn't need to ask, of course. Her face said she had been.

"Your orders are that I'm always supposed to listen." The way her hands became busy at inconsequentials—papers on the desk, staples, arranging two pencils in her top drawer—told Henry she was trying very hard not to look affected by the conversation. After arranging the pencils, she picked them both up and stuck them in her hair the way Mrs. Brunwig always did.

"You're upset."

"No!" she denied in an obvious tone. "What you do is your business."

"Did you know Clayton had cancer?"

She looked up, her lips pouting in the way that showed she was trying to pass judgement on the lie.

"He had a tumor in his right arm. Eventually it would have worked its way to his heart and clogged it with a blood clot. So I removed it forcibly to save his life."

"Oh," she said. She wasn't buying it, but it was the first thing that came to mind and he had to stick with it.

"You know how Clayton is. He and I discussed the tumor, but he couldn't decide if he should really go to the hospital. That's just like him. Look how long it's taken him to decide to take you out to dinner. Clayton is the sort of guy who takes no definitive action."

"He is like that," she said, and he could feel her mood begin to switch. "He's very stubborn about doing anything."

"So I took the liberty of forcing him into the hospital. I'm the best friend he ever had."

"You must think I'm a total idiot."

"Of course I do! I think *everyone* is a total idiot. But can't you see the logic behind my action?"

"I think it's kind of dramatic." But she believed him, at least. Dramatic was smack in the middle of where Julie Ward lived.

"Clayton would do *nothing* if I didn't take dramatic action. Not even save his own life." Yes, Henry thought. She was a total idiot. So self-absorbed that the mention of her trying to date Clayton won her over completely. "Now, I don't want you listening to my conversations. The monocom is for listening to Clayton. It's the only way I can make sure he takes care of himself. Understand?" He touched his fingers to her chin, leaned over, kissed her deeply.

Her face paled. "Henry! What . . . ! Henry?"

He was walking to Clayton's office. "Now just behave yourself," he said over his shoulder. He slammed the door.

Imagining his father again, dead in the blood puddle. Standing him up. Cleaning him. Grooming him.

What now, Henry?

"I don't know why I did that. I kissed her, and I hadn't expected to."

So you are impulsive.

"But I'm not! I'm studied, reasoned, careful, calculating . . ."

You just kissed her.

"If I had my arm, I'd know why I did it."

You have an arm. It is right there.

"It isn't the Urim. The Urim gave me intelligence and I removed it. I think since I had it removed I've been sinking into basic human impulse and emotion."

Is that so bad, Henri? Is it terrible to feel as human beings feel?

"It's a burden. It carries no inner logic. It's a random variable. And I can feel areas of knowledge slipping away."

That is bad. Knowledge is important, too.

"I go downstairs to the lab every day. When I hang on to the extracted bone, the Urim, everything I know comes back all at once. But then it fades again over the next few hours. Now I find myself going down there three or four times a day just to maintain an acceptable level of genius."

Why do you bother telling me these things? Why do you need to discuss your life with a dead man?

"You're my father. We have a closeness."

You and Papa Bear have a closeness.

"I know. That's strange. We have no shared biological ancestry, but he acts as if we did."

He is angry. He feels like a father to you.

"He shouldn't. The genes aren't that close."

Tell me about the girl. Elizabeth.

"She is beautiful! I almost tell her so each time I see her! I . . . now I'm speaking like a fool. I need to return to the Urim. Can you imagine such sentimentality from your own son?"

I am surprised. I almost felt myself deigning to be proud of you.

"Why must you always insult me? Why can't I earn your respect?"

What use would a dead man's respect be to you, Henri? Everything in your life is a tool. My respect would be nothing but a curiosity.

"You're a fool. If I had my own child, I would give him my respect. I would turn him into something I could be proud of."

So we all hope. Even so did I hope.

"If I were a father, I would not raise a child to associate fatherhood with death! I would not raise a child who could view the world only in terms of how best to control and destroy it!"

Just let me be dead, Henri. I tire of the father-son conflict dynamic. It is old. It is deader than I am.

"Not to me. I had a true father for only twenty minutes."

You were my son. You were useful while I lived. Why can you never let go?

"Useful! How can you reduce me to such objectivity? What a fine father you are! How can you say such things to your own child?"

Because I am imaginary. Because I really say nothing at all, Henri.

"Yes. Yes. I imagine you. That is true. You are no more than a mental exercise. A personal demon. I forgot. I forget so many things since I parted from the Urim."

Do you think so? Use your reason, Henri. The Urim is not you. It was not given to you to make you into anything. It was given to you because of what you already were in the womb of your mother. You allow your Urim too much credit. It did not make you. It simply suited you.

"Perhaps."

It is not perhaps. It is so. Think hard, Henri. Did your forgetting start after you had the arm removed?

"No."

When did it start?

"When . . . after I met the woman. Elizabeth."

After you began to feel a genuine emotion. Not the woman. The humanity.

"No. She has nothing to do with this. I need to go. I need to go to the Urim again."

Such faith in this Urim. Such faith for a man who has loved nothing but knowledge his entire life.

"You are a terrible father. You did not deserve to have even twenty minutes of me as your child." Henry laid the doctor down again in the blood puddle.

Henry left the office for the laboratories. He passed Julie Ward and observed her carefully. Had she been listening again? He couldn't tell. He couldn't read her face, her posture, her attitude. What was she? He grasped, struggled, even though she was the easiest of all of them to fully know. He categorized twenty-six emotional states for Julie Ward, and recited them, to keep his hold on waning knowledge: Affection; Anticipation; Apprehension; Boredom; Delight; Depression; Devotion; Doubt; Elation; Hate; Indignation; Languor; Levity; Mellowness; Outrage; Panic; Passion; Rage; Resentment; Satisfaction; Suspicion; Tenderness; Worry.

Faith. Hope. Love.

From the executive offices of the Christian Stewardship Ministry building to the Solutions laboratories in the same building was twenty-eight floors, twenty-three aboveground stories plus five belowground. The rational mode of transportation between one and the other was the elevator: down to street level in the public lifts, down to the laboratories in the private lift. The only other way down was the fire stairwells, two flights of fifty-six steps per story of the building, a total of three thousand twenty-four steps, not counting the landings at floor levels and mid-levels.

Henry walked the stairwell. He passed seventy-six fire extinguishers.

The six-inch steel door of sublevel five had three key locks, a thumbprint identification scanner, and a three-digit combination bolt release. Henry fumbled with the keys for half a minute, trying twelve of the possible one thousand combinations before remembering the right one. A thumbprint was a thumbprint, so that went smoothly. He struggled against mental inertia, and for the bolt release finally dialed three sixes.

The door opened to the smell of smoke, or at least to the residual odor of fumes several hours old.

"Henry!" said Lawrence Bourne, but Henry pushed past him to the glass encasement that held the forearm bone that was Urim. He slid the encasement door and grabbed the bone with his right hand.

Nothing.

"That's the radius, Henry," said Lawrence Bourne. "You want the next case. But—"

Henry's mind scrambled. There were two bones in the forearm. Two, yes, radius and ulna. Henry's Urim was the ulna, not the radius. He spun to the next case and opened it, reached inside, grasped the ulna.

The world became a contradiction for Henry Albert. There was a totality that can best be described as a Complete Yes coexisting with a Complete No; an Infinite Positive and an Infinite Negative.

Then blackness.

Then he was being lifted by Lawrence Bourne. "No, Henry. That was Thummim. You grabbed Clayton's forearm."

Clayton's? That was right. He'd had Clayton's forearm removed, brought here. He'd grabbed Thummim, not Urim. Lawrence Bourne walked him across the laboratory. They stopped at a table, a small side table beside the lab bench. There was nothing on it but a petri dish holding reddish-orange tissue. "There," said Lawrence Bourne, and Henry was confused. No bone? Where was his ulna? But he let Bourne put his fingers in the tissue, and the knowledge began to flow. This was the lab. This was where his ulna, his forearm bone, was. The tissue in the petri dish—that would be from his ulna. That would be part of Urim. He was Henry Albert, and he was the chosen one, the one who would end the world.

Once again, Henry knew.

"Thank you," he said to Lawrence Bourne. He was about to say it again, but censored himself before the redundancy.

"You're back to normal?"

"Quite. I apologize for the lapse."

Lawrence Bourne said nothing to that.

"How does it proceed?" Henry asked.

"It proceeds with three men dead. Drilling the calciums was nearly impossible. We had an explosion. Fortunately, we've breached the shell. That's myeloid tissue you're soaking in."

An explosion. That accounted for the smoke, the static

charge of ozone odor. And myeloid; bone marrow. The core of Urim. "You've removed all the marrow from the Urim?"

"Not all. It keeps replenishing itself. No sooner do I extract a single cc than another cc of myeloid develops inside the bone. Same thing with the Thummim."

"Go on," said Henry. "What's the analysis?"

"I'm sure you can deduce it. I contrasted genotypes between your radius samples and the ulna constituents. Calcium phosphate, calcium carbonate, gelatin, lamellae, collagen, elastin, so on. All of them matched your base genetic structure."

"The myeloid is the unique constituent?"

"Exactly. It's foreign. Your ulna bone marrow couldn't possibly be yours. It's the unattributable variable."

It made sense. It all became clear to Henry Albert as his fingers soaked in the myeloid tissue. He'd directed Bourne to breach the outer shell of the ulna at any cost. No laser approach had worked, and they had switched to standard diamond-bit drilling. Bulky machinery, primitive approach. There'd been an explosion, and three men died. A part of Henry felt as if he should acknowledge that, but it was a part of him that was fading quickly. That part had something to do with feelings and emotions, but what was all that in light of research? In light of discovery?

"You've done well," said Henry Albert.

"Not well enough." Lawrence Bourne was disturbed. "I should have foreseen the explosion. We were pushing the envelope. Three deaths is a significant loss of mind power."

"I'll replace them," Henry said. He took his fingers from the petri dish and looked around the table for the cover.

"Don't worry about closing it," said Lawrence Bourne. "Nothing will happen to the myeloid tissue. It doesn't decay, it doesn't take on bacterial parasites, it doesn't show aging in any traditional way I can measure. For all I know, it may be entirely antientropic."

Henry stooped to look closer at the material in the dish. It looked like standard tissue, any other myeloid. "Have you done analysis on Clayton's ulna?"

"I was about to start when you arrived. I've removed three cc's of Thummim marrow. It's over in the fourth encasement. But I haven't fully explained my analysis of your Urim yet."

Each time Bourne said the words "myeloid" or "marrow," there was the briefest hesitation in his voice. "I'll read the report," said Henry.

"Of course. But one thing you should know now. The marrow. It isn't."

"Isn't what?"

"Isn't marrow. Isn't tissue cells at all. The cells are undifferentiated. And they're haploid."

"Haploid?"

"Yes. They only have single DNA strands, like spermata or ova."

"Thank you, I know what haploid means. Are you certain?"

Bourne frowned; Henry knew that questioning Bourne's certainty was akin to a direct insult.

But *haploid*?

"Get out," said Henry Albert in a way that clearly closed the discussion. Bourne got out; Henry waited until he heard the bolt latch and the three keys turn.

Item One: Petri dish A, contents pseudo-myeloid tissue consisting of undifferentiated haploid cells. Urim.

Item Two (he brought it from the glass encasement that held Clayton's ulna bone, set it on the table before him): Petri dish B, contents still unanalyzed, myeloid tissue. Thummim.

He placed the index finger of his right hand into the Urim myeloid. "Body of Henry," he said, feeling the stretch of his grin and the elasticity in his cheeks. "Body of Clayton," and he braced himself as he put the index finger of his left hand into the myeloid of Thummim.

Absolutely nothing happened, of course, since his left arm was artificial. Henry cursed himself—forgetting, still forgetting even while in direct contact with the Urim myeloid. He moved the petri dishes closer together and stretched his pinky finger over, into Thummim myeloid. Then he felt the doubt: This was ludicrous. He had no idea what he'd expected.

Then the power of the doubt.

There is a pseudo-mathematical philosophical concept which attests that an arrow shot at a tree can never reach the tree. This is the reasoning: To get to the tree, the arrow first has to travel half the distance. Then it must cover half of the remaining distance. Then half of the remaining distance of that. And no matter how many of the halves it travels, there will always be another half-of-a-distance to be achieved on the path toward the target, the tree. Smaller halves, to be sure, and smaller, and smaller, and smaller, but always another point called "halfway" between arrow and tree. Voilá, the arrow can never get there.

Henry Albert traveled half the distance to God. Then he traveled half the half. And half of that. And halfway again. And half and half and half and half and half almost there but still a half and a half that could be halved . . .

"Who?" said a Voice, a still Voice, small, and then Henry's doubt was gone.

"Come to me!" Henry yelled across the infinite regression of halves. "Come here!"

"For you?" Forever away. "For one man out of billions?"

Halfway halfway half.

"I am Urim and Thummim! Come to me! Face me!"

"I acknowledge Urim. I acknowledge Thummim. I move for faith alone. And who are *you*?"

"I have faith! I now have more faith than any man in creation!"

"No, Henri Elobert. What you have is knowledge. Faith is the substance of things not known. For a single moment, you believed without knowing, and now that you know, you can never believe again. Faith is not certainty. There is no belief apart from doubt."

Halfway again and no progress. Panic. No hope. "I'm destroying Your creation! You'll be forced to come for that!"

"I know," said the Voice. "Of that I'm certain."

Halfway and nowhere near. Not even moved. His hand was raised, fingers out of the petri dishes, and the lab came back, the halfways gone. He put his fingers in the dishes again. Nothing. And again. And nothing.

Because Henry Albert had no faith. Henry Albert had knowledge.

Out there in the world Henry Albert was going to destroy, there were people, there were books, there were articles, and more and more of them focused on Clayton Pinkes. "The Miracle of the Rain!" headlined the *New York Times*, the first occurrence in years of an exclamation point on their front page. "Prophet Against The Lions" cried the *Washington Post*, a picture of Clayton holding his arm aloft toward Heaven, bravely facing the crowd of Descartesians in the Piazza of San Pietro seconds before the downpour. And the *New York Post*, despairing the insufficiency of alliteration and kicky slang to capture the significance of the Roman miracle, ran a front cover picture of Clayton under the word "WOW" in six-inch letters.

There were converts. There were hundreds of thousands, even millions of them. More than a few were defecting Descartesians, both European and U.S. Calls came in to prayer lines at every Stewardship field office. Donations soared. Membership jumped and jumped and jumped, and people clamored to hear the wisdom of God's Chosen, Clayton Pinkes.

There were smaller articles, mostly unnoticed by the *hoi polloi*. "Tenth Asian State Signs Pact With Common Europe." "Eastern Troops Invited To Germany For Joint Exercises." "European Parliament Invites Arab Observers."

And by the end of a week, the first newspaper to wonder finally asked. "*¿Dónde Está El Profeta?*" queried *El Diario*.

"Where Is The Prophet?"

"He's in his office," said Julie Ward. "He hasn't come out for three hours." She was rhythmically banging her knee up against the bottom of her desk. That was Anger, but Henry didn't pursue the cause.

"Any visitors? Phone conversations?"

"Nothing. I've had the monocom open the whole time, and I don't think he's even moved." Now her shoulders drooped. Anger was off, Despair on. "He won't even look at his messages. I've got urgent notes from thirty-two senators, eighty-four representatives, and two from the President himself. If I could just say he'd had an accident and was recovering, they'd stop calling."

"No!" Henry said, realizing he'd yelled. He lowered his voice. "No one is to know. Not even hints. The media will be all over the story if there's the slightest rumor."

She played with a brown curl; Apprehension. "Neil Perrin made a statement to the press this morning saying that Clayton was deep in prayer for the coming week to learn God's will for the human race."

"I know. I approved that."

"The studio is going crazy about our canceling the next show."

"They can do a rerun."

"I think Clayton is very sad." Her eyebrows lowered. Tenderness. "Maybe he needs someone to talk to, someone who can listen to him. Should I ask him out to dinner?"

Henry didn't bother answering that. "Turn off the monocom. I'm going to have a heart-to-heart chat with him." She did, and her head drooped. Depression. Henry walked into Clayton's office.

Clayton was sitting there quietly reading the top sheet of a stack of wood-dark paper with gold print. He held the papers in his one remaining hand. Also standing there, very quietly, was Michael the Archangel.

"I guess it's safe to talk now, pal," said the archangel.

"Give me time," said Clayton. "I'm still reading."

Henry was acutely aware of the absence of Urim and Thummim, those things he'd always depended on to control Michael. He should have, Henry realized, taken some of the myeloid tissues to carry with him. He'd do that from now on, two small vials perhaps.

"You should be in the infirmary," Henry said. "I gave explicit orders for you to have preparatory surgery for a cybernetic arm."

Clayton glanced at the bulge made by the stump under his shirt where his right arm wasn't. Then he kept reading.

"What is this?" Henry demanded.

"It's none of your business." The dark shape loomed closer to Henry. "I'm handling a matter between Clayton and myself. With you I have other issues. Tell me the plan."

Henry didn't like to be told that anything with Clayton was none of his business. "You know the plan," he said, stepping toward Clayton's desk to see the pages Clayton was reading. The dark shape came between them, and Henry stopped on instinct. The archangel could do nothing physical, Henry knew that. But lately Henry's emotions had been vulnerable. An attack on the mental level could have serious effects.

"Of course I know the plan. It's *my* plan, after all. Let's see if you've got it straight."

Henry waved his arms, natural and cybernetic, in exasperation. "We build up the number of Clayton's followers past critical mass. On a day soon after, we declare a prophesy from Clayton to be announced live on all networks and PrivNet satellite links. Elizabeth opens with an appeal to all unbelievers to change their hearts. Clayton comes on and declares the beginning of the Great Tribulation. He leads all believers in prayer for the coming of the End of Time, and the subsequent return of God. The Urim and Thummim are joined, activated by the faith of the masses, the countdown to End of Time begins. Irreversibly. Seven years of war, pestilence, famine, destruction, and at last the universe is destroyed. This having happened, God is drawn back to address all souls and angels. The end."

Wherever Michael really was inside that black void, Henry could sense him smiling. "The new beginning," Michael said. "That is the plan. That's how it will go."

"Yes," said Henry. "That is your plan."

"What's all this about Lucifer?" Clayton asked, looking up from his reading. "I thought demons were just a thought experiment used to shift blame."

"That's true. He's no demon, and he's very sensitive about the poor press he's gotten over the centuries. But he's also one of the best damn debaters that side of the hereafter. He's been selected as defense attorney. It's the only reason I've come to you."

"What is this?" asked Henry. "What are you two discussing?"

They ignored him. "I'll need time to think," said Clayton. "You may have heard I've been through a bit of trauma." Clayton looked directly at Henry when he said that.

"Yeah, so I hear. Apparently, there are parts of my plan that are so secret, even I don't get to know what they are. But, Clayton—I need an answer today."

"Get back to me on it. Let me alone for now."

The angel disappeared. Again Henry asked, "What are you two discussing?" but Clayton kept on reading.

What Clayton was reading was a fifteen-page

transcript of Raphael's pre-trial arraignment. The most informative section recorded the following:

MICHAEL: I would like to begin these proceedings—

LUCIFER: Objection!

MICHAEL: How in blazes can you have an objection already? We've just started.

LUCIFER: Your role as judge in these proceedings is a considerable compromise of interest, Your Honor Prince of Angels. I object that your bias has predetermined the outcome of the case.

MICHAEL: Overruled. I would like to begin these proceedings by declaring the charges brought by this Council Most Holy against the archangel known as Raphael, who willfully—

LUCIFER: Objection! My client has been known by a number of aliases while performing duties on Earth for this Council Most Holy. Propriety demands that a full accounting of his names be formally entered into the records of these proceedings.

MICHAEL: I don't have—

LUCIFER: I've taken the liberty of drawing together all identities my client has used over the centuries. If Your Honor Prince of Angels pleases, you may use the list as a reference for your proceedings.

MICHAEL: There are thousands of names here!

LUCIFER: Indeed there are. Each is a piece of evidence telling the story of my client's faithful service to this Council Most Holy and to our Most High Lord Now Missing.

MICHAEL: Lucifer, I am not reading this list! Overruled.

LUCIFER: Objection!

MICHAEL: You can't object to an overruled objection!

LUCIFER: I most certainly can. This Council Most
            Holy acts through oligarchical rule in legal
            matters, each member having an equal
            vote. I appeal to the other members.

SURIEL: He has a point, Michael. This isn't your
            average business meeting.

URIEL: I concur.

MICHAEL: Oh, all right, then go on and overrule him
            yourselves.

SURIEL: Objection sustained.

MICHAEL: What!

URIEL: Sustained.

JEREMIEL: Overruled.

AZARIEL: Sustained.

GABRIEL: Um . . . pass.

SURIEL: The objection is sustained by a 3-2-1
            decision.

LUCIFER: If it pleases the Council Most Holy, which
            objection is sustained?

SURIEL: The objection to the overruling of your
            second objection, I believe.

GABRIEL: That's right. I've been keeping track.

LUCIFER: Then if it pleases the Council Most Holy,
            I should like to return to my original
            objection.

GABRIEL: Do we need to vote on that?

MICHAEL: Oh for goodness sake, just do it!

LUCIFER: Fine. I would direct the Council's atten-
            tion to the Scripture of our Lord, First
            Letter to the Corinthians, chapter six verse
            three, which reads, "Do you not realize
            that we shall judge angels?" The question,
            in its context, is implicitly answered "Yes."
            The "We" in the question refers to human
            beings, not other angels. I hereby make
            a motion that this Council Most Holy
            bring an appropriate human for the

judgement of my client, and that the
Council, while serving an advisory role,
submit itself to the decision of that human.

[[A LOT OF COMMOTION HERE. I MISSED MOST
OF THE WORDS. SORRY.—Mandi.]]

MICHAEL: This is utter nonsense! The motion is
           denied!

LUCIFER: If it pleases the Council, I should like to
           point out that the rash overruling of all
           my objections and motions by His Honor
           Prince of Angels is itself evidence of my
           suspicions that the trial's outcome is pre-
           determined. We talk no small matter here.
           If found guilty, my client, for millennia a
           loyal servant of the Council, faces total
           eradication of his personality throughout
           the space-time continuum. Utter destruc-
           tion with no chance of appeal. I simply
           request fairness. Justice.

GABRIEL: Motion sustained.

SURIEL: Sustained.

MICHAEL: This is insubordination!

AZARIEL: Sustained.

URIEL: I agree. Sustained.

JEREMIEL: Sustained.

MICHAEL: You've lost your heads! Who the hell in
           humanity is qualified to judge an archan-
           gel?

LUCIFER: If it pleases the Council, I am prepared
           to suggest such a man.

The intercom signaled, and Clayton practically
growled at it. Henry had found no place to sit—the
extra chairs gone again—so he perched atop the coffee table. "What is it?" Clayton said to the com. "I
said not to disturb me."

"It's really important, Clayton," said the electronically
hollow voice of Julie Ward. "I mean, I assume it is. Yes,

I'm sure it is. You'd want to know, so that makes it really important."

Henry wondered why he had kissed lips that tripped endlessly over basic thoughts.

"So I'll just send them in, okay?"

"Who, Julie? I have no idea what you're saying."

"Father Lanpher. I mean Richard Lanpher. Yeah, he's nodding to that. Richard Lanpher."

"All right. I'll see Dickie." Clayton set down the sheaf of papers and stood, looking uncertain about his balance as he rose. "Dickie doesn't know about my arm yet. I should have told him. Now he'll be shocked."

"Them," Henry said. Clayton stared dumbly. "Julie said 'them.' Who's with him? I don't want anyone saying anything to the press about your accident."

"Accident?" said Clayton. "Fuck you."

The door opened and they came in, Father Dickie Lanpher and a short, plump, serene-faced Amerasian woman who clung to his arm in what was, without question, an affectionate, loving, endearing, committed embrace.

"Oh, you're both here," said Father Lanpher. Henry studied the woman. Not at all beautiful, neither in a classic sense nor by the dictates of modern fad. Possibly as intelligent as typical people went, but that was hard to determine without hearing her voice. Layered, in a way, physically, that was. Not obese, but toying with the boundaries of fat. She shuffled a bit when she walked, but Henry couldn't determine if that was natural or due to the affection-lock she had on Father Lanpher's arm. Not at all up to standards, Henry concluded. Not at all like Elizabeth.

"I'd like you both to meet my bride, Lisa Imai. Sweetheart, this is Clayton Pinkes and Henry Albert."

At the handshaking, Father Lanpher noticed the arm Clayton didn't have. "Good God, Clayton! What happened? You . . . good God, Clayton!"

"I had an accident," Clayton said. "Your *bride*?"

"An accident! Are you hurt? Lord, what a stupid question. Of course you're hurt! Your arm!"

Clayton was still trying to offer his left hand to shake. "Your *bride*, Dickie? A *wife*?"

"Yes, of course. When did this happen? Is it *only* your arm? I don't mean only, that's horrible, but are you otherwise all right?"

"Perfect. Dickie, you're a priest. Priests don't have wives."

Henry wished both of them would commit to one of the two conversations.

"Well, *this* ex-priest has a wife now. Is there any way they can restore your arm? They have artificial ones that work almost like the real thing. Have you given that thought?"

"It's been discussed. What do you mean ex-priest? You've left the priesthood? Dickie, you can't do that!"

There was a break, so Henry interceded. "Clayton lost his arm in a car accident outside Rome. No, no one else was hurt. Yes, he'll be having a cybernetic limb installed. No, there are no other injuries to Clayton. And you, Clayton. This is former-Father Richard Lanpher. Beside him is his bride, Lisa Imai. They were married . . . help me here, Richard."

"Two days ago."

" . . . two days ago in what I assume was a touching, understated, private ceremony. Richard informed the Diocese of Rochester that he would be leaving the priesthood . . . when, Richard?"

"Two days ago."

" . . . on the same day he consummated his love for Lisa Imai, probably causing quite a stir down at the Bishop's office. There. Does anyone lack the basic information?"

Henry watched Clayton's eyes shift between Father and Mrs. Father Richard Lanpher. His face changed subtly with each shift: traitor, intruder, traitor, intruder, etc.

"Thank you very much, Clayton," said Richard Lanpher, his voice hard and even. "Most people give congratulations for the happiness of others. From you I get a mandate that I can't do this."

"But you can't! Everything we've worked for is coming to a head!"

To Henry it was all tangential. Richard Lanpher had no vital role in the closing events of the plan. He'd served his purpose years ago by providing Clayton a forum that was acceptable to the Roman Catholic Church. Why should Clayton feel so betrayed? Let the priest have his last few moments of fun.

Henry thought of Elizabeth again and became very bored with the present company.

"I'm quitting what we've worked for, Clayton. You've taken this end of the world twist, and now it all seems so ridiculous. This is *love* I have, real love. I'm not going to ignore it for your fantasies of apocalypse."

"Fantasies! I could show you things, Dickie. I could tell you things so incredible, you'd tremble."

"Spare me your homilies. Your world is a fantasy." His arm rose to the woman's shoulders. She looked frightened by the clash, and Richard Lanpher held her tighter. Elizabeth would never be frightened by conflict, thought Henry. But he was touched, nonetheless.

"I could show you things, Dickie . . ."

"I don't want your world! For God's sake, Clayton, look at the lot of you! *You're* unmarried because you're too busy with yourself; Henry's unmarried because he's too busy with everybody else; Papa Bear's unmarried because he's too busy with Henry; Neil Perrin, because he's out finding heroes; Julie Ward because she can't sustain an emotion for three consecutive minutes. And me? Too tied up in doing my duty as a piece of furniture in this charade. What are we, Clayton? We're nothing but a band of celibates to our own emotions, too frightened to just step out in faith and claim a little bit of happiness. We've spent our entire lives hoping to connect to something. Anything! And now you tell me I can't love. How does that hurt you, Clayton? Is it just jealousy? Is it just that you're pissed off because I've stopped searching? Because I've found?"

Henry tried to follow all the words, but there was far too much emotion in them to understand. What would Elizabeth say to all this? How would she answer Richard Lanpher? Would she scold Clayton?

"You have an obligation," Clayton said. "Remember back at Saint Catherine's? The day your arm was torn from its socket playing Smear the Queer with the Football? There was a kid named Paolo Diosana."

"I remember. What the hell does—"

"And Paolo Diosana healed your arm. Completely. Well, listen to this, Dickie. Paolo was an angel. He was an angel of God. You were touched by an angel of God because you were a part of the plan. A part of this life. You were spared pain for that reason alone, and that obligates you."

Richard released his wife and stepped closer to Clayton, right to the edge of what Henry determined to be Clayton's personal space. "It was just a dislocated shoulder, Clayton." He glanced at the stump of Clayton's right arm, but continued against the reservation his face showed. "Do an arm and a miracle commit me until my dying day? Am I a slave to a single incident from my past?"

Clayton's mouth was open, trying to form a sufficient response. None came. Henry stepped gradually toward the door, feeling as if he had nothing to do with anything being said here.

"You're all emotional adolescents," Richard said. "I can't have a part in this circus any more. You're thirty-nine years old, Clayton, almost forty, and there's not a solid relationship in your life! Not even with God."

Now Clayton seemed to find words. "That's low, Dickie. I've shared things with you in confession that aren't to be mentioned in the presence of others."

"Shared? You've announced. You've delivered. You've never shared a single thing in your life."

Dull. It would go on for hours. Henry was through the door, now, and closed it, walked past Mrs. Brunwig's desk to Julie Ward's.

"Should I start listening again?" she asked. Bright and cheery.

"If you like. Nothing useful is being said in there. Where is Elizabeth Goddard?"

"The show for this week is cancelled. I assume she's at home." Betrayed and depressed.

Where did she live? He knew that, or at least knew he knew it, but he couldn't remember. In hotels. But, no, that was when he'd first met her. She'd gotten a townhouse here. He'd bought it with Solutions money. "Call her. Tell her it's vital for her to meet me here at the fifth sublevel. Say that it has to do with Clayton." What was the cliché? "A matter of life and death."

"Fine. I'll call her." Distance. Jealousy.

Henry forced it away. So much raw emotion around these offices, such bursts of unchecked feeling. Feelings: inhibiting and destructive. Distracting, at least. Very distracting.

She stepped off the elevator, her hair pulled back in a bun that Henry didn't like. He walked over to her and, without greeting her, undid the curved clip and removed the two barrettes. The blonde hair fell, not settling as gracefully as if she had intended to wear it down, but beautiful still. And for the first time, he said it.

"You're beautiful."

She looked away from him, crossed her arms. "Henry—"

"Don't say it."

"Don't say what?"

"Don't say you're not beautiful. Don't say you're too old to be what the world declares beautiful. Don't say you're too heavy, you're too plain, you have too many wrinkles. That's all beneath you. Just pull away from the self-criticism. Don't be like other women who spend life in doubt of how they measure up to others' standards of beauty."

She glanced at him over her turned shoulder. "That wasn't what I was going to say."

"No? What then?"

"I wanted to say that you sound like a pseudo-gallant, chauvinist bastard."

Henry thought about that. "Do I?" He worked through the definitions of the words bastard, gallant, and chauvinist, the prefix pseudo. "I do, don't I? Isn't that wonderful?" She was so strong, had such self-possession. She brought out parts of him forever dormant: protection; a desire to own; a need to conquer; a drive to play a subservient role until that moment he could reveal that he was, in fact, in complete control of her.

He unlocked and unlatched the door to the sublevel five laboratory.

The lab quivered with the kinetics of human activity: nurses, three of them, and an elderly man in a traditional white doctor-coat, who would be the gynecologist Henry had ordered; all L-3's, knowing their current task but ignorant of its further implications. There was Lawrence Bourne, directing the preparations; Neil Perrin and two other Solutions operatives to supervise and direct the procedures. And there, far in the back, slumped in the deepest corner with his right hand under his chin and his left hand supporting the elbow of his left arm, a young man with baby-smooth skin, thin, long, peroxide hair. The man—the *angel*—who had nearly allowed Henry to die.

Elizabeth noticed him—Henry read the surprise in the tilt of her eyebrows—and she walked across the lab directly toward him.

"Gabe?" she said. "Gabe Angelo?"

The young man with white hair nodded.

"You're a part of this operation, then?"

"Not really."

"Then why are you here? Christ, every time I run into you, something drastic happens that changes the course of my life."

Gabe Angelo covered his face with both hands. "Yes," he said. "But I'll be with you all the time from now on. Until you want me to leave."

Henry came between the two of them. "You're not welcome here." The others in the lab turned at the sound of Henry's voice. They began to come closer, squinting and intrigued by this individual whose presence had escaped their notice until now.

"She's my client," Gabe Angelo said. "I'm staying with her. Move Heaven and Earth and Urim and Thummim to get rid of me, if that pleases you. I'm not leaving without a fight."

Henry considered this. He could banish him by Urim alone. But why bother? Just another emotional struggle that would cost time and strength of will.

"You look exactly the same," said Elizabeth. "I thought it was my imagination the last time we talked, but now I'm certain. You're not aging."

The staff was murmuring, and Henry shushed them. "What the hell are you?" Elizabeth asked.

The angel's face began to shine, just like the time he'd barely—reluctantly?—saved Henry's life. "Hail, Elizabeth," he said. "Full of grace. The Lord shall be with thee. Blessed art thou among all women." Gabe Angelo turned and stared a deadly look at Henry. "And blessed is the fruit of her womb."

"We have work to do," Henry said.

"None of this is part of the plan."

"Then how do you know about it?"

"Because I take care of her. I'm indebted to her."

"This is a better plan. If you try to interfere, I'll deal with you harshly."

"I have no doubt of that. I only hope—" He stepped

nearer to Elizabeth now, but she drew away, closer to Henry. Henry liked that. She was holding his arm, the way Lisa Imai had held Richard Lanpher's. "I only hope you'll be able to laugh about this one day, Elizabeth. That you'll find ways in it to make others laugh."

Elizabeth's full weight leaned into Henry now. Her knees buckled, and he put both arms around her for support. "Henry?" she said, her eyelids half-closed and the pupils beginning to dilate. He walked her to the table in the middle of the room, set her down gently.

Neil Perrin was putting the pentathol hypodermic back in its case. "Bourne says that will only keep her for half an hour."

"True," said Bourne. "Let's get general anesthesia going." His staff was already rolling a cot toward the table, sheeting it with bright, white linen. Henry kept holding Elizabeth's hand, even after he'd set her on the table.

"Neil."

"Henry?"

"You've got another task you should be about."

"Yeah, I'll . . . yeah." Neil Perrin walked from the room. There was the clicking of turning keys, the hollow echo of the latching bolt.

Neil's eyes had shown terror, Henry thought. Another burst of useless emotion.

Elizabeth was still fighting the injection, Henry could tell. Her eyes tried to open again, but only managed to flutter. "Clayton?" she said.

"Shh," said Henry, feeling gentle, kind, protective. "Don't worry. Clayton and I both love you. You're safe. We love you."

"Henry?" The grip of her hand lightened.

"Please, leave now," Henry said over his shoulder to the angel. "This is a very personal moment." He turned to look, but Gabe Angelo had already disappeared.

❖   ❖   ❖

At that moment, the bottom-line readout of the
Population Numerics Data Base in Heaven, Management
Information Systems, read:

FAITHFUL:

TARGET PERCENTAGE FOR URIM/THUMMIM: 2.760%
CURRENT PERCENTAGE OF WORLD POPULATION: 2.639%

And still rising.

ZETA:
The Trial of Raphael

"Michael?" Clayton said to the coffee pot. He got no response, so he tried the electric pencil sharpener. "Michael?"

The room darkened.

"I accept."

"Thank you," Michael said, and he almost sounded relieved, genuinely grateful.

"So how do I get to Stockholm?"

"No time to use an airport. Would you mind an out-of-body trip? It'll feel like the same thing from your point of view. I'd carry you there physically, if I could, but my physical limitations, you know. . . ." There was a hint of embarrassment in his tone.

"I don't know how to do that," said Clayton.

"It's easy. Just do it. Better sit down first or the body will collapse when you leave."

Clayton sat. Just do it? He tried, and he could feel Michael helping, tendrils of touch against his consciousness. Then Clayton stood up next to his own body. "Wow. It feels like I'm here, not sitting there." He went back into the body, came out again, went in, out. Each time it felt like nothing more than moving around; no sense of doubling, of wispy etherealness, of shedding skin.

"Don't do that too much. It takes a lot of energy out of you."

Clayton didn't feel any less energetic, but he obeyed the instruction.

"Fine," said Michael. "Let's go to Sweden."

It was a perfect time of year in Stockholm; for everything a season, and this was a time to be conventioneering—if you happened to be a metaphysical manifestation serving in the devoted corps of Our Lord Most Missing. The convention schedule was, of course, packed with enough lectures, seminars, and entertainments to keep a curious angel busy all week, but to make sure there was something for everyone, the convention committee scheduled cultural events outside the hotel. There were expeditions to the concert hall in Hötorget, canal trips down the Göta. And there were plenty of special interest group activities, including a group that amused itself by manifesting in the guise of international celebrities on the streets of Stockholm, attracting some human attention, then disappearing around a corner to change back. Winners were declared to be those who caused the most stir, attracted the biggest crowd, in a seven-minute appearance.

The convention hotel stood in front of the concert hall in the Hötorget district, giving conventioneering angels a breathtaking window view of the concert hall's immense, pillared façade and the sculptures positioned on the walkway before it. The committee was free to put the hotel anywhere they wished, since it wasn't real in any physical sense and took up almost no room as far as any Swede or tourist would perceive. But year after year, this area was voted as the favorite spot.

At the height of this year's activities, the word went out: The trial was on, and *really* on. Not just an *in absentia* trial. They'd captured Raphael.

The reaction was mixed. The trial had been billed as an exciting event, the most entertaining of the entertainments. The angels, especially the union workers, had been laboring hard to prepare for the End of Time, and they were ready for any sort of entertainment they could get. But an archangel on trial? *This* archangel? Threatened with nonexistence if found guilty? It had all been quite exciting when it was a mock event. No one expected Raphael to be found, at least not before the return of God. No one had expected to see a real defendant.

No one had wanted to. For Raphael was the Angel of Touch, the only spirit granted by God the gift of physical contact with the material universe. This gave him particular status, earned him respect. He could be testy, of course, and he could often spoil a good party with his glib and ponderous moods. But in tight situations, Raphael was something that Michael often appeared not to be: Raphael was committed to fairness and justice and comfort for the weary. Just as he often healed humans physically, so he edified angels spiritually.

To be fair—all angels wished to be fair—that was, of course, Raphael's role. Michael's was administration. He had a great deal to keep organized, and his role demanded a level of precision and hard-headedness for which no other angel was qualified. A leader couldn't be soft, argued some of the angels.

Others were not so moved. Perhaps not soft, they said, but at least fair.

Still, said some, Raphael had abandoned his station at a critical moment. Could that be ignored? Was that fair?

No, said others, but neither does the situation need to be dealt with by an act of total eradication, destruction of an angel. An *arch*angel.

Duty is duty, said the some. Do you think Michael feels nothing at all about this? He has to maintain law and order. His directions are sometimes harsh, but they are, in the last analysis, always appropriate.

Appropriate? said the others. Who died and left him God?

God left and left him God, said the some.

And then more rumors spread. It was claimed that the angel Lucifer had maneuvered the Council Most Holy into deferring their authority to a human judge, and that the human judge had accepted the offer. Clayton Pinkes, *the* Clayton Pinkes, Prophet for the End of Time. This led to even more bitter disputes. A wise choice, said those who felt the Thummim would bring the wisdom of God to the courtroom. Foolishness, said those who insisted that the rumor about Pinkes having lost the Thummim was no mere rumor. Improper, cried those who stubbornly clung to their loyalty for Michael, appointed Prince of God. Confusing, admitted those who tried to think it through clearly, reasonably. A sad day, an extremely sad day, said those who held deep respect for the Archangel Raphael, and who feared for his very existence.

It was still at a tense and solely verbal level, but it was clear: War was breaking out in Heaven.

The chamber for the trial was packed for as far as Clayton could see. To his left hand was a semicircle oaken table, the top fully a foot thick, its outer edge ornately carved with representations of acts of angels: the pillar of fire, Suriel blocking Pharaoh's army at the parting of the Red Sea; the ladder of angels ascending and descending from Jacob's vision; Michael crowned as Prince of Angels; Gabriel announcing the conception of Christ to the Virgin; Uriel and Azariel tending to Christ in the wilderness; Jeremiel conversing with St. Augustine about the nature of the Trinity; even Raphael, curing the blindness of Tobit of Old. Astoundingly detailed carvings, and, even more unnerving to Clayton, astoundingly real archangels seated around the table.

In the center, right in front of Clayton where he sat at the judge's bench, was the court stenographer, a slender woman with an enormous, pasted-on smile. The nameplate before her read MANDI, STENOGRAPHER, JUSTICE SYSTEM OF THE COUNCIL MOST HOLY. Clayton thought about saying hello to her, decided against it at second thought.

To Clayton's right hand—right stump, he reminded himself—was a simple desk for defending attorney Lucifer and his client, the Archangel Raphael. Raphael's arms were still merged with those of the gargoyle called Abaddon.

At the moment, Lucifer wasn't behind the desk. He was standing on the floor before the bench, nose-to-nose with Michael (if Michael had had a discernible nose). "I oughta wrap you up in chains, pal, and toss you in a pit of fire!" Michael hollered.

"Oh, *wonderful* tactic!" Lucifer shouted back. "Making vague references to myths we ourselves invented to keep human beings in line! Well, it doesn't work, Prince of Pomposity! In this court, you're not the law!"

Clayton rubbed the one hand he had against his forehead. What was he even doing here? He should be back with Elizabeth. He hadn't seen her since the first day he'd awoken after the accident. He should be back with Dickie, trying to . . . to what? Talk him out of being happily married for the last few weeks—months?—of the world? Maybe Dickie was right in what he did. Maybe the only truly human response to the terrifying immensity of the universe was to huddle in comfort with another human being. Not sitting as a judge of angels. Let the angels bury their own angels.

Clayton felt guilty.

The trial: he had to concentrate. This was something immense, something important. An archangel was under indictment.

"If the prosecutor and the defender would kindly stop pissing and moaning for a moment," he said, "I think we could establish a little order." Both Michael and Lucifer did stop, and Clayton was surprised. Perhaps he *was* the law here. Perhaps the authority was real.

The courtroom was crowded to capacity. No, far beyond capacity. The gallery was packed with spectator angels all the way back to the farthest wall, and the walls themselves shivered gently. Clayton could feel ten million more sets of eyes beyond those walls. It wasn't paranoia. He knew that there really were millions more watching. The courtroom's physical manifestation was a courtesy extended to him by the Council Most Holy.

"Please," said Clayton, "is there a written copy of your procedures that I could look over? I'd like to be able to determine when one of you is out of line. This shouting match is less organized than a brawl."

"Actually," said Michael, "we don't have any procedures."

"What?"

"No procedures, no precedents," Lucifer answered. "We've never had a Council trial before, Your Honor Pinkes. There are rules here and there, but most of it we're making up as we go along."

Wonderful. Improvisation in the name of justice. "Okay, let me think. First I want to hear the formal charges from Michael. Then I want rebuttal from Lucifer. After that we'll proceed through the witnesses, prosecution first, then defense."

"Witnesses?" both Michael and Lucifer said. Lucifer deferred to the archangel. "We don't need any witnesses, pal. Everybody knows the facts."

"Michael, I don't want you hamstringing Lucifer's defense—"

"But he's not," Lucifer said. "We all really do know the facts. Raphael told us, and they've been well published."

No witnesses? Raphael told the whole story? What sort of trial had no witness testimony? "Did it ever occur to you gentlemen"—too late Clayton decided he should have said "gentleangels"—"that maybe Raphael *lied* about the facts?"

There was a very short, very empty silence, and then the prosecuting attorney, the defense attorney, the Council, the visible audience, and the invisible millions of angels began to laugh. Loud, crackling laughter, painful laughter because of sheer volume. Clayton tried to put his hands over his ears, discovering he could only cover the left side. He shrugged his right shoulder and tilted his neck to cover the other ear, but it didn't do much good. His head pounded in rhythm with the laughter. It finally subsided; Clayton's head buzzed dully.

Raphael sat quietly. He had not laughed with the others.

"Why would he lie, Your Honor Pinkes?" Lucifer sounded baffled.

"The facts aren't in question, Clayton," Michael explained. "You're here to determine what the facts *mean*, whether Raphael is guilty or innocent based on those facts. We don't need to uncover truth. Only to decide justice. And my position"—Michael's volume increased steadily—"is that any act of mutiny is a betrayal of an archangel's position, entrusted to him by God—"

"Save it," said Clayton. "We'll skip the witnesses, then. After I hear from Lucifer, I want to hear from Raphael."

Again a commotion, but not laughter. Some of the voices from the gallery and beyond sounded angry. Others cheered.

Michael kept at it. "That's preposterous! How can he speak in his own defense? It's an outrage!"

"If you don't settle down, I'll find you in contempt of court and have you . . . I don't know, have you looking really contemptible." That didn't sound very threatening to Clayton himself, but many in the crowd applauded and Michael settled down. He began to speak more reasonably.

"Clayton, how can Raphael testify to the meaning of his own actions? No angel does what he *thinks* is wrong or bad. It may be bad nonetheless, but he's incapable of believing so."

"How do you know, Michael? Maybe Raphael will come up here and say, 'On second thought, I've really screwed up.' I'm not making any decision until I hear from everybody, including Raphael himself."

More reactions from the multitude of angels: whispers, small debates erupting, cheering, hissing. The walls that were quivering gently before were now humming with steady vibration.

"You may start, Michael."

"Thanks, Your Honor Pinkes. As you know, the Archangel Raphael was assigned to you as a Managing Angel, part of a new program—"

"No," said Clayton, ignoring Michael so that he could try to read the audience, the millions and millions of them. "Don't tell me. Tell them. The Council and the masses."

"A speech? Look, pal, you're the one who's supposed to decide the—"

"You'll give it to them, and I'll learn from their reactions. And *you*—" Clayton indicated Lucifer. "If I hear so much as a single squawk of objection from you, I'll figure out how to toss you into that pit of fire myself." Lucifer bowed politely and took his seat beside Raphael.

"Geez," Michael muttered, turning toward the Council and the crowd. "Give a guy a little power . . ."

[[TRANSCRIPT NOTES: MICHAEL'S TESTIMONY]]
MICHAEL: Ahem. I guess you all know me, and I'm real happy so many of you could turn out for the trial. Shows a lot of solidarity, and, uh, that's good. Because solidarity and working together, that's what this trial is all about. You know the facts, but I gotta read the charges formally into the record.

Charge One: That Raphael did willfully neglect to report Managing Angel activities and other vital information that was essential to the End of Time project, and having done so, endangered the project.

Charge Two: That Raphael did willfully abandon his post, an act of mutiny against the authority invested by our Most Missing Lord in the Council Most Holy, His Executive Staff, and particularly toward, uh, Michael Prince of Angels. That's me.

Charge Three: That when presented with an opportunity by Clayton Pinkes—currently His Honor for these proceedings—to return from the realm of limbo, Raphael continued to refuse and spoke traitorously against the End of Time plans that he himself had voted for when the issue first came to the Executive Council.

Charge Four: By hindering the plans of the Council to bring back to the knowable universe our Most Missing Lord, the Archangel Raphael has proved himself to be in enmity with the Almighty, forsaking the one method we know can truly bring God back.

These charges—neglect of duty, abandonment of task, traitorous utterances, and enmity with God—can only carry one sentence. Annihilation.

Okay, that's pretty much the formal stuff. They got the facts in there, and they've got interpretations of the facts, all those "willfully" and "refused" accusations. It's pretty clear-cut, I think.

Let me talk straight with all of you. I like my job. I took it because I felt I could do it. It's a heck of a chore, organizing Heaven and Earth. I know a lot of you think I ride you too hard now and again. What would *you* do? What would you do if God went on vacation or something and said to you, "Hey, take care of the shop, I'll be back whenever"? You'd want to do it right. You'd want the best of all possible universes. And that's what I've wanted, what I've always tried to do. Geez, I ain't omnipotent or nothing, but I think I've done a pretty bang-up job so far. God believed I could do it. He *believed* in me.

But here we got Raphael. When Lucifer stands up to toss off his little schtick, he'll be a lot more eloquent than me. He'll tell you all the wonderful things Raph has done over the millennia. How faithful he's always been. How effective. But that ain't the point! The point is that when times got toughest, Raphael disappeared. While you and me and the angels sitting next to you were toiling for the Greatest Good, getting God back into the knowable universe, Raph was off doing as he pleased. Is that what God would want from you? From me? It's true that Raph believes he was searching for God in his own way. But he knows that our way would work—*will* work—much better. Raphael *had* a way to find God, *our* way, and the meaning behind the facts of this case is that he turned his back on us and on the God who made us.

I feel like I'm supposed to say more. But it's all that simple. Listen, I miss God. We all do, even Raphael, I guess. But when we get God back here, I want Him to be proud of the order and flow we've kept up. Of our sense of duty. Raphael went against that duty. He did things that could have ruined our plan. He might very well have kept God away from us.

That's all.

[[TRANSCRIPT NOTES: LUCIFER'S TESTIMONY]]
LUCIFER: My esteemed colleagues: seraphim and cherubim; thrones, dominions and powers; principalities and fellow laborers in the Kingdom of Heaven. Our exalted Prince of Angels has just passionately, touchingly, and quite admirably delivered to you . . . complete garbage. For underlying his every word was the assumption that my client, well known and well loved by you, is already declared guilty. I need to tell you that I do not disagree with a single fact in any of the four charges brought against my client. But I violently contest the way Michael has skimmed over their specifics to try to play with your sense of honor and duty to Our Deity Most Unfindable.

Charge One indicates that the Archangel Raphael neglected his duties, thereby hurting the plan for the

End of Time. But I say to you that failure to *perform* his duty and failure to *report* his performance are two entirely different issues. Raphael has been a Managing Angel to Clayton Pinkes quite effectively. For do we not see before us the Prophet for the End of Time, prepared at the conclusion of this trial to set in motion the conclusion of the plan itself? Against Charge One and its assumptions, I say that the specifics of reporting were only incidental; the output of the duty is seated before you in the person of His Honor Clayton Pinkes.

Charge Two is abandonment of post, called an act of mutiny. I urge you all to remember that while Our Lord of Valorous Absentia has, in fact, invested authority in the Council as a whole, He has also invested autonomy in each individual angel. Free will. Free minds. Our glorious Prince of Angels himself indicated that God has placed trust in him. But Michael is not the only spirit in whom God has placed trust. I say to you that if Raphael is guilty of mutiny because he disregarded the authority invested in the Council by God, then Michael himself is guilty of mutiny by disregarding the autonomy invested by God in Raphael or any other archangel.

[[SIGNIFICANT COMMOTION FROM THE GALLERY. REAL NOISY. NOW RAPHAEL GETS UP AND APPROACHES THE BENCH, SORT OF DRAGGING ABADDON BEHIND HIM. I DON'T THINK ABADDON WAS TRYING VERY HARD TO HOLD HIM BACK. —Mandi.]]

RAPHAEL: Stop this, Pinhead. He's gone too far.

LUCIFER: Your Honor, I'd like to point out that my opponent suffered no interruptions. I should be granted the same liberty.

CLAYTON: This is your *client*, Lucifer.

LUCIFER: C'mon, Raph! I was just getting warmed up.

RAPHAEL: Michael isn't on trial. I am.

LUCIFER: [[TO THE GALLERY]] Do you see how uncompromising my client is in the pursuit

of justice? Even in his hour of deepest
need, he seeks only fairness for his greatest enemy! How like the man David of
old! How like—

RAPHAEL: You're fired.

LUCIFER: Eh?

CLAYTON: Your client has dismissed you, Counselor.

LUCIFER: Objection!

CLAYTON, RAPHAEL, and MICHAEL:
                Overruled.

[[THEY SAID IT JUST LIKE THAT, AT THE SAME
TIME! IT WAS REALLY FUNNY, SORT OF ANYWAY,
EXCEPT THAT IT WAS A TRIAL AND REALLY
SERIOUS AND EVERYTHING. —Mandi.]]

"Do you want to address the gallery?"

"I want to address you, Pinhead. I think you've had
enough time to absorb how they're feeling."

Clayton had. The feelings in the gallery were strong,
incensed: anger toward the speakers countering admiration for the speakers countering scrutiny of the
speakers fighting anger toward the defendant fighting
respect for the defendant battling incredulity toward the
judge. Millions of minds, a mess. There was no way, no
way at all, to satisfy the entire group. The feeling was
more than just conflict. To Clayton, it felt like a single
step away from chaos and war.

"Kind of a tough crowd," said Clayton, his voice
lowered.

"Yeah. It's my fault." Raphael whispered, too. "Look,
Pinhead, just decide against me. I'll admit full guilt to
the assembly, and Michael will be able to bring Heaven
back under control. What we're seeing here, this can't
be. This is very wrong. More wrong than the destruction
of the entire material universe."

"Is it?" Clayton asked, rhetorically. There was contra-
dictory shouting and chanting from the crowd, and
Michael, sitting at the ornate table of the Council, was

beginning to fidget, glancing over his shoulder at the gallery, the edges of his blackness and void noticeably twitching. "Release him," Clayton said to the gargoyle Abaddon. "Raphael, give him your word of honor in the name of God that you won't flee."

Raphael nodded, and the gargoyle, without hesitation, unmerged the arms of his prisoner. Abaddon stepped back to the defense table.

"Tell me, Raphael. No, *Paolo*. Tell me, old friend Paolo, why'd you go against the orders in the first place?"

The adult Raphael faded, and the brooding, dark-skinned child form of Paolo Diosana stood before Clayton. His head was down, shamed. "For the exact reasons Michael charged. Because I didn't want the plan to work. I didn't think it was worth destroying the material world to drag back a reluctant God. I'm a minority here, Pinhead. I'm the only angel with a physical bias. And quite frankly, I'd miss the Earth. I'd miss the physical. I wasn't willing to forfeit it. Not for a God who abandoned it and all of us in the first place."

Clayton nodded. Then stopped nodding. Then leaned closer to Paolo. "But you've changed your mind. Now you're willing not only to see the material universe destroyed, but also to allow yourself to be annihilated. Why is that, Paolo?"

The boy guise of the angel waved a hand toward the gallery. "Look at that, Pinhead. Look what I've done. That's not just a bunch of carefully arranged atoms falling into chaos. That's the very essence of my world falling apart."

You bastard, thought Clayton. You sneaky little son of a bitch. But Clayton only said, "I see."

"Declare me guilty, Pinhead."

"You're brave. Standing in the face of total eradication, willing to acknowledge what is best. I could learn a lot from you, Paolo Diosana."

"Clayton—"

"No, let me finish. When I was young, I had reservations about destroying the whole world just to fulfill my longing for God. As an adult, I stopped worrying about it. It was too hard to imagine. I let myself get lulled into complacency with the idea of ending the world. There's a part of Clayton Pinkes inside me that I like to think of as the Totally Other. It's a very clever part of me that faces all the difficulties and contradictions of living by convincing me it's too hard to face them. I thought I finally controlled that part of me, but you've helped me see it differently. I've been a coward and a fool. I ought to just leave now and end the world, like a man."

Paolo Diosana looked at him, pupils rolled up to the tops of his eyes, whole body immobile, fully on guard. Yup, thought Clayton. I'm scaring the shit out of him.

"Here, today, watching you, Paolo, I realize I have to face my responsibility. Who am I to keep the human race away from God because of my own fears? Who am I to secretly, deep down, oppose the plans of fate and history? If the world must be destroyed for a greater good, then I'll face that fact with resolve and courage."

He let Paolo stew, gazing gravely down at him and trying to appear resolute over what he'd just said. Paolo composed himself rather quickly, but not quickly enough to hide it from Clayton. Because Clayton was looking for it. Because Clayton had figured it out, Thummim or no Thummim.

"You little archweasel," said Clayton Pinkes. "You *want* Heaven in chaos."

Paolo Diosana visibly relaxed. Why not? thought Clayton. Paolo knew his entire hand was exposed to Your Honor Pinkes.

The gallery around them advanced from vibration to violent shaking, millions arguing, shouting in impatience, awaiting the decision.

"This is all part of your own little plan. You have no

intention of declaring Michael right and accepting a guilty sentence."

" 'Then war broke out in Heaven,' " quoted Paolo. " 'Michael and his angels battled against the dragon. Although the dragon and his angels fought back, they were overpowered and lost their place in Heaven. The dragon was hurled down to Earth, and his minions with him.' "

"And you get to play the dragon?"

"Of course not. Lucifer does. He's got the leadership skills. Me, I'm just a highly placed minion."

"The beast. Part of the Unholy Trinity. The dragon, the beast, and the false prophet. All symbols from the Book of the Apocalypse. I suppose I get to be the third in that little trio."

Paolo Diosana smiled . . . angelically, although Clayton decided the description was redundant. "It's a biased text, Pinhead. You know, like the charges read against me. All the facts correct, but assumptions imposed about what the facts mean. You and I, we seek God. With all our hearts. But neither of us can accept a God who doesn't accept us back. One who *has* to believe in us. I don't want God to be forced back to the knowable universe on a technicality of Urim and Thummim. I want Him to come back when He's good and ready. Don't you think the Father of All deserves at least that much flexibility?"

"You'll lose this war. That's written, too."

"Will we? I don't know. Think back to 'Born Free.' Remember, when you were young? You led an entire group of human children through an exercise that proved 'Born Free' was a satanic song. It was all in jest, of course, but what was the point?"

Yes, Clayton remembered. The point was that anyone could bend words to reveal a truth. That Scripture could say anything you wanted it to. Michael had faith in the way he read the words. Paolo had faith in his own interpretation. But no one, it seemed to Clayton, was being reasonable anymore.

"We're on God's side, Pinhead. We support His right to make His own decisions. And we don't want the physical world destroyed. I think it's worth a fight." He turned to look at the gallery—screams now, verbal violence, and Clayton's ears again began to hurt. Even the table of the Council Most Holy was embroiled in dispute, Azariel shouting at Uriel, Jeremiel at Suriel. The dark shape of Michael sat motionless, slumped, emanating resignation and despair. Gabriel—

Gabriel was gone.

"It doesn't even matter what you decide now. If you declare me guilty, a third of them will rally against the decision. If you declare me innocent, two-thirds will oppose the verdict. Now it's inevitable."

Clayton stood and held up his arm, waving to the gallery and beyond. "Hey!" he shouted, the voice pretty much lost in the noise. "If you're interested, I've got the verdict! Verdict, everybody! Verdict here!"

The first few rows of the audience heard him, and a cry of "Verdict! Verdict!" worked its way back to the walls of the gallery, beyond.

"No verdict without complete silence!"

Eight thousand cries of "Quiet!" made it noisier still, but after about three minutes, Clayton standing there patiently, ten million angels were hushed and waiting.

"My judgement is final in this matter. What I declare, by the authority of the Council Most Holy, shall stand as law in the courts of Heaven."

A siren sounded then, an amplified, piercing wail that caused murmurs throughout the gallery. Clayton's heart jumped when it kicked in.

"Hello? Am I on? Hello?" The voice was tinny and obscurely familiar to Clayton.

Michael rose from the Council table. "Yes? What is it?"

"Oh, good. Hi, this is Bob, Manager, Management Information Systems. Sorry to cut in like this, folks, heh, heh, but I'm under strict orders to report. We've just gotten the hourly readout with the news. In the past hour, the 2.76% Believing Population of Earth target was achieved and surpassed. It's still going up as I speak. We're at 109.3% of plan for raw numbers of believers."

"Why the latest surge?" Michael asked.

"There's an announcement being broadcast by Christian Stewardship Ministry on all satellite networks and PrivNets. Clayton Pinkes and Elizabeth Goddard are appearing live in two hours to declare to the world the Will of God."

Twenty million eyes of ten million angels turned toward Clayton Pinkes. He shrugged (as well as any one-armed man could shrug, he supposed). "News to me."

"Thanks, Bob," Michael said, slowly lowering himself to his chair. They still stared, waiting.

"My goodness," said Clayton, "that certainly does add to the tension. Where was I?"

"'What I declare, by the authority of the Council Most Holy, shall stand as law in the courts of—'"

"Yes, thank you, Mandi. I hereby declare the Case of Archangel Raphael an appellate issue."

There were still those miles of silence through the gallery and out beyond. They expected more.

Lucifer stood. "If Your Honor Pinkes would explain the decision—"

"Certainly. In my opinion, everybody is right. You're also all wrong, every one of you. So my mind is a hung jury. I declare a mistrial, or whatever the hell it's supposed to be."

"If Your Honor finds insufficient evidence to declare my client guilty—"

"Oh, no. He's guilty, all right. But he's justifiably innocent, if you know what I mean."

They didn't. And still no commotion broke out.

"Since I, as highest authority present for the resolution of this matter, cannot find sufficient resolution, the issue will be appealed to a higher authority still. No action will be taken in this case until there is a decision from God Himself. Anyone disagreeing with this decision is against both the authority of the Council, from whom my own authority is derived, and against the right of God Almighty to declare a verdict in an issue that is splitting Heaven asunder."

Then the silence ended, but not in a tumult. Quiet discussion began throughout the gallery. Subdued talk. Laughter in a few areas.

Michael stood and approached the bench without permission. "What are you doing?" The whisper wasn't as harsh as Clayton had expected.

"Stalemate, Michael. Which means you win. Look at that crowd. Defused. There's not a one of them who will argue that God is unqualified to pass judgement."

Michael did look at the crowd—studying, musing, finally chuckling. "Good answer," he said.

Lucifer also stormed to the bench, Raphael/Paolo with him. "You can't leave this without resolution!" he shouted. "My client deserves to know—"

"Your client will be judged by God. Are you denying God His right to make decisions? If you claim that too loud, I suspect you'll lose a hefty chunk of your following." Lucifer fidgeted. "Face it, Lucifer. There'll be no war in Heaven." The defense attorney glanced quickly, nervously, at Michael, but still said nothing.

"When?" asked the Archangel Raphael. "When does God come back to settle the matter? That's the real issue, Clayton. We all know it and aren't discussing it."

"You heard the announcement," Michael growled. "It's in less than two hours."

Raphael looked thoughtful, ignoring Michael and watching Clayton. "Is it? Is it really?"

"I wasn't aware," said Clayton Pinkes, "that the issue in question had anything to do with this court any more." Raphael nodded, and Clayton said, "Go ahead. Say it."

"Say what?"

"Say the phrase. All my life I've had my visions, and all but one have been fulfilled. A single phrase from a vision far back in my childhood. It's the one I'm waiting for."

"How should I know what it is?"

"Say the first thing that comes into your head."

Raphael considered for a moment, then cleared his throat. "You've had twenty-six years to think about it, Pinhead. I'm just the angel, you're the prophet. Your world, not mine; your choice, not mine. Is it the end of the world?"

"Thank you. And the answer is: None of your fucking business." Clayton willed himself back to his body in Rochester, New York, disappearing from their presence.

Poof. Like that.

ETA:
Clayton Makes a Decision

Clayton came to be sitting in his chair; immediately, the
twinkling of an eye. Sitting on the edge of the coffee
table, tailored Italian suit with sharp creases and
bloodstains soiling his jacket, was Neil Perrin.

There was a pistol hanging limply from Neil's right
hand. His head was bowed and he was sobbing.

"Neil! What the hell happened?" The act of jumping up threw Clayton off balance—still the goddamn
missing arm playing gravity tricks with him.

"Oh. Hi, Clay. You're awake. I thought you were dead."

There was no move with the handgun, something
Clayton had half-expected. Clayton chanced moving from
behind the desk next to Neil. "Talk to me, Neil. Stop
crying. Talk to me."

Neil looked up, his eyes swollen and dark, his cheeks
damp in places and stained with dried, earlier tears. How
long had he been sitting here?

"I did it, Clay. I killed Papa Bear. Just like Henry
wanted."

Oh, Jesus. Sweet God in Heaven, not quite in Heaven.
"Where is he? We'll call an ambulance."

350

"Oh, he's dead, Clay. He's really dead. I put him in my office. Henry said to. He even told me how to set the body down just right. I had to put one of his legs up on a chair, and bend his arm backwards at a ninety-degree angle, and make a pool of blood form on his left-hand side. I had to muss up his hair and untuck his shirt. I had to, Clay. Henry told me to." Then the words were lost in another bout of sobs.

"Uh, the police," Clayton said. "We've got to call the police."

"You can't. Henry didn't plan on that." Neil's face was distorted, the face of an infant trying to draw breath for a piercing scream. He was soundless, though.

Clayton threw the door open. "Mrs. Brunwig!"

"She's gone for the day, Clay," Julie Ward called from her desk.

"Julie. Get in here!"

She got in there.

"Did you see him like this?"

She became defensive. "Of course I did! I'm not stupid, Clayton."

"Why didn't you do something?"

"Henry said not to. When you're not around, Henry's in charge."

"Well, now I'm around! Call the police."

"All outside communications are disconnected. Henry's orders."

Henry's orders. Henry said so. Henry's in charge. "Where is that scrawny son of a bitch? Tell me!"

Now she started to cry. "You don't have to get mad at me, Clayton. I just try to follow orders. I just want to make people happy."

"I'm upset, Julie! I'm not mad at you!"

The crying stopped immediately. She beamed. "Oh. Okay."

She was useless to him. "Look, sit here with Neil. Keep him talking. Don't let him get crazy."

"We can't stay in here. Henry's having the cameras brought up for the live broadcast. He thinks it would be best from your office. Sort of the way the President does it from the Oval Office".

"Then take Neil someplace else! Stay with him, will you?"

Confident, dependable: "Sure, Clay, I won't let you down."

"Clayton?" asked Neil's broken voice, muffled behind his hands. "Can we be friends again? I don't think I like Henry."

Clayton ran from the office, past the secretarial area, the reception lounge, and down the halls toward the elevators. Two armed security guards stood in front of the doors.

"Let me guess," Clayton said to them. "No one is to leave the floor. Henry's orders."

Both security guards looked at him sheepishly. "I'm sorry, Mr. Pinkes," one said. "It's for your own protection. Ever since the announcement, reporters and other folks have been crowding around the bottom floor. There's been quite a few scuffles down there."

"Well there's been a fucking *murder* up here!"

They looked uneasy. "We wouldn't know anything about that, Mr. Pinkes. We're ordered to remain at this post."

"Bastards," Clayton said. "Bastards." But the elevator doors opened just then. Out of them came two cameras, each supported by its own technician, and Henry Albert, his arm supporting Elizabeth Goddard.

"Ah, Clayton! Just in time, too! We'll be broadcasting a little earlier than expected. It adds to the tension, don't you think?"

"If you've hurt her, you'll die."

When Clayton said that, the two security guards put their hands on the butts of their weapons.

"She's fine. She'll be out of it in under five minutes. Right, honey?" He hugged her, rocking back and forth with her in his arms. Then he started singing: "She's my honey, she's my honey, she's my, she's my, she's my honey."

Elizabeth squinted over Henry's shoulder toward Clayton, a bleary expression of having just risen from a deep sleep. "Hi, Clay. I love you." Then she kissed Henry Albert.

Clayton tapped the heel of his right foot against the floor; steady, insistent, a surge of wanting to explode and rip Henry apart. "I want . . . " slowly, controlled "—to speak with you about—" looking at Elizabeth "—a certain matter."

Henry looked at him queerly, then slowly showed a semblance of understanding. "Oh, that? My reduction in staff? He never deserved to be my father. Whatever made Papa Bear think so?"

Why was Henry acting so strangely? Clayton'd grown accustomed to subdued brilliance, the calculating solemnity. Not to this . . . this unwinding maniac.

Henry started down the hall with Elizabeth; the technicians followed. "C'mon, Clayton! Time to preach your greatest sermon!"

Clayton followed—slowly, dazed, trying to convince the fight-or-flight response of his body that he was neither going to fight nor flee. He would not be swayed. He was the Prophet for the End of Time. Halfway down the hall, he stopped next to her—the portrait of her, the copy of la Tour's painting. *Mary Magdalen With Oil Lamp*. He grabbed it with his left arm—his remaining arm, his only arm—and lifted it from the wall.

Then he beat it against the floor. The frame cracked, broke. The print tore. He tore it some more, and then more, to as many pieces as he could using one arm and his teeth for grasping. As hand and teeth tore, his feet continued kicking and splintering the wooden frame.

In the reception area, he stopped at Julie Ward's desk. She was typing a memo on the computer. SUPPLIES

REQUEST: 15 BOXES PAPER CLIPS. 10 PACKAGES PENCILS. Beyond where she sat, back in Clayton's office, Henry and the crew were setting up the cameras and lights.

"Where's Neil?" Clayton hissed to Julie. "I told you to stay with him!"

"Well, he told me to leave him alone. Honestly, Clay, I just don't know who to listen to anymore!"

"Where is he?"

"I took him to his office."

"His *office*?"

"Yeah, it's a real mess. There's a dead guy in there. It's really very horrible." She finished the memo, printed off a hard copy.

Clayton walked back to his office, where three extension lights were already blazing. The cameras were set on tripods and pointed toward his desk. "Come in, come!" said Henry, patting him on the shoulder. "I've got wonderful news! Wonderful!" Henry glanced toward the door, out toward Julie Ward. "Shut that, would you? You're about to find out what you're announcing to the world in a few minutes."

Clayton shut the door. The studio lights were already making the office warm.

"Now sit down, over here." He sat Clayton next to Elizabeth on the edge of the coffee table. I've got to get some chairs in here, Clayton thought. Elizabeth looked somewhat more awake now, but still dazed, as if coming out of shock. When he sat, she reached over and took his hand. She didn't look at him.

"Clayton, my friend, I'm proud to announce that you and I"—Henry blushed—"well, we're going to be a father."

Clayton thought he'd just heard Henry say . . .

"What the hell sort of scheme is this?"

"Not a scheme at all! It's done! Well, almost done." Henry bent down and gave Clayton a hug. "Congratulations! It's a boy!"

Extreme vertigo, very, very extreme. Elizabeth's hand

tightened around Clayton's, so he was able to focus there, on her.

"Elizabeth?"

"He raped me."

The fight-or-flight response again.

"Don't be ridiculous," Henry chuckled, and Clayton could hear the words "silly little woman" in the tone. "It was done by machine! That's not rape. We used one of her ova, but it was, of course, drained of all genetic material. Then we merged a haploid Urim strand with a haploid Thummim, implanted the cell, and bingo! We're daddies!"

"Bingo?" Clayton stood up. "Bingo?"

"All right, I make it sound a little easier than it was. But it's a living cell, and it's human, it really is! It was one of the secrets of Urim and Thummim we'd been missing all along. The heart of religion is sex!" Henry hugged Clayton again, and Clayton shoved him away. He would kill him, now. He would take Henry's neck between his hands, squeeze with every ounce of frustration and hatred he'd accumulated since the car bombing, and drop Henry limp to the floor.

Elizabeth's hand rested softly on his shoulder. "Don't," she said. Her face pressed against his neck. There were no tears. "Please don't, Clayton."

All right, Clayton wouldn't do that. He couldn't, anyway. He only had one hand.

"Now the next steps are very important," Henry rambled, oblivious to the hatred he should be feeling from Clayton. "Elizabeth goes on first and makes the appeal for faith. Then you go on after her and declare that God is coming to Earth in the flesh. We'll lead the faithful in a prayer for the coming of God—we both have to be touching her, I think—and then the entire spirit of God flows into that growing embryo! Our son! We'll be the Fathers of God!"

Henry walked behind the desk and flopped down in Clayton's chair. The technicians glanced at him—they were efficient men, so all they did was glance and go back to arranging their multitude of cables.

"Fathers of God! Now there's a son you can be proud of."

Three apparitions, then: first Gabriel, standing by the office door. He called out, "Here," and Michael was with him, then Raphael. One of the technicians swore and jumped away, tripping over the pile of cables as he did.

"What do you think you're doing?" Michael said, frozen words.

"Praying," said Clayton Pinkes. It was true.

"This is not the plan."

"No," said Clayton. "It's not your plan, Michael. And it's not yours, Paolo. It's a third plan. Everybody's got a plan." He walked over to the Archangel Gabriel. "What's your plan?"

"I don't have one. I just want to be with Elizabeth. She's very funny, you know. I admire that. I aspire to it. I have a great passion for Elizabeth Goddard."

Clayton sighed. "Yeah. Everybody's got one of those."

Henry jumped up from the desk chair. He was pointing . . . what? Bones. Bones? Then Clayton understood. Urim. Thummim. One of those was *his* bone.

"Nobody move," said Henry. "These things are loaded." Then he giggled, hysterically approving his own joke.

"That's not funny," said Gabriel. He crowded a little closer to the dark shape of Michael.

"Are we set to broadcast?"

The technicians didn't say anything.

"Broadcast, you incompetents! Let's go!"

They scurried behind their cameras, trying to stay clear of the three archangels. Henry walked to Elizabeth, gently taking her by the arm and leading her to the desk chair. "Knock them dead, my love. Make them want to believe what Clayton says. Make them need faith. You are the best." He kissed her on the cheek.

"Ten seconds," said one of the technicians. "Rolling lead-in. Five seconds to live."

"You're just going to let it happen, aren't you?" Paolo had drawn up alongside Clayton.

"I can't think. I don't know what to do."

"At this very second, the Descartesians have rallied the armies of Europe. Asia is starting a massive recruitment as well. Ever since your friend Henry stopped funding them, they've gotten their leaders and politics in order."

"Thanks," said Clayton. "That really clears things up."

"We're live!"

Elizabeth sat up. She smiled. When Clayton wasn't looking, all the weariness and shock had drained from her. He knew why, of course. There was a crowd to address. There were millions, maybe tens of millions, all fixed to her image at this very second. The Audience.

"Hi!" she said, radiant. "My name is Elizabeth Goddard, and I'm the last moral comedienne in the world."

Henry took a step toward the desk, but stopped before coming into the view of the camera.

"I've been thinking about the Mother of God lately. You know, the Virgin Mary, how she conceived by the Holy Spirit?"

Henry's shoulders relaxed. She was back on track, so he'd let her continue.

"Well, that got me thinking: She's the only woman in history ever to have had sex with God. Think about it: that must have been one fucking, magnificent orgasm! Cripes, if only our men could perform like that."

"Cut!" screamed Henry. "Stop transmitting!"

Around the world, television screen and PrivNet consoles flashed the message: "PLEASE STAND BY."

Henry was frozen where he stood, and no one said a thing. Except Gabriel. He was laughing. He was applauding.

"You're my best audience, Gabe Angelo." Elizabeth

walked from the desk, right past Henry and Clayton. "I could hug you."

"No, you couldn't, but the sentiment is appreciated. I'm proud of you, Elizabeth. You know what life is really supposed to be about."

The door flew open, then, sort of passing through Michael and Gabriel, missing Elizabeth by inches. Neil Perrin stood there, handgun raised. *Neil's got his pistol*, part of Clayton's mind said, but the rest was numb. There were three loud cracks, almost as if Neil had fired, which was silly, why would Neil fire? And a quick movement then, Elizabeth moving, but moving in the wrong direction.

"I hate you, Henry Albert!" Neil screamed. That made sense. Neil *should* hate Henry.

But it was still ridiculous, the sound of the shots and Elizabeth still moving the wrong way, ridiculous. But blood was flying and Elizabeth Goddard was all bloody, falling to the floor, the side of her head gone. What an impossible, ridiculous thing to think you were seeing. Then Neil Perrin falling to the floor. Somebody tackling him? Julie Ward, with a body check to the back of Neil's knees, and then one of the technicians jumping, grabbing the gun, the other pinning Neil down. And Elizabeth on the floor.

Silly.

Julie stood and stared at the mess on the floor. "How depressing," she said, and then she walked over to Clayton. "But you should have picked me!" Julie Ward's voice was reasonable. "Why should she get to be the Mother of God? *I'm* the one who's the virgin. I'm better qualified!" She put her arms around Clayton's neck, suddenly becoming coy and seductive. "Now you can use me. I've made up my mind. And . . . I'm glad about it, Clayton. I'm really happy now."

It wasn't silly anymore.

He pushed Julie away and ran to Elizabeth. Blood. Blood blood blood blood blood. "Do something!" he screamed back at Raphael. "Do something to heal her!"

"It's too late."

"You're the one who's supposed to heal! Do something!"

Raphael—now Paolo again, the boy guise—kneeled down next to Clayton. Small, dark, slender, serious Paolo Diosana. He unbuttoned the cuffs of his white, parochial school shirt, and slowly, meditatively rolled up the sleeves, one by one, as if there were no act in the universe of greater importance at the moment. It was a gesture Clayton had never forgotten.

Paolo raised both hands and set them on Clayton's shoulders. Clayton could feel them, angel hands, warm with comfort. "You're my friend, Clayton. Listen. Her death was immediate. It's too late."

Clayton didn't want comfort. He wanted Elizabeth healed. He wanted to back up three minutes and play it all over again. "Do something," he pleaded, his voice weak.

"I'm trying. You won't let me."

"Do something."

"We'll all keep living, Clayton. It's not . . ."

And Clayton looked up, the fury burning in his face, down his spine. "Not *what*, Paolo? What were you going to say? 'It's not the end of the world'?"

From behind Clayton, Gabriel's voice whispered to Michael, although Clayton heard it, "I'll escort her."

Clayton was on his feet, stepping around the still catatonic form of Henry Albert. "What was that? You'll escort her? You mean to death, don't you? To the other side where only the dead go? No you fucking won't, Gabriel. I'll do it. I'll escort her." Clayton grabbed the two bones from Henry Albert's stiff hands and clenched them in his left fist. Henry blinked once, and his eyes followed Clayton, but he made no move.

"Link the camera. Broadcast."

The technicians looked to Henry, then to anyone else

who might have something to say about it, but no one said anything to them. Clayton stood behind the desk, and they had to tilt the cameras upward to center him in the viewer.

"Ten seconds."

"Clayton," said Paolo.

"My world!" Clayton screamed. "Not yours! My world that you've done nothing but make crazier since I was a boy! The whole, fucking, lunatic, desperate planet! Mine!"

"Five seconds."

"Blessed be God," said the voice of Michael. "Blessed be His Holy Name."

"We're live."

Clayton stared at the world.

"Listen," he said. "Listen for a moment. It will only take a minute, so listen closely. The world is screwed up. It isn't working. You know that, deep down. So maybe we need the courage to admit it. It's not worth living in. I need you to agree to that. It's not worth living in. Say that with me. It's not worth living in."

Clayton glared beyond the cameras at Michael. At Raphael. At Gabriel, who had a great passion for Elizabeth Goddard.

"So we're just going to settle down for a while. Seven years. Not seven weeks or seven minutes or seven seconds. Seven years. Total peace. Total harmony. It doesn't have to go on forever. We could try it once a century or so. At the end of it, we can all go back to our fighting and hating and wars and rumors of wars. I just . . . dammit, I don't want to sound sentimental. All you have to do is agree it should happen. Say it with me: Everybody, settle down! Everybody, just settle down!"

There was a groan from Michael. Gabriel stepped forward, his eyes fixed on Clayton, hopeful.

Clayton agreed silently with the look in Gabriel's eyes. "And while we have peace, let's try to laugh as much as possible. Laughter is a good thing."

When he said it, he was crying.

"Cut," said Raphael gently. The cameras stopped.

Around the globe, 3.28% of the human race agreed, sincerely believed, that what Clayton Pinkes said was a very good idea.

The Urim and Thummim fell from his hands, now too hot to hold. They landed on the carpet, bursting in sparks and flames and a wind that Clayton remembered from long ago, when Sister Leo Agnes' soul had migrated from the universe, into that place that angels and living humans could not go.

"You declared the global peace!" said Raphael. "You archweasel, yourself! You reinstituted the global peace."

But Clayton was staring at the body of Elizabeth Goddard, there on his office floor, and she forever away. "I guess the laughter can start tomorrow."

And Clayton wept.

Inside the mind of Henri Elobert:

He stood back there, on Kerguélen, in the viewing room in the secret part of the compound.

On the screen was Dr. Elobert in his puddle of blood.

"Why did she turn on me? What happened?"

I do not know, said Father in French. *I suppose she does not like you.*

"But what happened?"

I don't know, said Roland in English. *I guess she doesn't like you.*

"Please tell me. Please tell me what happened."

Don' be knowin', boy, said Papa Bear. *Spose she jus' plain don' like ya.*

THETA:
Seven Years Later;
Latitude 63° N, Longitude 6° W

This stretch of the Rio Carrao was calm, perhaps the calmest, Clayton liked to imagine, anywhere in the stretch of the Gran Sabana through which the river fumbled. He had the motor of the boat at the lowest setting. He'd never, in fact, taken it faster than this. He wanted to disturb the wildlife, the flora, the water itself, as little as possible. There was the hacienda built above the cliff, of course, and he had regretted having the small area cleared just so he could live here. There was a twinge of guilt. Maybe he shouldn't use a motorboat. But a man with one arm couldn't row.

Human progress was working its way south, he knew, down from Caracas, but he'd be long dead before actual land development, real civilization, got this far south. In the meantime . . .

In the meantime he lived. He lived watching the world down here in this still-unsettled area of Venezuela where the SouthAmer machine of progress had yet to stake a claim. He watched the flamingo, the heron, the ibis, even the gaurcharo, that hideous thing. He'd go off the river, inland, to watch the anteater, the armadillo, the sloth (poor fellow, named for a deadly sin Clayton now enjoyed and called existence). Sometimes he'd head to the llanos to see the grasses, or to the Orinoco delta for the mangroves. But that was rare; it meant an overnight trip, a night in a hotel near civilization.

On this particular trip he watched a young boy, dark-skinned, slender, walking on the water of the Carracao. The boy was careful to step over the few bewildered crocodiles who'd ventured away from the shore.

"¿Quién eh?" called Clayton. "¿Qué quiere?"

"Speak English, Pinhead. Your accent is terrible."

The boy stepped in the boat.

"As I live and breathe," said Clayton. "Have a seat. Not safe to stand in a boat."

Paolo—Raphael—sat down. "Happy birthday."

Clayton coughed. "Fifty," he said, shaking his head. "Fifty."

"You're hard to find. What are you doing down here?"

Clayton shrugged. "Wasn't staying in the U.S. Where else could I go? Europe? I'm certain they'd simply love me there. Asia? No thanks. Don't like feudalism."

"Africa."

Clayton considered it. "Africa? Might go there next. Of course, there's still the plagues."

"Nope. They petered out in the first few months of your Seven Years of Peace. Might come back, though."

"Always do," said Clayton. "Somewhere."

They coasted for a while, watching the banks, the screaming colors of nature at rest in flowers, the mangoes, the palms and brazilwoods.

"Now that the Peace is over, it's all starting up again. Same old human history. American patriotism is resurging. Asia is feuding. Europe is trying to formulate a group as strong as the old Descartesians."

Clayton snorted. "Guess they could use Henry."

The angel nodded.

"How is he?" Clayton asked.

Paolo made a circular gesture with his hand, the equivalent of a verbal, "Well, ya know."

"Is he eating by himself yet?"

"He'll chew when a nurse sticks a spoon in his mouth."

They didn't say anything more about it.

The boat maneuvered a curve of the river that took them out of the dense overgrowth. The world expanded into the cliffs of the higher plain, the open sky clear and blue above them. "See that?" Clayton pointed to a cliff far in the distance. A thin stream of falling water dropped thousands of feet to the base. "I can see that from my hacienda. Gorgeous view. That's why I stay."

Paolo smiled.

"It's called *Salto Angel*. Angel Falls. Get it? I like that. The Angel Falls."

"I get it."

"Pretty glib, huh?"

"No. It's just cute."

Clayton scratched his beard and spit in the water. "I think it's glib. Glib enough."

There was a jaguar watering by the bank, and Clayton patted Paolo on the arm, pointing it out. "Look at that, would you. She's beautiful."

"Yeah," said Paolo, and then he chuckled. "Honestly, Clayton. This back-to-nature stuff. You wanna be an archetype when you grow up?"

"Ah, go to hell. You're not human. What do you know?"

They'd gone a little farther before Clayton asked, "How is it? Up there, I mean."

"Routine. Michael runs a neat ship. He's good at what he does."

Clayton leaned closer to him. "No rebellion or anything?"

"No reason for it. I got what I wanted." He looked around the water, the banks, toward the cliffs. "All this.

With the Urim and Thummim gone, there's no effort to drag God back."

"Oh, yeah. God." Clayton caught himself throttling the motor a little faster than he usually did. He stopped, felt bad about it, even apologized silently to the waters.

"I'm suspended from active duty, of course. Until the case is . . . resolved. I'm enjoying it. Getting a lot of writing done."

"You got books up there?"

"I'm writing it for humans. I'm trying to compose a Third Testament. You know, Old, New, Mine."

"Yeah?" said Clayton. "What for?"

"For the new age. The Age of Recurring Peace. You really don't realize what you've done, do you? Your declaration by Urim and Thummim was binding. Every century will have seven years of peace from now on. It's an entirely new religious dispensation."

Clayton dismissed the idea with a wave of his one hand. "You know human beings. They'll make up for it during the other ninety-three years." And then, curious, he asked, "They really gonna let you add a Third Testament to the Bible?"

"I don't know. That would need unanimous Council approval and agreement by at least three-quarters of the entire angel population. I've asked Lucifer to help me argue the case."

"The two of you?" Clayton chuckled. "You'll get it, then."

The air felt hotter, thicker to Clayton, but he didn't want to go home yet. How many people got to live as he lived? How many would trade their souls to get away? "It's getting hot out," he said to Paolo, as if sharing it would divide the temperature by two.

"I've brought you a birthday present."

"Shouldn't have. I really don't need anything."

"I think you'll like it. I've had a lot of free time, and I've made headway in my search for God. I've gotten a couple letters."

"From God?" That was silly. But life was silly.

"Yeah. He still won't come, but at least He's willing to carry on a sporadic message exchange with me."

"Well, that's fine for you. Just fine." Clayton stared at the bottom of the boat. Paolo held out a sealed sheet of paper, folded, freshwood brown with CLAYTON embossed on the front. Clayton felt a shiver start at the base of his spine that spread through the rest of his body.

"Take it, Pinhead. I'm dying of curiosity."

It took a long time for Clayton to decide to accept the letter. He fumbled with the seal in an awkward, one-handed manner. Paolo looked away politely until it was opened.

"Dear Clayton," it said, the letters in the same embossed gold as his name had been on the cover side of the page.

Dear Clayton,
    I really do believe in you.
                              Warmest regards,
                              The Almighty

"You wrote this, didn't you?"

Paolo's expression didn't change. "I could have. Sure. But the fact is, maybe I didn't. I can't be trusted, but this time I really might be on the level. I guess that's what faith comes down to."

Clayton read the letter again, then folded it gently. He tucked it inside his shirt, careful not to wrinkle it. "That's nice," he said. "That's goddamn nice."

Paolo put his arm around Clayton's shoulder, and Clayton ran the engine a little faster than usual.

Epilogue/Apologue

And it came to pass that Clayton Pinkes, Prophet for the End of Time, brought Sabbath Peace to all the Earth, seven years a century;

Outside of the Peace, men's wars continued, as they shall until the coming of Our Blessed Lord in Hiding, may He be forever sought;

And men continued in love and faith and hope, and in hate and doubt and despair, in marrying and giving in marriage, in pillaging and taking by pillage, in being born and dying;

But through doubt, Clayton Pinkes clung to faith, choosing to know what he could not see. And so he carried the burden of the world.

May his sacrifice be praised in Heaven. Blessed be the name of Clayton Pinkes.

[[MANDI,
COULD YOU PROOFREAD THIS FOR ME? WE'RE PRESENTING THE WHOLE TESTAMENT TO THE COUNCIL NEXT WEEK FOR FINAL APPROVAL. THANKS.

—Raphael.]]

DAVID WEBER

<u>The Honor Harrington series:</u> *(cont.)*

Field of Dishonor

Honor goes home to Manticore—and fights for her life on a battlefield she never trained for, in a private war that offers just two choices: death—or a "victory" that can end only in dishonor and the loss of all she loves....

Flag in Exile

Hounded into retirement and disgrace by political enemies, Honor Harrington has retreated to planet Grayson, where powerful men plot to reverse the changes she has brought to their world. And for their plans to suceed, Honor Harrington must die!

Honor Among Enemies

Offered a chance to end her exile and again command a ship, Honor Harrington must use a crew drawn from the dregs of the service to stop pirates who are plundering commerce. Her enemies have chosen the mission carefully, thinking that either she will stop the raiders or they will kill her . . . and either way, her enemies will win....

In Enemy Hands

After being ambushed, Honor finds herself aboard an enemy cruiser, bound for her scheduled execution. But one lesson Honor has never learned is how to give up! One way or another, she and her crew are going home—even if they have to conquer Hell to get there!

continued ☞

MORE PRAISE FOR
LOIS MCMASTER BUJOLD

What the readers say:

"My copy of *Shards of Honor* is falling apart I've reread it so often.... I'll read whatever you write. You've certainly proved yourself a grand storyteller."
—Liesl Kolbe, Colorado Springs, CO

"I experience the stories of Miles Vorkosigan as almost viscerally uplifting.... But certainly, even the weightiest theme would have less impact than a cinder on snow were it not for a rousing good story, and good storytelling with it. This is the second thing I want to thank you for.... I suppose if you boiled down all I've said to its simplest expression, it would be that I immensely enjoy and admire your work. I submit that, as literature, your work raises the overall level of the science fiction genre, and spiritually, your work cannot avoid positively influencing all who read it."
—Glen Stonebraker, Gaithersburg, MD

" 'The Mountains of Mourning' [in *Borders of Infinity*] was one of the best-crafted, and simply best, works I'd ever read. When I finished it, I immediately turned back to the beginning and read it again, and I can't remember the last time I did that."
—Betsy Bizot, Lisle, IL

"I can only hope that you will continue to write, so that I can continue to read (and of course buy) your books, for they make me laugh and cry and think ... rare indeed."
—Steven Knott, Major, USAF

What Do You Say?

Send me these books!

Shards of Honor	72087-2 ✦ $5.99	☐
Barrayar	72083-X ✦ $5.99	☐
Cordelia's Honor (trade)	87749-6 ✦ $15.00	☐
The Warrior's Apprentice	72066-X ✦ $5.99	☐
The Vor Game	72014-7 ✦ $5.99	☐
Young Miles (trade)	87782-8 ✦ $15.00	☐
Cetaganda (hardcover)	87701-1 ✦ $21.00	☐
Cetaganda (paperback)	87744-5 ✦ $5.99	☐
Ethan of Athos	65604-X ✦ $5.99	☐
Borders of Infinity	72093-7 ✦ $5.99	☐
Brothers in Arms	69799-4 ✦ $5.99	☐
Mirror Dance (paperback)	87646-5 ✦ $6.99	☐
Memory (paperback)	87845-X ✦ $6.99	☐
Falling Free	65398-9 ✦ $4.99	☐
The Spirit Ring (paperback)	72188-7 ✦ $5.99	☐

 LOIS MCMASTER BUJOLD
Only from Baen Books

If not available at your local bookstore, fill out this coupon and send a check or money order for the cover price(s) to Baen Books, Dept. BA, P.O. Box 1403, Riverdale, NY 10471. Delivery can take up to ten weeks.

NAME: _____

ADDRESS: _____

_____

I have enclosed a check or money order in the amount of $ _____